Roles and Rituals Of Indian Women

Roles and Rituals Of Indian Women

Vijay Kumar Gupta

MD PUBLICATIONS PVT LTD
NEW DELHI
www.mdppl.com

Published by :

MD Publications Pvt Ltd
"MD House", 11, Darya Ganj,
New Delhi-110 002
Phone : +91-11-41563325 (Customer Service)
+91-11-41562846 (Editorial)
E-mail (orders) : **order@mdppl.com**
Website : **www.mdppl.com**

ISBN : 978-81-7533-268-3

Published and Printed by Mr. Pranav Gupta on behalf of **MD Publications Pvt Ltd** at Printext, New Delhi.

PREFACE

As a female subject in the modern world, experiential life involves a constant mediation between modernity and the cultural excrescences of tradition. The influences of ideology and those of religion continue to percolate into our lives. Within the domestic sphere, in the even more contested realm of private belief and practice.

At first glance women's rituals in contemporary India show that they uphold patriarchal values while encouraging blatant market oriented urban commercialization and seem to further underline male preference in a society that already encourages male domination.

Most of the significant rituals like Karva Chauth, celebrated annually with great fervour every year, are geared towards upholding the long life of favoured male relatives-husband and sons, or for the brothers in festivals like Rakshabandhan and Bhaiduja. However, a closer look at the festivals reveals that the practice of performing vratas involving fasting and rigours followed by celebrations and feasting allowed women to create ritual spaces for themselves, spaces that had been denied to them in brahmanical and institutional rituals.

In household religious ceremonies even today, it is not uncommon to see women take the lead role in organizing the entire function. There is no domestic ritual in which women cannot participate, whereas there are several popular Hindu rituals where the presence of men is either debarred, or is not desirable. The sacred rituals are said to bear the desired fruit only if men and women perform it as a pair. In religious rituals and customs, females are barred from taking part in all worship. In Kerala, females are not allowed to enter in the Ayeppa temples. They are also barred from worshiping the God Hanuman and in some regions they are barred from even touching the 'linga' idol of Lord Shiva.

I am very grateful to Mr. Pranav Gupta, Director of MD Publications Pvt Ltd, New Delhi, for his kind cooperation and support for this book.

Vijay Kumar Gupta

CONTENTS

1

Roles and Rituals of Indian Women

An Introduction

Women have fought for their status and role in communities, religions, and the nation for years. And women in Hinduism are no different. Women traditionally would live the life of a mother and a wife following the footsteps of their ancestors. Women's roles were laid out in Hindu law books such as the Dharma-Sastras, however basic rules in the Laws of Manu (200 C.E.) lays out how a women or wife should behave in the household and towards her husband. Nevertheless women's roles have evolved over time and women are going against the social norm of their tradition and even their way of life. Hinduism is a complex religion and unlike many western religions it is also a way of life. Family is very important in Hinduism and as keeper of the household women play an important role in the tradition.

Women are revealed in the sacred scriptures as presenting a duality of being benevolent and malevolent exposing her with great contrasting powers. "In times of prosperity she indeed is Laksmi, [goddess of wealth] who bestows prosperity in the homes of men; and in times of misfortune, she herself becomes the goddess of misfortune, and brings about ruin". Because of this changing power that a women possesses it is rational that man should want to control this mysterious power. Then, perhaps it may have been interpreted that women should remain stagnate, running the household, rearing the children, and participate in religious rituals as an assistant to their husband. It is the female's role as a wife to bear her husband's children and educate them in their traditional practices.

To maintain there dominance over the women men have their wives maintain the home and the family that he has made and provided for. The female's prakrti, (nature), is like the soil where the male plants his seed to grow into "conjoined images". And therefore "the male controls the female; that Nature is controlled by Culture". Culture or society controls nature as it is motivated to change and evolve just as the man tries to control the women. Prior to marriage the female is regulated by her father and then when she is married she is controlled by her husband. During the marriage the wife must then be truly devoted to her husband and it is believed that she is able to transfer her natural female power to the husband for daily rituals and caring for his family.

Daily roles and activities of the wife involve more than just caring for the household; they also involve religious rituals. Although, only Brahman men can do the Vedic rituals women still play an important role in devotional rituals. The wives of Brahmin priests can act as assistants to their husbands on ritual occasions because there are no scriptural sanctions against such female ritual behavior. Many Hindu scriptures say women are to be honored, "religious deeds are said to be useless if women are not honored and cherished". So, in a small village in North India, "women instigate and participate in twenty-one of the thirty-three annual rites… [and] dominate nine of the twenty-one annual rites".

Although women have developed a stronger religious status they are still considered dangerous to men; whether it is because their inner power or another reason we cannot be certain and therefore they are accepted as active participants in the Vedic rituals. Hindu women's traditional roles in the household in India have changed a great deal over the past fifty or even hundred years. Western countries have had an influence on these changes. Scholars traveling to India want to learn and study the Indian Hindu culture. And, therefore they have written many articles and books on the sacred scriptures including reviews on the Vedas and other religious scriptures that were once restricted from women. Because of these reviews a new age has come and has been recognized by the world bring scholars from all over the world.

The ongoing reconstruction of the social status of women has brought about many new changes in, "Education, health measures, rural and industrial welfare schemes, problems of early marriage, purdah, and the positions of widows, women's franchise rights, and the representation of women in governing bodies". The schools now allow young women to learn the Vedas and sacred scriptures that were formally restricted to only men of a certain class/caste. With this new revelation many people have spoke out saying, "No society can prosper without education for its women. By treating women as the lowest caste... you don't raise them to a level of vidya Shakti [educated power]; they will end up being avidya Shakti [ignorant power]".

Due to this modification of women roles in society infant mortality has reduced with better health measures. Young girls are no longer forced to marry before they hit puberty, and widows are able to re-marry. Although there is more men then women being born in India the change in women's status as independent women in governing bodies is expected bring a change to this as well. To most women these changes seem radical and the feel that they are disrespecting their tradition. By accepting the changes as a new improvement to their past traditions they can keep their traditional values as well as become revolutionalized. Many women have accepted the lifestyles of their ancestors as the social norm.

Many women have stepped out of the norm and made a difference in their village, society, and their country giving other women everywhere someone the look up to and follow in their leadership. The life of asceticism is now not only a part of coming of age for a man but women are more commonly choosing this lifestyle as well. An example of this growth and leadership is evident through the rise of the female guru. Female guru's are not traditionally accepted and the social norm in Hinduism. "The most radical challenge of the female gurus is not directed toward the received guru tradition but rather the received social expectations".

For instance, many female gurus are or married that are some that have not been married which has created some conflict with their families who want them to adopt the traditional role of women to be a wife and mother. Instead they live an ascetic lifestyle and do not try to define the difference between female or male gurus. Both are trying to attain the same goal, and gender does not affect how they come to their attainment. However, "all of the female gurus is associated with the Goddess through the concept of shakti, for they, like the Goddess, are paramount embodiments of Shakti". Female gurus are, for the most part, understood and accepted by their followers. The work they do with the people teaching and connecting with their students, illustrates the growing influence of women in Hinduism.

Although change has challenged the idea of the proper wife who remains under her husband's control, change has also brought about many beneficiary factors. Women are much more able think and act independently should they choose to. They may better educate themselves not only in the religious texts, such as the Vedas, but in social inclement and activities as well. Women have a choice between becoming a wife who obeys her husband's wishes and or "the Mother, the goddess who epitomizes the dual character of the Hindu female". Although most Hindu women will probably continue to follow their tradition and be a proper wife change has created possibilities for those women who want a different lifestyle involving religious power or as business women, for example, should they choose it. The opportunity for change is among us all should we choose it, "women as [a] mother in Hindu thought controls others and becomes the Hindu woman in control of her".

Women's rituals comprise an important part of practical Hinduism. Some male-authored Hindu scriptures limit women's religious roles, consider women more subject than men to bodily impurities, and subordinate them to their fathers and husbands. Priests in temples and other public spaces are predominantly- though not exclusively- male. Most domestic Hindu rituals, however, lie in the hands and hearts of women. Women perform their own *seva* and *puja* at permanent or temporary domestic shrines, are the chief ritual experts at many calendrical festivals, and are responsible for many ritual aspects of weddings and other life-cycle celebrations. Women more frequently than men undertake personal vows (*vrata*)- individually or collectively- to ensure the well-being of their families. The elements of a *vrata* usually include a partial fast, simple worship in a domestic space temporarily purified for this purpose, and often the retelling of one or more stories honouring the deities and exemplifying the rewards or describing the origins of the ritual.

The event may conclude with the consumption of special food to break the fast. Vows are often associated with calendrical cycles, whether solar, lunar, or both. For example, each day of the week is identified with a particular deity: Monday with Shiva, Tuesday with Hanuman, Wednesday with Ganesha, and so forth. If a woman undertakes a Monday *vrata*, she will fast and worship Shiva and tell his story every Monday. Or, a person may do an eleventh *vrata*, a vow for the eleventh day of the lunar calendar, which would come twice a month in the waxing and waning halves of the moon. Some vows are undertaken for the occasional potent convergence of both calendrical systems, such as *somavati amavasa*, a Monday dark moon. Women's ritually performed stories feature heroines who may be devotees of the deity being honoured, daughters of female devotees, or persons ignorant of that particular deity who then learn about its power and blessings in the course of severe tribulations.

Notably, the heroines of women's devotional stories exemplify moral virtues, ritual knowledge, devotional fervour, and transformative agency. The power accumulated by women through their ritual actions should never be used exclusively for their own well-being. Selflessness is a very important virtue that is exemplified by self-denial in fasting. Nonetheless, because women's well-being is connected to familial well-being, women see their rituals as productive of better circumstances for themselves and their loved ones. For women, practical Hinduism is a space where they express their competence, self-respect, and power and see themselves as protectors of husbands, brothers, and sons. Even while critiquing the ways in which some Hindu traditions disadvantage women, Indian feminists have located important resources for women in goddess" worship, in *vrata* narratives, and in the sense of gender solidarity and self-worth that woman's rituals produce.

Pilgrimage in Hinduism, as in other religions, is the practice of journeying to sites where religious powers, knowledge, or experience are deemed especially accessible. Hindu pilgrimage is rooted in ancient scriptures. According to textual scholars, the earliest reference to Hindu pilgrimage is in the Rigveda (*c.* 1500 BCE), in which the "wanderer" is praised. Numerous later texts including the epic *Mahabharata* (*c.* 300 BCE –300 CE) and several of the mythological Puranas (*c.* 300–750 CE) elaborate on the capacities of particular sacred sites to grant boons, such as health, wealth, progeny, and deliverance after death. Texts enjoin Hindu pilgrims to perform rites on behalf of ancestors and recently deceased kin. Sanskrit sources as well as devotional literature in regional vernacular languages praise certain places and their miraculous capacities.

Pilgrimage has been increasingly popular since the 20th century, facilitated by ever-improving transportation. Movement over actual distance is critical to pilgrimage, for what is important is not just visiting a sacred space but leaving home. Most pilgrimage centres hold periodic religious fairs called *melas* to mark auspicious astrological moments or important anniversaries. In 2001, for example, the Kumbh Mela in Allahabad was attended during a six-week period by tens of millions of pilgrims. Because of shared elements in rituals, a pilgrim from western Rajasthan does not feel alienated in the eastern pilgrimage town of Puri, even though the spoken language, the landscape and climate, the deities' names and appearances, and the food offerings are markedly different from those the pilgrim knows at home. Moreover, pilgrimage works to propagate practices among diverse regions because stories and tales of effective and attractive ritual acts circulate along with pilgrims.

Pilgrimage sites are often located in spots of great natural beauty thought to be pleasing to deities as well as humans. Environmental activists draw on the mythology of the sacred landscapes to inspire Hindu populations to adopt sustainable environmental practices. The Sanskrit and Hindi word for pilgrimage centre is *tirtha*, literally a river ford or crossing place. The concept of a ford is associated with pilgrimage centres not simply because many are on riverbanks but because they are metaphorically places for transition, either to the other side of particular worldly troubles or beyond the endless cycle of birth and death.

SACRIFICE AND WORSHIP

Although, the Vedic fire rituals were largely replaced in Puranic and modern Hinduism by image worship and other forms of devotionalism, many Hindu rites can be traced back to Vedism. Certain royal sacrifices- such as the *rajasuya*, or consecration ritual- remained popular with Hindu kings until modern times. Other large-scale Vedic sacrifices (*shrauta*) have been regularly maintained from ancient times to the present by certain families and groups of Brahmans. The surviving rituals from the Vedic period, however, tend to be observed at the level of the domestic (*grihya*) ritual.

SAMSKARAS: RITES OF PASSAGE

The *samskaras* are transitional rites intended to prepare a person for a certain event or for the next stage in life by removing taints (sins) or by generating fresh qualities. If the blemishes incurred in this or a previous life is not removed, the person is impure and will not be rewarded for any ritual acts. The *samskaras* sanctify critical moments and are deemed necessary for unfolding a person's latent capacities for development. In antiquity there was a great divergence of opinion about the number of rites of passage, but in later times 16 were recognized as most important. In modern times most *samskaras* (except those of impregnation, initiation, and marriage) have fallen into disuse or are performed in an abridged or simplified form without Vedic *mantras* or a priest.

The impregnation rite, consecrating the intended time of conception, consists of a ritual meal of pounded rice (mixed with various other things according to whether the married man desires a fair, brown, or dark son; a learned son; or a learned daughter), an offering of rice boiled in milk, the sprinkling of the woman, and intercourse; all acts are also accompanied by *mantras*. In the third month of pregnancy the rite called *punsavana* (begetting of a son) follows. The birth is itself the subject of elaborate ceremonies, the main features of which are an oblation of ghee (clarified butter) cast into the fire; the introduction of a pellet of honey and ghee into the newborn child's mouth, which according to many authorities is an act intended to produce mental and physical strength; the murmuring of *mantras* for the sake of a long life; and rites to counteract inauspicious influences.

There is much divergence of opinion as to the time of the name-giving ceremony; in addition to the personal name, there is often another one that should be kept secret for fear of sinister designs against the child. The defining moment comes, however, when the father utters the name into the child's ear. A hallmark of childhood *samskaras* is a general male bias. In the birth ritual (*jatakarman*), the manuals direct the father to breathe upon the child's head, a practice transparently designed to supplant the role that biology gives to the mother. In practice, however, the mother may join in this breathing ritual. There is also an array of life-cycle rites that focuses specifically upon the lives of girls and women. In South India, for instance, one finds an initiation rite (*vilakkitu kalyanam*) that corresponds roughly to *upanayana*, the male initiation, and that gives girls the authority to light oil lamps and thereby to become full participants in proper domestic worship. Other rites celebrate first menstruation or mark various moments surrounding childbirth. Typically women act as officiants.

The important *upanayana* initiation is held when a boy is between the ages of 8 and 12 and marks his entry into the community of the three higher classes of society. In this rite he becomes a "twice-born one," or *dvija*. Traditionally, this was also the beginning of a long period of Veda study and education in the house under the guidance of a teacher (*guru*). In modern practice, the haircutting ceremony- formerly performed in a boy's third year- and the initiation is usually performed on the same day, the homecoming ceremony at the end of the period of study being little more than a formality. Wedding ceremonies, the most important of all, have not only remained elaborate- and often very expensive- but have also incorporated various elements- among others, propitiations and expiations- that are not indicated in the oldest sources.

Already in ancient times there were great divergences in accordance with local customs or family or caste traditions. However, the following practices are considered essential in the performance of the wedding rite. The date is fixed only after careful astrological calculation; the bridegroom is conducted to the home of his future parents-in-law, who receive him as an honoured guest; there are offerings of roasted grain into the fire; the bridegroom has to take hold of the bride's hand; he conducts her around the sacrificial fire; seven steps are taken by bride and bridegroom to solemnize the irrevocability of the unity; both are, in procession, conducted to their new home, which the bride enters without touching the threshold. Of eight forms of marriage recognized by the ancient authorities, two have remained in vogue: the simple gift of a bride and the legalization of the alliance by means of a marriage gift paid to the bride's family. In the Vedic period, girls seem not to have married before they had reached puberty.

Child marriage and the condemnation of the remarriage of widows, especially among the higher classes, became customary later and have gradually, since the mid-19th century, lost their stringency. The traditional funeral method is cremation. Burial is reserved for those who have not been sufficiently purified by *samskaras* (i.e., children) and those who no longer need the ritual fire to be conveyed to the hereafter, such as ascetics who have renounced all earthly concerns. An important and meritorious complement of the funeral offices is the *sraddha* ceremony, in which food is offered to Brahmans for the benefit of the deceased. Many people still perform this rite at least once a year, even when they no longer engage in any of the five obligatory daily offerings discussed below.

Daily Offerings

There are five obligatory offerings: (1) offerings to the gods (food taken from the meal), (2) a cursory offering (*bali*) made to "all beings," (3) a libation of water mixed with sesame offered to the spirits of the deceased, (4) hospitality, and (5) recitation of the Vedas. Although some traditions prescribe a definite ritual in which these five "sacrifices" are performed, in most cases the five daily offerings are merely a way of speaking about one's religious obligations in general.

Other Private Rites

The morning and evening adorations (*sandhya*), being a very important duty of the traditional householder, are mainly Vedic in character but have become lengthy because of the addition of Puranic and Tantric elements. If not shortened, the morning ceremonies consist of self-purification, bathing, prayers, and recitation of *mantras*, especially the Gayatri-mantra (Rigveda 3.62.10), a prayer for spiritual stimulation addressed to the Sun.

The accompanying ritual includes (1) the application of marks on the forehead, characterizing the adherents of a particular religious community, (2) the presentation of offerings (water, flowers) to the Sun, and (3) meditative concentration. There are Shaiva and Vaishnava variants, and some elements are optional. The observance of the daily obligations, including the care of bodily purity and professional duties, leads to earthly reward and helps to preserve the state of sanctity required to enter into contact with the divine.

TEMPLE WORSHIP

Image worship in sectarian Hinduism takes place both in small household shrines and in the temple. Many Hindu authorities claim that regular temple worship to one of the deities of the devotional cults procures the same results for the worshiper as did the performance of one of the great Vedic sacrifices, and one who provides the patronage for the construction of a temple is called a "sacrificer" (*yajamana*). Building a temple, this belongs to whoever paid for it or to the community that occupies it, is believed to be a meritorious deed recommended to anyone desirous of heavenly reward.

The choice of a site, which should be serene and lovely, is determined by astrology and divination as well as by its proximity to human dwellings. The size and artistic value of temples range widely, from small village shrines with simple statuettes to great temple-cities whose boundary walls, pierced by monumental gates (*gopura*), enclose various buildings, courtyards, pools for ceremonial bathing, and sometimes even schools, hospitals, and monasteries.

Temple services, which may be held by any qualified member of the community, are neither collective nor carried out at fixed times. Those present experience, as spectators, the fortifying and beneficial influence radiating from the sacred acts. Sometimes worshipers assemble to meditate, to take part in chanting, or to listen to an exposition of doctrine. The *puja* (worship) performed in public "for the well-being of the world" is, though sometimes more elaborate, largely identical with that executed for personal interest. There are, however, many regional differences and even significant variations within the same community.

SHAIVA RITES

Ascetic tendencies were much in evidence among the Pashupatas, the oldest Shaiva tradition in northern India. Their Yoga, consisting of a constant meditative contact with God in solitude, required that they frequent places for cremating bodies. One group that emerged out of the Pashupata sect carried human skulls (hence the name Kapalikas, from *kapala*, "skull"). The Kapalikas used the skulls as bowls for liquor into which they projected and worshipped Shiva as Kapalika, the "Skull Bearer," or Bhairava, the "Frightful One," and then drank to become intoxicated. Their belief was that an ostentatious indifference to anything worldly was the best method of severing the ties of *samsara*.

The view and way of life peculiar to the Virashaivas, or Lingayats (Lingam-Bearers), in southwestern India is characterized by a deviation from common Hindu traditions and institutions such as sacrificial rites, temple worship, pilgrimages, child marriages, and inequality of the sexes. Initiation (*diksa*) is, on the other hand, an obligation laid on every member of the community. The spiritual power of the *guru* is bestowed upon the newborn and converts, who receive the eightfold shield (which protects devotees from ignorance of the supremacy of God and guides them to final beatitude) and the lingam (phallic symbol). The miniature lingam, the centre and basis of all their religious practices and observances, which they always bear on their body, is held to be God himself concretely represented.

Worship is due it twice or three times a day. When a Lingayat "is absorbed into the lingam" (i.e., dies), his body is not cremated, as is customary in Hinduism, but is interred, like ascetics of other groups. Lingayats who have reached a certain level of holiness are believed to die in the state of emancipation. Shaivism, though inclined in doctrinal matters to inclusiveness, inculcates some fundamental lines of conduct: one should worship one's spiritual preceptor (*guru*) as God himself, follow his path, consider him to be present in one, and dissociate oneself from all opinions and practices that are incompatible with the Shaiva creed. Yet some of Shiva's devotees also worship other gods, and the "Shaivization" of various ancient traditions is sometimes rather superficial.

Like many other Indian religions, the Shaiva-siddhanta has developed an elaborate system of ethical philosophy, primarily with a view to preparing the way for those who aspire to liberation. Because *dharma* leads to happiness, there is no distinction between sacred and secular duties. All deeds are performed as services to God and with the conviction that all life is sacred and God-centred. A devout way of living and a nonemotional mysticism are thus much recommended. Kashmir Shaivism developed the practice of a simple method of salvation: by the recognition (*pratyabhijna*) - direct, spontaneous, technique-free, but full of *bhakti*- of one's identity with God.

VAISHNAVA RITES

The faithful Shrivaishnava Brahman arranges his day around five pursuits: purificatory rites, collecting the requisites for worship, acts of worship, study and contemplation of the meaning of the sacred books, and meditative concentration on the Lord's image.

Lifelong obligations include the performance of sacrifices and other rites, restraint of the senses, fasting and soberness, worship, recitation of the scriptures, and visits to sacred places. Ramanuja, the great theologian and philosopher of the 12th century, recommended, in addition to these practices, concentration on God, a virtuous way of living, and insensibility to luck and misfortune.

According to Madhva (*c.* 1199–*c.* 1278), faithful observance of all regulations of daily conduct- including bathing, breath control, etc. will contribute to eventual success in the quest for liberation. Devout Vaishnavas emphasize God's omnipotence and the far-reaching effects of his grace. They attach much value to the repetition of his name or of sacred formulas (*japa*) and to the praise and commemoration of his deeds as a means of self-realization and of unification with his essence. Special stress is laid on *ahimsa* ("non injury"), the practice of not killing or not causing injury to living creatures.

SACRED TIMES AND FESTIVALS

Hindu festivals are combinations of religious ceremonies, semi-ritual spectacles, worship, prayer, lustrations, processions, music, dances, magical acts- participants throw fertilizing water or, during the Holi festival, coloured powder at each other- eating, drinking, lovemaking, licentiousness, feeding the poor, and other activities of a religious or traditional character. The original purpose of these activities was to purify, avert malicious influences, renew society, bridge over critical moments, and stimulate or resuscitate the vital powers of nature (hence the term *utsava*, meaning both the generation of power and a festival). Because Hindu festivals relate to the cyclical life of nature, they are supposed to prevent it from stagnating. These cyclic festivals- which may last for many days- continue to be celebrated throughout India.

Such festivals refresh the mood of the participants, further the consciousness of their own power, and help to compensate for their sensations of fear and inferiority concerning the forces of nature. Such mixtures of worship and pleasure require the participation of the entire community and create harmony among its members, even if not all contemporary participants are aware of the festival's original character. There are also innumerable festivities in honour of specific gods, celebrated by individual temples, villages, and religious communities. An important festival, formerly celebrating Kama, the god of sexual desire, survives in the Holi, a saturnalia connected with the spring equinox and in western India with the wheat harvest. Although commemorated throughout India, the rituals associated with Holi vary regionally.

Among the Marathas, a people who live along the west coast of India from Mumbai (Bombay) to Goa, the descendants of heroes who died on the battlefield perform a dance, sword in hand, in honour of their ancestors until they believe themselves possessed by the spirits of the heroes. In Bengal swings are made for Krishna; in other regions a bonfire is also essential. The tradition that accounts for the festival of Holi describes how young Prahlada, in spite of his demonic father's opposition, worshipped Vishnu and was carried into the fire by the female demon Holika, the embodiment of evil, who was believed to be immune to the ravages of fire. Through Vishnu's intervention, Prahlada emerged unharmed, while Holika was burned to ashes.

The bonfires are intended to commemorate this event or rather to reiterate the triumph of virtue and religion over evil and sacrilege. This explains why objects representing the sickness and impurities of the past year- the New Year begins immediately after Holi- are thrown into the bonfire, and it is considered inauspicious not to look at it. Moreover, people pay or forgive debts, reconcile quarrels, and try to rid themselves of the evils, conflicts, and impurities they have accumulated during the preceding months, translating the central conception of the festival into a justification for dealing anew with continuing situations in their lives.

Hindus celebrate a number of other important festivals, including Diwali, in which all classes of society participate, though it is believed to have been given by Vishnu to the Vaishyas (traders, et al.). It takes place in October and features worship and ceremonial lights in honour of Lakshmi, the goddess of wealth and good fortune; fireworks to chase away the spirits of the deceased; and gambling, an old ritual custom intended to secure luck for the coming year. The nine-day Durga festival, or Navaratri, is, especially in Bengal, splendid homage to Shakti; in South India it is a celebration of Rama's victory over Ravana.

SOCIAL STRUCTURE

The caste system, which has organized Indian society for millennia, is thoroughly legitimated by and intertwined with Hindu religious doctrine and practice. Four social classes, or *varnas*- Brahmans, Kshatriyas, Vaishyas, and Sudras- provide the simplified structure for the enormously complicated system of thousands of castes and subcastes. According to a passage from the Purusha hymn (Rigveda 10.90), the Brahman was the Purusha's mouth, the Kshatriya his arms, the Vaishya his thighs, and the Sudra his feet. This depiction of the Purusha, or cosmic man, gives an idea of the functions and mutual relations of the four main social classes. The three main classes in the classic division of Indian society are the Brahmans, the warriors, and the commoners.

The Brahmans, whatever their worldly avocations, claim to be by virtue of their birth a perpetual incarnation of the *dharma*, guardians and dispensers of divine power, entitled to teach the Veda, sacrificing for others and accepting gifts and subsistence. The term *alms* are misleading; the *daksina* offered at the end of a rite to a Brahman officiant is not a fee but an oblation through which the rite is made complete. Brahmans are held to be the highest of all human beings because of the superiority of their origin, their sanctification through the *samskaras* (rites of passage), and their observance of restrictive rules. The main duty of the nobility (the Kshatriyas) is to protect the people that of the commoners (the Vaishyas) to tend cattle, to trade, and to cultivate land.

Even if a king (theoretically of Kshatriya descent) was not of noble descent, he was still clothed with divine authority as an upholder of *dharma*. He was consecrated by means of a complex and highly significant ritual; he was Indra and other gods (*deva*) incarnate. The emblems or paraphernalia of his office represent sovereign authority; the white umbrella of state, for example, is the residence of Shri-Lakshmi, the goddess of fortune. All three higher classes, claiming Aryan descent, had to sacrifice and to study the Veda, although the responsibilities of the Vaishyas in sacred matters were less demanding. While this tripartition seems to have been inherited from Indo-European times, the fourth class (the Sudras), whose sole duty was "to serve meekly" (*Manava dharma-shastra* 1.91), is partly descended from the subjugated non-Aryans, a fact that accounts for its many disabilities and exclusion from religious status.

According to Hindu tradition, the Veda should not be studied in their presence, but they may listen to the recitation of epics and Puranas. They are permitted to perform the five main acts of worship (without Vedic *mantra*s) and undertake observances, but even today they maintain various ceremonies of their own, carried out without Brahmanic assistance. Yet a distinction is often made among Sudras. Some are purer and have a more correct behaviour and way of living than others, the former tending to assimilate with higher castes, the latter to rank with the lowest in the social scale, who, often called Chandalas, were at an early date charged with sweeping, bearing corpses, and other impure occupations.

Ritual purity was and is an important criterion; impure conduct and neglect of Veda study and the rules regarding forbidden food might suffice to stigmatize the "twice-born" as a Sudra. On the other hand, in later times the trend of many communities has been toward integrating all Sudras into the Brahmanic system. The Brahmans, who have far into modern times remained a respected, traditional, and sometimes intellectual upper class, were (until the 1930s) much in demand because of their knowledge of rites and traditions. Although Kshatriya rank is claimed by many whose title is one of function or creation rather than of inheritance, this class is now rare in many regions. Moreover, for a considerable time none of the four *varna*s represented anything other than a series of hierarchically arranged groups of castes.

CASTES

The origin of the caste system is not known with certainty. Hindus maintain that the proliferation of the castes (*jati*s, literally "births") was the result of intermarriage (which is prohibited in Hindu works on *dharma*), which led to the subdivision of the four classes, or *varna*s. Modern theorists, however, assume that castes arose from differences in family ritual practices, racial distinctions, and occupational differentiation and specialization. Scholars also doubt whether the simple *Varna* system was ever more than a theoretical socioreligious ideal and have emphasized that the highly complex division of Hindu society into nearly 3,000 castes and subcastes was probably in place even in ancient times.

In general, a caste is an endogamous hereditary group of families bearing a common name, often claiming a common descent, as a rule professing to follow the same hereditary calling, clinging to the same customs, especially regarding purity, meals, and marriages, and often further divided into smaller endogamous circles. Moreover, tribes, guilds, or religious communities characterized by particular customs- for example, the Lingayats- could easily be regarded as castes. The status of castes varies in different localities. Although social mobility is possible, the mutual relationship of castes is hierarchically determined: local Brahman groups occupy the highest place, and differences in ritual purity are the main criteria of position in the hierarchy. Most impure are the untouchables, referred to as scheduled castes in the constitution of modern India and popularly called Harijans.

Among the scheduled castes, however, there are numerous subdivisions, each of which regards itself as superior to others. Traditional Hindus maintain that the ritual impurity and "untouchability" inherent in these groups does not essentially differ from that temporarily associated with mourners or menstruating women. This, and the fact that some exterior group or other might rise in estimation and become an interior one or that individual outcastes might be well-to-do, does not alter the fact that the spirit of exclusiveness has been carried to extremes at times. The scheduled castes were subjected to various socioreligious disabilities before mitigating tendencies helped bring about reform. After independence, social discrimination was prohibited, and the practice of preventing access to religious, occupational, or civil rights on the grounds of untouchability was made a punishable offense.

Despite these prohibitions, scheduled castes were barred from the use of temples and other religious institutions and from public schools. These groups also had many disabilities in relations with private persons. From the traditional Hindu point of view, this social system is the necessary complement of the principles of *dharma*, *karma*, and *samsara*. Corresponding to hells and heavenly regions in the hereafter, the castes are the mundane social frame within which *karma* is manifested. A low social status is the inevitable result of sins in a former life but can, by virtue and merit, is followed by a better position in the next existence.

SOCIAL PROTEST

For many centuries certain Indian religious communities have been dedicated in whole or in part to the elimination of caste discrimination. Many have been guided by *bhakti* sentiments, including the Virauaivas, Sikhs, Kabir Panthis, Satnemis, and Remnemis, all of whom bear a complicated relation to the greater Hindu fold. A major theme in *bhakti* poetry throughout India has been the ridicule of caste and the etiquette of ritual purity that relates to it. This element is stronger among the *bhakti* poets who accept the concept of *nirguna*, which holds that *brahman* is to be characterized as without qualities, than the poets who advocate the idea of *saguna*, which maintains that *brahman* possesses qualities.

Other religions have provided members of low-ranked castes with a further hope for escaping social hierarchies associated with Hindu practice. Sikhism has traditionally rejected caste, a position clearly emphasized in the *gurdwaras*, where access to sacred scripture, the *Adi Granth*, is granted without regard to caste and communal meals are served to all Sikhs. Islam played this role in Kerala from the 8th century onward and elsewhere in India since the 12th century, but some convert groups have retained their original caste organization even after embracing Islam. Christianity has exercised a similar force, serving for centuries as a magnet for disadvantaged Hindus. In 1956 B.R. Ambedkar, the principal framer of the Indian constitution and a member of the scheduled Mahar caste, abandoned Hinduism for Buddhism, and millions of his lower-caste followers eventually also converted to Buddhism.

Yet many Ambedkarite Dalits (the "Oppressed") continue to venerate saints such as Kabir, Cokhamela, and Ravidas, who figure in the general lore of Hindu *bhakti*. Other Dalits, especially members of the Camer caste (traditionally leather workers), have gone further, identifying themselves explicitly as Ravidasis, creating a scripture that features his poetry and building temples that house his image. Still other Dalit communities have claimed since the early 20th century that they represent India's original religion (*adi dharma*), rejecting caste-coded Vedic beliefs and practices as perversions introduced by Aryan invaders in the 2nd millennium BCE.

RENUNCIANTS AND THE REJECTION OF SOCIAL ORDER

Another means of rejecting the social order, which forms the background for significant portions of Hindu belief and practice, is renunciation (self-denial and asceticism). The rituals of *sannyasa*, which serve as a gateway to a life of religious discipline, often mimic death rituals, signifying the renouncer's understanding that he (or, less typically, she) no longer occupies a place in family or society. Other rituals serve to induct the initiate into a new family- the alternative family provided by a celibate religious order, usually focused on a *guru*. In principle this family should not be structured along the lines of caste, and the initiate should pledge to renounce dietary restrictions.

In practice, however, some dietary restrictions remain in India's most influential renunciant communities (though not in all), and some renunciant orders are closely paired with specific communities of householders. This follows a pattern that is loosely present everywhere. Householders and renunciants offer each other mutual benefits, with the former dispensing material substance to the theoretically propertyless holy men and women while the latter dispense religious merit and spiritual guidance in return. Such an enactment of the values of *dharma* and *moksha* is symbiotic to be sure, but that does not serve to domesticate renunciants entirely. Their existence questions the ultimacy of anything tied to caste, hierarchy, and bodily well-being.

RELIGIOUS ORDERS AND HOLY MEN

Members of the various denominations who abandon all worldly attachment enter an "inner circle" or "order" that, seeking a life of devotion, adopts or develops particular vows and observances, a common cult, and some form of initiation.

INITIATION

Hindus are free to join a religious order and must submit to its rites and way of living after joining it. The initiation (*diksha*), a rite of purification or consecration involving the transformation of the aspirant's personality, is regarded as a complement to, or even a substitute for, the previous initiation ceremony (the *upanayana* that all twice-born Hindus undergo at adolescence), which it strikingly resembles. Such religious groups integrate ancient, widespread ideas and customs of initiation into the framework of either the Vaishnava or Shaiva patterns of Hinduism. Vaishnavism emphasizes their character as an introduction to a life of devotion and as an entrance into closer contact with God, although happiness, knowledge, a long life, and a prospect of freedom from *karma* are also among the ideals to which they aspire. Shaivas are convinced of the absolute necessity of initiation for anyone desiring final liberation and require an initiation in accordance with their rituals.

All communities agree that the authority to initiate belongs only to a qualified spiritual guide (*guru*), usually a Brahman, who has previously received the special *guru-diksha* (initiation as a teacher) and is often regarded as representing God himself. The postulant is sometimes committed to a probationary period, to training in Yoga mysticism, or to instruction in the esoteric meaning of the scriptures. The initiate receives a devotional name and is given the sacred *mantras* of the community. There are many complicated forms of initiation: the Vaishnavas differentiate between the members of the four classes; the Shaivas and Tantrists take into account the natural aptitude and competency of the recipients and distinguish between first-grade initiates, who are believed to obtain access to God, and higher-grade initiates, who remain in a state of holiness.

YOGA

The initiate guided by a *guru* may practice Yoga (a "methodic exertion" of body and mind) in order to attain, through mortification, concentration, and meditation, a higher state of consciousness and thereby find supreme knowledge, achieve spiritual autonomy, and realize oneness with the Highest (or however the ultimate goal is conceived). Yoga may be atheistic or theistic and may adopt various philosophical or religious principles.

Every denomination attempted to implement Yogic practices on a theoretical basis derived from its own teachings. There are many different forms of Yoga, and the practices vary according to the stage of ádvancement of the adepts. All serious yogis, however, agree in disapproving the use of Yogic methods for worldly purposes.

SECTARIAN SYMBOLS

The typical Hindu ascetic (*sadhu*) usually wears a distinctive mark (*pundra*) on his forehead and often carries some symbol of his religion. A Vaishnava might possess a discus (*chakra*) and a conch shell (*sankha*), replicas of Vishnu's flaming weapon and his instrument of beneficent power and omnipresent protection, or a *shalagrama* stone or a tulsi plant, which represent, respectively, Vishnu's essence and that of his spouse Lakshmi. A Shaiva might impersonate Shiva and carry a trident (*trishula*), denoting empire and the irresistible force of transcendental reality; wear a small lingam; carry a human skull, showing that he is beyond the terror inspired by the transitoriness of the world; or smear his body with apotropaic (supposed to avert evil) and consecratory ashes. These emblems are sacred objects of worship because the divine presence, when invoked by *mantra*s, is felt to be in them.

CULTURAL EXPRESSIONS

The structure of Indian temples, the outward form of images, and indeed the very character of Indian art are largely determined by the religion and unique worldview of India, which penetrated the other provinces of culture and welded them into a homogeneous whole. Moreover, the art that emerged is highly symbolic. The much-developed ritual-religious symbolism presupposes the existence of a spiritual reality that may make its presence and influence felt in the material world and can also be approached through its representative symbols.

The production of objects of symbolic value is therefore more than a technique. The artisan can begin work only after entering into a state of supranormal consciousness and must model a cult image after the ideal prototype. After undergoing a process of spiritual transformation, the artisan is believed to transform the material used to create the image into a receptacle of divine power. Like the artisan, the worshiper (*sadhaka*, "the one who wishes to attain the goal"), must grasp the esoteric meaning of a statue, picture, or pot and identify his or her self with the power residing in it. The usual offering, a handful of flowers, is the means to convey the worshiper's "life-breath" into the image.

Types of Symbols

If they know how to handle the symbols, the worshipers have at their disposal an instrument for utilizing the possibilities lying in the depths of their own subconscious as well as a key to the mysteries of the forces dominating the world.

Yantra and Mandala

The general term for an "instrument [for controlling]" is *yantra*, which is especially applied to ritual diagrams but can also be applied to cult images, pictures, and other such aids to worship. Any *yantra* represents some aspect of the divine and enables devotees to worship it immediately within their hearts while identifying themselves with it. Except in its greater complexity, a *mandala* does not differ from a *yantra*, and both are drawn during a highly complex ritual in a purified and ritually consecrated place. The meaning and the use of both are similar, and they may be permanent or provisional.

A *mandala*, delineating a consecrated place and protecting it against disintegrating forces represented in demoniac cycles, is the geometric projection of the universe, spatially and temporally reduced to its essential plan. It represents in a schematic form the whole drama of disintegration and reintegration, and the adept can use it to identify with the forces governing these.

As in temple ritual, a vase is employed to receive the divine power so that it can be projected into the drawing and then into the person of the adept. Thus, the mandala becomes a support for meditation, an instrument to provoke visions of the unseen.

A good example of a mandala is the shrichakra, the "Wheel of Shri" (i.e., of God's shakti), which is composed of four isosceles triangles with the apices upward, symbolizing Shiva, and five isosceles triangles with the apices downward, symbolizing Shakti. The nine triangles are of various sizes and intersect with one another. In the middle are the power point (bindu), visualizing the highest, and the invisible, elusive centre from which the entire figure and the cosmos expand.

The triangles are enclosed by two rows of (8 and 16) petals, representing the lotus of creation and reproductive vital force. The broken lines of the outer frame denote the figure to be a sanctuary with four openings to the regions of the universe. A "spiritual" foundation is provided by a yantra, called the mandala of the Purusha (spirit) of the site that is also drawn on the site on which a temple is built. This rite is a reenactment of a variant of the myth of Purusha, an immortal primeval being who obstructed both worlds until he was subdued by the gods; the parts of his body became the spirits of the site.

Lingam and Yoni

One of the most common objects of worship, whether in temples or in the household cult, is the lingam (phallus). Often much stylized and representing the cosmic pillar, it emanates its all-producing energy to the four quarters of the universe. As the symbol of male creative energy it is frequently combined with its female counterpart (yoni), the latter forming the base from which the lingam rises. Although the lingam originally may have had no relation to Shiva, it has from ancient times been regarded as symbolizing Shiva's creative energy and is widely worshipped as his fundamental form.

Visual Theology in Icons

The beauty of cult objects is believed to contribute to their power as sacred instruments, and their ornamentation is held to facilitate the process of inviting the divine power into them. Statues of gods are not intended to imitate ideal human forms but to express the supernatural. A divine figure is a "likeness" (*pratima*), a temporary benevolent or terrifying expression of some aspect of a god's nature. Iconographic handbooks attach great importance to the ideology behind images and reveal, for example, that Vishnu's eight arms stand for the four cardinal and intermediate points of the compass and that his four faces, illustrating the concept of God's fourfoldness, typify his strength, knowledge, lordship, and potency.

The emblems express the qualities of their bearers- e.g., a deadly weapon symbolizes destructive force, many-headedness omniscience. Much use is made of gestures (*mudras*); for example, the raised right hand, in the "fear-not" gesture (*abhaya-mudra*), bestows protection. Every iconographic detail has its own symbolic value, helping devotees to direct their energy to a deeper understanding of the various aspects of the divine and to proceed from external to internal worship. For many Indians, a consecrated image is a container of concentrated divine energy, and Hindu theists maintain that it is an instrument for ennobling the worshiper who realizes God's presence in it.

Religious Principles in Sculpture and Painting

Like literature and the performing arts, the visual arts contributed to the perpetuation of myths. Images sustain the presence of the god: when Devi is shown seated on her lion, advancing against the buffalo demon, she represents the affirmative forces of the universe and the triumph of divine power over wickedness. Male and female figures in uninterrupted embrace, as in Shaiva iconography, signify the union of opposites and the eternal process of generation. In Hindu sculpture the tendency is toward hieratic poses of a god in a particular conventional stance (*murti*; image), which, once fixed, perpetuates itself.

An icon is a frozen incident of a myth. For example, one *murti* of Shiva is the "destruction of the elephant," in which Shiva appears dancing before and below a bloody elephant skin that he holds up before the image of his horrified consort; the stance is the summary of his triumph over the elephant demon. A god may also appear in a characteristic pose while holding in his multitudinous hands his various emblems, on each of which hangs a story. Lovers sculpted on temples are auspicious symbols on a par with foliage, water jars, and other representatives of fertility. Carvings, such as those that appear on temple chariots, tend to be more narrative; even more so are the miniature paintings of the Middle Ages. A favourite theme in the latter is the myth of the cowherd god Krishna and his love of the cowherdesses (*gopis*).

Religious Organization of Sacred Architecture

Temples must be erected on sites that are *shubha*- i.e., suitable, beautiful, auspicious, and near water- because it is thought that the gods will not come to other places. However, temples are not necessarily designed to be congenial to their surroundings, because a manifestation of the sacred is an irruption, a break in phenomenal continuity. Temples are understood to be visible representations of a cosmic pillar, and their sites are said to be navels of the world and are believed to ensure communication with the gods. Their outward appearance must raise the expectation of meeting with God. Their erection is a reconstruction and reintegration of Purusha-Prajapati, enabling him to continue his creative activity, and the finished monuments are symbols of the universe that is the unfolded One.

The owner of the temple (i.e., the individual or community that paid for its construction)- also called the sacrificer- participates in the process of reintegration and experiences his spiritual rebirth in the small cella, aptly called the "womb room" (*garbhagriha*), by meditating on the God's presence, symbolized or actualized in his consecrated image. The cella is in the centre of the temple above the navel- i.e., the foundation stone- and it may contain a jar filled with the creative power (*shakti*) that is identified with the goddess Earth (who bears and protects the monument), three lotus flowers, and three tortoises (of stone, silver, and gold) that represent earth, atmosphere, and heaven. The tortoise is a manifestation of Vishnu bearing the cosmic pillar; the lotus is the symbol of the expansion of generative possibilities.

The vertical axis or tube, coinciding with the cosmic pillar, connects all parts of the building and is continued in the finial on the top; it corresponds to the mystical vertical vein in the body of the worshiper through which his soul rises to unite itself with the Highest. The designing of Hindu temples, like that of religious images, was codified in the Shilpa-shastras (craft textbooks), and every aspect of the design was believed to offer the symbolic representation of some feature of the cosmos. The idea of microcosmic symbolism is strong in Hinduism and comes from Vedic times; the Brahmanas are replete with similar cosmic interpretations of the many features of the sacrifice. The Vedic idea of the correspondence (*bandhu*) between microcosm and macrocosm was applied to the medieval temple, which was laid out geometrically to mirror the structure of the universe, with its four geometric quarters and a celestial roof.

The temple also represents the mountain at the navel of the world and often somewhat resembles a mountain. On the periphery were carved the most worldly and diverse images, including battles, hunts, circuses, animals, birds, and gods. The erotic scenes carved at Khajuraho in Madhya Pradesh and Konarak in Orissa express a general exuberance that may be an offering of thanksgiving to the gods who created all. However, that same swarming luxuriance of life may also reflect the concern that one must set aside worldly temptations before entering the sacred space of the temple, for the carvings decorate only the outside of the temple; at the centre, the sanctum sanctorum, there is little if any ornamentation, except for a stark symbol of the god or goddess. Thus, these carvings simultaneously express a celebration of *samsara* and a movement toward *moksha*.

Theatre and Dance

Theatrical performances are events that can be used to secure blessings and happiness; the element of recreation is indissolubly blended with edification and spiritual elevation. The structure and character of classical Indian drama reveal its origin and function: it developed from a magico-religious ceremony, which survives as a ritual introduction, and begins and closes with benedictions. Drama is produced for festive occasions with a view to spiritual and religious success (*siddhi*), which must also be prompted by appropriate behaviour from the spectators; there must be a happy ending; the themes are borrowed from epic and legendary history; the development and unraveling of the plot are retarded; and the envy of malign influences is averted by the almost obligatory buffoon (*vidusaka*, "the spoiler"). There are also, in addition to films, which often use the same religious and mythic themes, *yatras*, a combination of stage play and various festivities that have contributed much to the spread of the Puranic view of life.

Dancing is not only an aesthetic pursuit but also a divine service. The dance executed by Shiva as king of dancers (Nataraja), the visible symbol of the rhythm of the universe, represents God's five activities: he unfolds the universe out of the drum held in one of his right hands; he preserves it by uplifting his other right hand in *abhaya-mudra*; he reabsorbs it with his upper left hand, which bears a tongue of flame; his transcendental essence is hidden behind the garb of apparitions, and grace is bestowed and release made visible by the foot that is held aloft and to which the hands are made to point; and the other foot, planted on the ground, gives an abode to the tired souls struggling in *samsara*. Another dance pose adopted by Shiva is the doomsday *tandava*, executed in his destructive Bhairava manifestation, usually with 10 arms and accompanied by Devi and demons.

The related myth is that Shiva conquered a mighty elephant demon that he forced to dance until he fell dead; then, wrapped in the blood-dripping skin of his victim, the god executed a horrendous dance of victory. There are halls for sacred dances annexed to some temples because of this association with the divine. The rhythmic movement has a compelling force, generating and concentrating power or releasing superfluous energy. It induces the experience of the divine and transforms the dancer into whatever he or she impersonates. Thus, many tribal dances consist of symbolic enactments of events (harvest, battles) in the hope that they will be accomplished successfully. Musicians and dancers accompany processions to expel the demons of cholera or cattle plague. Even today, religious themes and the various relations between humans and God are danced and made visual by the codified symbolic meanings of gestures and movements.

2

Hindu Rituals and Women

RITES AND RITUALS IN HINDUISM

Hinduism prescribes both ritual and spiritual practices for the liberation of men from the cycle of births and deaths. The ritual aspect is meant to make man more spiritual in the end, not vice versa. Each and every important event in the life of a Hindu, who has chosen to lead a normal householder's life, calls for the performance of certain rites. Most of the rites are caste and gender specific. In other words not all are required to perform them all. These rites are considered to be part of man's obligatory duties depending upon the profession and caste of each individual and intended mainly to invoke the blessings of various gods to ensure success in earning merit and gaining a safe passage to the heavenly world and the continuation of family lineage. The Hindu rites also add structure and purpose to the human life as they are required to be performed at various stages in the life of an individual, as a part of one's dharma and obligatory duty towards oneself, one's family, society, ancestors, other living beings and gods. Some of the important rites of Hinduism are described here.

1. Rites performed before the birth of an individual, invoking gods to make a woman of the household conceive.
2. Rites performed during the third month of pregnancy invoking gods for the birth of a male child. (Hindu women please take note. The Aryans were chauvinistic

and wanted more male children).

3. Rites performed at the time of the birth of a child.
4. Rites performed at the time of name giving ceremony.
5. Rites performed six months after the birth of the child.
6. The hair cutting ceremony.
7. Rites performed at the time of "upanayana" to make the individual a "dvija" or twice born".
8. Rites associated with marriage ceremony, starting from the time the marriage is fixed till the ceremony is concluded.
9. Rites associated with marriage life involving both the couples.
10. Rites associated with entry into a new house or construction of a new house.
11. Rites associated with the death and funeral of an individual.

It must be noted that in the present world the practice of Hinduism is changing gradually. While rituals are still performed by certain sections of society, especially the higher castes, according to the established tradition, in case of majority of people, ritualism is giving way spiritualism. Many Hindus, especially those who live in the urban areas and brought up on modern education are liberal and spiritual, rather than conventional and ritualistic. Many of them turn to rituals only under peer pressure. Performance of rituals takes time and effort. They also cost considerable sums of money. Ritualism implies also honoring the age old social structure and caste system, which too many modern Hindus is rather an unacceptable outdated practice.

In following spiritual ideals of Hinduism such considerations usually do not arise besides many spiritual practices attempt to alleviate problems such as stress and anxiety. Therefore many Hindus willingly take to the spiritual path and participate in yoga classes and meditation camps. For the reasons mentioned above, Hindus presently perform the rites very selectively. Some rites, such as the upanayana ceremony are meant exclusively for the higher castes. So a good number of Hindus are excluded from the obligation of performing them.

The rites that are most commonly observed are the ceremonies associated with events such as marriage, the birth of a child, the naming ceremony and the death of an individual. Even these are not performed uniformly due to a number of a regional variations and local traditions.

A special note on sraddha ceremony:

According to Hindu scriptures, when a person dies, he either travels to heavenly worlds or to the ancestral worlds depending upon his previous deeds. We are told that the departed souls can be elevated to higher planes of existence and pushed further on the scale of evolution if their direct descendents on earth, especially the male progeny perform some annual rites and make sacrificial offerings to them. With such rites, not just one but the entire family of ancestors would be benefited and spiritually uplifted.

So when a Hindu departs from this world, his descendents make ritualistic offerings as prescribed in the sacred texts so that the departed one makes further spiritual progress in those worlds also. The obligation towards the departed souls is thus a part of ones ordained duties, or obligatory karma, the performance of which brings happiness not only to the departed soul, but also to the ones who performed it.

Sraddha ceremony is way of repaying ones debt towards ones parents and ancestors. A person is indebted to his parents and ancestors because they were responsible for his birth on earth. Without even one of them in the ancestral line, he would never have been. He is thus greatly indebted to them for his corporeal existence. He can repay this debt only by performing annual rites for the departed ancestors. He is therefore expected to perform these ceremonies without fail and save himself and every one before him from misery.

HINDUISM AND RELIGIONS OF INDIAN ORIGIN

Hinduism, Buddhism, and Jainism originated in the same milieu: the circles of world renouncers of the 6th century BCE. All share certain non-Vedic practices (such as renunciation itself and various Yogic meditational techniques) and doctrines (such as the belief in rebirth and the goal of liberation from perpetual transmigration), but Buddhists and Jains do not accept the authority of the Vedic tradition and therefore are regarded as less than orthodox by Hindus. From the 6th to the 11th century there was strong and sometimes bloody competition for royal patronage between the three communities- with Brahmans representing Hindu values- as well as between Vaishnavas and Shaivas.

In general, the Brahman groups prevailed. In a typically absorptive gesture, Hindus in time recognized the Buddha as an incarnation of Vishnu, usually the ninth; it was often held, however, that Vishnu assumed this form to mislead and destroy the enemies of the Veda. Hence, the Buddha avatar is rarely worshipped by Hindus, though it is often highly respected by them. At an institutional level, certain Buddhist shrines, such as the one marking the Buddha's enlightenment at Bodh Gaya, have remained partly under the supervision of Hindu ascetics and are visited by Hindu pilgrims.

Hinduism has much in common with Jainism, which until the 20th century remained an Indian religion, especially in social institutions and ritual life; for this reason, many Hindus still consider it a Hindu sect. The points of difference- e.g., a stricter practice of *ahimsa* ("noninjury") and the absence of sacrifices for the deceased in Jainism- do not give offense to orthodox Hindus. Moreover, many Jain laypeople worship images as Hindus do, though with a different rationale. There are even places outside India where Hindus and Jains have joined to build a single temple, sharing the worship space.

HINDUISM AND ISLAM

Hindu relations with Islam and Christianity are in some ways quite different from the ties and tensions that bind together religions of Indian origin. Hindus live with a legacy of domination by Muslim and Christian rulers that stretch back many centuries- in North India, to the Delhi Sultanate established at the beginning of the 13th century. It is hardly the case that Muslim rule was generally loathsome to Hindus. Direct and indirect patronage from the Mughal emperors Akbar and Jahângîr (1569–1627), whose chief generals were Hindu Rajputs, laid the basis for the great burst of Krishnaite temple and institution building that transformed the Braj region beginning in the 16th century. Moreover, close proximity and daily interaction throughout the centuries has led to efforts to accommodate the existence of the two religions.

One manifestation of such syncretism occurred among mystically inclined groups who believed that one God, or the "universal principle," was the same regardless of whether it was called Allah or *Brahman*. Various syntheses between the two religions that emphasize nonsectarianism have arisen in northern India. Yet there were periods when the political ambitions of Islamic rulers took strength from iconoclastic aspects of Muslim teaching and led to the devastation of many major Hindu temple complexes, from Mathura and Varanasi (Banaras) in the north to Chidambaram and Madurai in the far south; other temples were converted to mosques. Episodically, since the 14th century, this history has provided rhetorical fuel for Hindu warriors eager to assert themselves against Muslim rivals.

The bloody partition of the South Asian subcontinent into India and Pakistan in 1947 added a new dimension. Mobilizing Hindu sensibilities about the sacredness of the land as whole, extremists have sometimes depicted the creation of Pakistan as a rape of the body of India, in the process demonizing Muslims who remain within India's political boundaries. These strands converged at the end of the 20th century in a campaign to destroy the mosque built in 1528 by a lieutenant of the Mughal emperor Babur in Ayodhya, a city that has traditionally been identified as the place where Rama was born and ruled. In 1992 Hindu militants from all over India, who had been organized by the Vishwa Hindu Parishad (VHP;

"World Hindu Council"), the Rashtriya Swayamsevak Sangh (RSS; "National Volunteer Alliance"), and the Bharatiya Janata Party (BJP; "Indian People's Party"), destroyed the mosque in an effort to "liberate" Rama and establish a huge "Rama's Birthplace Temple" on the spot.

In the aftermath, several thousand people- mostly Muslims- were killed in riots that spread across North India. The ritual world of Hinduism, manifestations of which differ greatly among regions, villages, and individuals, offers a number of common features that link all Hindus into a greater Indian religious system and influence other religions as well. The most notable feature in religious ritual is the division between purity and pollution. Religious acts presuppose some degree of impurity or defilement for the practitioner, which must be overcome or neutralized before or during ritual procedures. Purification, usually with water, is thus a typical feature of most religious action. Avoidance of the impure—taking animal life, eating flesh, associating with dead things, or body fluids—is another feature of Hindu ritual and is important for repressing pollution.

In a social context, those individuals or groups who manage to avoid the impure are accorded increased respect. Still another feature is a belief in the efficacy of sacrifice, including survivals of Vedic sacrifice. Thus, sacrifices may include the performance of offerings in a regulated manner, with the preparation of sacred space, recitation of texts, and manipulation of objects. A third feature is the concept of merit, gained through the performance of charity or good works that will accumulate over time and reduce sufferings in the next world.

DOMESTIC WORSHIP

The home is the place where most Hindus conduct their worship and religious rituals. The most important times of day for performance of household rituals are dawn and dusk, although especially devout families may engage in devotion more often. For many households, the day begins when the women in the house draw auspicious geometric designs in chalk or rice flour on the floor or the doorstep. For orthodox Hindus, dawn and dusk are greeted with recitation from the Rig Veda of the Gayatri Mantra for the sun—for many people, the only Sanskrit prayer they know. After a bath, there is personal worship of the gods at a family shrine, which typically includes lighting a lamp and offering foodstuffs before the images, while prayers in Sanskrit or a regional language are recited.

In the evenings, especially in rural areas, mostly female devotees may gather together for long sessions of singing hymns in praise of one or more of the gods. Minor acts of charity punctuate the day. During daily baths, there are offerings of a little water in memory of the ancestors. At each meal, families may set aside a handful of grain to be donated to beggars or needy persons, and daily gifts of small amounts of grain to birds or other animals serve to accumulate merit for the family through their self-sacrifice.

For the vast majority of Hindus, the most important religious path is bhakti (devotion) to personal gods. There is a wide variety of gods to choose from, and although sectarian adherence to particular deities is often strong, there is a widespread acceptance of choice in the desired god (ishta devata) as the most appropriate focus for any particular person. Most devotees are therefore polytheists, worshiping all or part of the vast pantheon of deities, some of whom have come down from Vedic times. In practice, a worshiper tends to concentrate prayers on one deity or on a small group of deities with whom there is a close personal relationship.

THE PUJA OR WORSHIP

Puja (worship) of the gods consists of a range of ritual offerings and prayers typically performed either daily or on special days before an image of the deity, which may be in the form of a person or a symbol of the sacred presence. In its more developed forms, puja consists of a series of ritual stages beginning with personal purification and invocation of the god, followed by offerings of flowers, food, or other objects such as clothing, accompanied by fervent prayers. Some dedicated worshipers perform these ceremonies daily at their home shrines; others travel to one or more temples to perform puja, alone or with the aid of temple priests who receive offerings and present these offerings to the gods.

The gifts given to the gods become sacred through contact with their images or with their shrines, and may be received and used by worshipers as the grace (prasada) of the divine. Sacred ash or saffron powder, for example, is often distributed after puja and smeared on the foreheads of devotees. In the absence of any of these ritual objects, however, puja may take the form of a simple prayer sent toward the image of the divine, and it is common to see people stop for a moment before roadside shrines to fold their hands and offer short invocations to the gods.

GURUS AND SAINTS

Since at least the seventh century A.D., the devotional path has spread from the south throughout India through the literary and musical activities of saints who have been some of the most important representatives of regional languages and traditions. The hymns of these saints and their successors, mostly in vernacular forms, are memorized and performed at all levels of society. Every state in India has its own bhakti tradition and poets who are studied and revered. In Tamil Nadu, groups called Nayanmars (devotees of Shiva) and Alvars (devotees of Vishnu) were composing beautiful poetry in the Tamil language as early as the sixth century.

In Bengal one of the greatest poets was Chaitanya (1485-1536), who spent much of his life in a state of mystical ecstasy. One of the greatest North Indian saints was Kabir (ca. 1440-1518), a common leatherworker who stressed faith in God without devotion to images, rituals, or scriptures. Among female poets, Princess Mirabai (ca. 1498-1546) from Rajasthan stands out as one whose love for Krishna was so intense that she suffered persecution for her public singing and dancing for the lord. A recurring motif that emerges from the poetry and the hagiographies of these saints is the equality of all men and women before God and the ability of people from all castes and occupations to find their way to union with God if they have enough faith and devotion. In this sense, the bhakti tradition serves as one of the equalizing forces in Indian society and culture.

A detailed series of life-cycle rituals (samskara, or refinements) mark major transitions in the life of the individual. Especially orthodox Hindu families may invite Brahman priests to their homes to officiate at these rituals, complete with sacred fire and recitations of mantras. Most of these rituals, however, do not occur in the presence of such priests, and among many groups who do not revere the Vedas or respect Brahmans, there may be other officiants or variations in the rites.

PREGNANCY, BIRTH, INFANCY

Ceremonies may be performed during pregnancy to ensure the health of the mother and growing child. The father may part the hair of the mother three times upward from the front to the back, to assure the ripening of the embryo. Charms may serve to ward off the evil eye and witches or demons.

At birth, before the umbilical cord is severed, the father may touch the baby's lips with a gold spoon or ring dipped in honey, curds, and ghee. The word vak (speech) is whispered three times into the right ear, and mantras are chanted to ensure a long life. A number of rituals for the infant include the first visit outside to a temple, the first feeding with solid food (usually cooked rice), an ear-piercing ceremony, and the first haircut (shaving the head) that often occurs at a temple or during a festival when the hair is offered to a deity.

UPANAYANA: THE THREAD CEREMONY

A crucial event in the life of the orthodox, upper-caste Hindu male is an initiation (upanayana) ceremony, which takes place for some young males between the ages of six and twelve to mark the transition to awareness and adult religious responsibilities. At the ceremony itself, the family priest invests the boy with a sacred thread to be worn always over the left shoulder, and the parents instruct him in pronouncing the Gayatri Mantra. The initiation ceremony is seen as a new birth; those groups entitled to wear the sacred thread are called the twice-born.

In the ancient categorization of society associated with the Vedas, only the three highest groups - Brahman, warrior (Kshatriya), and commoner or merchant (Vaishya) - were allowed to wear the thread, to make them distinct from the fourth group of servants (Shudra). Many individuals and groups who are only hazily associated with the old "twice-born" elites perform the upanayana ceremony and claim the higher status it bestows. For young Hindu women in South India, a different ritual and celebration occurs at the first menses. The next important transition in life is marriage. For most people in India, the betrothal of the young couple and the exact date and time of the wedding are matters decided by the parents in consultation with astrologers.

At Hindu weddings, the bride and bridegroom represent the god and the goddess, although there is a parallel tradition that sees the groom as a prince coming to wed his princess. The groom, decked in all his finery, often travels to the wedding site on a caparisoned white horse or in an open limousine, accompanied by a procession of relatives, musicians, and bearers of ornate electrified lamps. The actual ceremonies in many cases become extremely elaborate, but orthodox Hindu marriages typically have at their center the recitation of mantras by priests. In a crucial rite, the new couple takes seven steps northward from a sacred household fire, turn, and makes offerings into the flames.

Independent traditions in regional languages and among different caste groups support wide variations in ritual. After the death of a family member, the relatives become involved in ceremonies for preparation of the body and a procession to the burning or burial ground. For most Hindus, cremation is the ideal method for dealing with the dead, although many groups practice burial instead; infants are buried rather than cremated. At the funeral site, in the presence of the male mourners, the closest relative of the deceased (usually the eldest son) takes charge of the final rite and, if it is cremation, lights the funeral pyre. After a cremation, ashes and fragments of bone are collected and eventually immersed in a holy river. After a funeral, everyone undergoes a purifying bath. The immediate family remains in a state of intense pollution for a set number of days (sometimes ten, eleven, or thirteen).

At the end of that period, close family members meet for a ceremonial meal and often give gifts to the poor or to charities. A particular feature of the Hindu ritual is the preparation of rice balls (pinda) offered to the spirit of the dead person during memorial services. In part these ceremonies are seen as contributing to the merit of the deceased, but they also pacify the soul so that it will not linger in this world as a ghost but will pass through the realm of Yama, the god of death. Hindus recognize multiple sources of power in the world about them, sacred forces in rivers and rocks, in village temples and on hilltop shrines, even in holy women and men. It has been noted that time, like physical space, also reveals an abundance of spiritual meanings and events.

There is the time of nature, a cosmic time of seasons and universal changes, measured by celestial bodies and monsoon winds, and evident in the alternations of light and darkness, warmth and cold, rain and drought, growth and decay. But there is also the time of an individual in the hoped-for span of a hundred years between birth and death. Like cosmic time, carefully segmented into memories of important events of the seasons and the deities, so too personal time is ritually marked. The marks are called *samskaras,* rites of passage and transformation. Some ritual manuals consider as many as forty *samskaras* to be worthy of performance, but a more traditional set of ten to eighteen is characteristic.

A *samskara* is literally an accomplishment, perfection, or refinement, and therefore the ritual advancement of a lifebody from its moment of conception to the moment just beyond its bodily death. Since many of the symbols are agricultural, the metaphor of ripening is often employed: A single cycle of life proceeds from seed planting to harvest sacrifice and beyond to rebirth in the succeeding cycle. Therefore food and its transformation, both material- in processes within the body- and spiritual- in ritual exchanges- remain dominant expressions. Every culture, every religion pays ritual attention to the life cycle. Not all of them, however, place as great an emphasis as Hinduism does upon the substantive transformations that occur in such procedures. There are several significant features of Hinduism to keep in view during a survey of the *samskaras.*

First, because of unquestioned acceptance of the concept of transmigration, the personal journey from conception to cremation or burial is not a singular one. Rather, each life is one of a great number of rebirths for that self until the achievement of its final state of liberation from the birth-and-death cycle. Second, this personal journey of a lifebody is not a lonely one. It begins, obviously, as an extension of an existing parental family with all of its remembered forebears. It ends, ideally, with a living son, one further extension of the lineage, acting as performer of the last rites, the final sacrifice of the used-up body. If our own cultural image of a family tree is a great spreading oak or chestnut with many branches, the Hindu image is a slender bamboo, tall and undeviating, with regularly spaced joints (*vamsa,* "lineage") to represent an unbroken descent from father to son.

The masculine character of this lineage is one of the central features of Hindu ritual and kinship: Every attention is given to producing a son to keep the lineage and its ritual structure intact. A daughter is only a temporary member of the family, since she will be assumed into her husband's lineage, first during the marriage ceremony itself, and then, after her life in *his* village or town, again at death when she may join the company of his ancestors. From the point of view of the personal journey of each lifebody, however, it is important to remember this wider community that is involved in every ritual. It is composed not only of all the visible relatives, but the invisible ones as well.

The participant presence of the deceased, both male and female, is never forgotten, and offerings of food with accompanying *mantras* are invariably shared with them, as with the living. Third, there is in the series of *samskaras,* to borrow a current media expression, an apparent front-loading. The majority of the rites occur before the age of six months and, in fact, several are accomplished before the severance of the umbilical cord. Since a dominant concern of thesamskaras throughout a lifetime is refinement, that is to say, the elimination of impurities, attention is drawn once more to the previous career of this self, including its dangerous passage from body to body. What follows is the orderly sequence of samskaras, the ritual passage from conception through childhood, initiation, marriage, death, and beyond.

FROM CONCEPTION THROUGH CHILDHOOD

Vedic manuals for domestic rituals begin the life cycle with marriage procedures. It is on the fourth night of the wedding ceremony that consummation should occur, and sexual union is actually the rite of impregnation. According to the *mantra* of a famous wedding hymn in the *Atharvaveda,* the bride is earth and the groom is heaven. This notion of woman as crop field and man as provider of seed remains throughout Hindu myth and experience. Furthermore, the embryo that grows in the bride as a consequence of the marriage rite is itself a new being composed partly of the father's semen- the source of bones, teeth, bodily channels, and semen- and partly of the mother's uterine blood- the source of blood, flesh, and internal organs. If the father's contributing substance predominates, the new being will be male; if the mother's is stronger, then female.

The next *samskara,* however, performed in the third month of a woman's first pregnancy, is the "generation of a male." This indicates that ritual action may still determine the sex of the fetus. Beans, barley, berries, or banyan tree shoots may all play a part in the ritual. In the fourth or a later month is the ritual "parting of the hair" in which the father-to-be parts his wife's hair three times upward, from front to back, using for a "comb" a porcupine quill, tufts of sacred grass, or a full spindle. Ripening fruits are also employed in this ceremony that, like the others, takes place at the hearth fire of the home and involves special *mantras*.

In some parts of India the mother-to-be looks at cooked rice, envisioning the child yet to be born.The ritual of birth itself is performed immediately upon delivery, before the umbilical cord is severed. The first part of this *samskar*a concentrates on the "production of wisdom" in the newborn; the father touches the baby's lips with a gold spoon or ring dipped in honey, curds, and clarified butter. The name of the goddess of sacred speech, Vach, is whispered three times into the infant's right ear. The second part of the rite includes *mantras*, for "long life." After the cutting of the cord the infant may be given a secret name, known only to the mother and father, before being placed at the mother's breast.

In the Vedic period several mysterious feminine powers were in attendance during birth, functioning as midwives of the child's destiny as well as its physical arrival into the world. Worship of the goddess Shasthi ("Sixth") on the sixth day of life is a contemporary survival of such ancient feminine guardian figures. Ten or twelve days after the delivery (or in some areas, one year later), the baby undergoes the name-giving *samskara* and receives an everyday name, often that of an astrologically appropriate deity, by which she or he will be known. This name serves as a "cover" or distraction from the real one, still a secret from the evil eye or other dangerous elements.

Amulets, black threads around the wrist, lampblack marks on the body, and other devices may also guard the child from now until puberty or later. Some time in the fourth month the newest addition to the family may be taken out of the house for the first time. That event, witnessing the sun and the moon, is a *samskara*, as is the moment of first feeding with solid food (cooked rice), usually in the sixth month. A month or so later is the ear-piercing ceremony, the earlobes being ringed with wire, the right ear first for boys, the left one first for girls.

Ritual shaving of the head and direct removal of impurities held by the hair is an important procedure throughout life in Hinduism and is often connected with special pilgrimages and vows as well as standard rites of passage. Thus the first such tonsure is the forerunner of a continuing voluntary ritual. When the hair is shaved away a small lock is left at the back of the bare skull, a twist of hair as a visible reminder of this consecration. Incidentally, the first tonsure rite is the only *samskara* that may be performed in a temple, often an ancestral goddess temple, as well as in the home. A secondary tonsure for males in their sixteenth year is sometimes considered a *samskara,* this one including the first shaving of facial hair as well as the scalp.

EDUCATION, MARRIAGE, AND ADULTHOOD

The most powerful of *samskaras* between birth and marriage is certainly the initiatory thread-ceremony known as the *upanayana,* the ritual "leading near" of a student to his guru for religious instruction. Nowadays only the most exacting Brahman families request such a performance for a son; more frequently an abbreviated version serves as a preliminary to the marriage vows. Through the Vedic era and on into classical Hinduism the *upanayana* was the indispensable second birth for all twice-born classes, that is, the Brahmans, Kshatriyas, and Vaishyas, who received their threads at the ages of eight, eleven, and twelve, respectively. Being "born again," bound for a lifetime by a sacred thread worn over the left shoulder, was a transition of great community as well as personal significance.

An initiate was not merely introduced to the Vedic tradition, both textual and sacrificial, when he heard from his guru the first *mantra* (the *gayatri,* which is *Rigveda* 3.62.10) and learned from him the procedures for offering into the sacrificial fire (the standard *homa*). At that moment he became a link in the ageless transmission of knowledge and assumed his part of human responsibility for maintaining cosmic truth and order. No small step was that. The elaborate ritual itself opened the door to the first stage of life, that of the student "living according to *brahman*," the *brahmacarin*, receptive to his guru and all that this spiritual father would turn over to him in this lengthy birthing process.

The *Atharvaveda* speaks with awe of the Vedic student more powerful than a thousand suns. Still today a few Brahman boys from special families follow the ancient tradition, living in the home of the guru for a period of years, learning daily the Vedic texts, orally, one line at a time, reciting the line back until the entire Veda, or significant parts of several *Vedas*, are committed to memory. Another *samskara* marked the other end of the *brahmacarin's* career, the "return" to the parental home after a ritual bath signifying graduation. The second stage of life of the married householder became the focus of ritual attention. The ancient student received his entire education during the years with his teacher; nowadays, of course, a Brahman boy will normally be in public schools like everyone else.

Today the tradition has been trimmed down to a symbolic studenthood of the religious life: the investiture with the thread, whispering of the *gayatri mantra*, instructions in domestic sacrifice, and the ritual bath and "return" all occur on the same day in the boy's own home, usually on the day before his departure for the marriage ceremony that takes place in the village or town of the bride. The marriage arrangements, for all castes, are the responsibilities of parents, and preparations may take a great many months. The ceremony proper, a *samskara* transforming both bride and groom, occurs at night in the house of the bride's father. It is embedded in a wide range of other rituals and local practices that may go on for several days and usually have all the traits of a community festival.

One preliminary ritual of significance, done in the privacy of the respective bride's and groom's homes well in advance, is the anointing of their bodies with an oil of turmeric, the yellow root known for its powers of fertility. Already in the ancient period there were many variations of procedures and levels of symbolism in this union of two individuals, two cosmic principles, male and female. Modern India has even greater diversity in this universally observed *samskara,* but a number of features have carried over from the Vedic manuals and may be recognized in most parts of India and the wider Hindu world today.

These include construction of a ritual booth of auspicious banana and mango leaves, tying of a thread around the wrist of the bride, first gazing of the couple at one another after the removal of a separating cloth, placing the bride's foot three times on the family grinding stone as a vow of fidelity, the important seven steps northward from or around the ritual fire, and an initial offering into the hearth of the new home. The *homa* that the boy learned in his initiation is now performed with the bride as the pair assumes the role of householders in the community.

Together they observe the pole star, Dhruva, and the nearby star, Arundhati (wife of the sage Vasistha), who is, like Dhruva, a model of loyalty and steadfastness. Usually there is a ritual marking of the part in the bride's hair with a stroke of vermillion, a signal to all of her marital status but also the symbol and promise of her powerful new role as mother-to-be.

DEATH AND BEYOND

The last *samskara* in the journey of a lifebody is the ritual disposal of the material body after death, either by cremation or by burial. This is a "final offering," as the *samskara* is named. Cremation and burial are both known from the time of the *Rigveda,* and both are widely practiced in Hinduism today (although the tendency for higher caste groups is to burn, for lower caste groups in South India to bury their dead). Funerary rites highlight once again Hinduism's claim that death is a continuing experience in the long course toward liberation, while the self in process remains indestructible. This *samskara* declares the same ends as all the previous ones. It celebrates the completion of a stage of life, in this case, the end of the lifebody. It refines, by eliminating impurities and rendering the entire material body to ashes or earth.

And it promotes, by liberating the subtle body for another birth in the long course. Again, this set of rituals, like the preceding ones, is subject to wide variation, but the traditional ritual sequence includes preparation of the body in or just outside the home; a procession to the burning-ground or cemetery, both usually found together at a river bank in or just outside the village or town; a ritual lighting of the pyre or placing of the body in the grave; circumambulation of the pyre or grave by the chief mourner, usually the eldest living son, who is the "offerer" of his father's body; the breaking of a large ceramic pot of water over the fire or grave; ritual bathing by the mourners along with shaving and tonsure of the men; the symbolic or actual gifting of a cow. If cremation is the means of disposal, a bone-gathering ceremony follows; later these fragments are dispersed in a sacred river.

More or less elaborate preparations, depending upon the ritual and financial status of the mourners, are immediately begun to promote the deceased on to a new journey. No longer technically samskaras, these shraddhas, as they are called, constitute a whole ritual enterprise in itself and an important dimension of Hindu life and thought. To summarize and reflect upon what can be learned from this review of a life cycle according to Hinduism, a number of insights into the tradition as a whole become available. For example, there are correspondences between cosmic time and personal time, as well as an apparent symmetry of generation and regeneration. The seed of a lifebody is ritually placed in the field-womb, where it germinates after ten lunar months ("days"). After death the used-up body is ritually devoured by the funeral fire or the earth and a new temporary body is ritually begun, one that also germinates after ten days, then functions to carry the self to the company of ancestors.

The clustering of essential rituals at the points of birth and death-rebirth is best understood in this light. Throughout these rituals there are strong continuities with the oldest layers of Hinduism. It is perhaps in the *samskaras* and ancestor rites that India best remembers its ancient Vedic heritage. Basic *samskaras* have endured through centuries of change in doctrine and practice.

They proved to be an all-Indian template, a unifying pattern that countered the regional diversities and popular innovations that inevitably sprang up across the subcontinent. Of course not every householder today performs the entire set of *samskaras*, but everyone knows the system, participates in the most essential ones, and attempts, even if the scale is abbreviated or several rites are telescoped into a single performance, to accomplish as many as possible on the oldest surviving male child.

Here, too, we learn of the ritual need for continuing lineage, a link in the living present to connect the ancestors to those not yet born, a link who must by long tradition be male provider of seed. And as noted more than once, in these rituals there is an underlying spiritual basis for Hindu physiology. Above all, a lifebody does not begin, nor does it remain, whole, pure, or safe. It requires ritual prescriptions in a lifelong process of ripening and refinement.

This process is accomplished within the context of the family and its sacred hearth. Household deities may be invoked or mentioned, but no one of them is credited with these mysterious transformations. The male head of the household or an invited Brahman priest is the outward visible performer, but it is the ritual "work" itself that succeeds in refining, shaping, perfecting the ongoing lifebody and advancing it on yet another step on the path toward ultimate liberation.

Hindu Marriages are performed according to Vedic rites described in the Sam Veda and the Yadur Veda. This page is being developed to assist in planning Hindu Marriages. In general Vedic marriage requires the wedding to be conducted in front of a fire (Agni). Agni is considered the main Priest in

Vedic rites as the first sloka of the Rig Veda is dedicated to Agni: Agneya mile Purohitam or Agni is the Priest. Couples go around the fire seven times together to confirm their vows and by putting something in the fire such as Khai or pop corn to ignite the flames. When a couple marries according to Vedic rights and with mutual consent, it is called Prajapati Vivah.

This is the most complete wedding ceremony with all the frills and it requires the consent of parents or guardians because the protection of the bride or daughter is handed over by the father to the bridegroom during the Panigrahan ceremony or the acceptance of the bride's hands. The actual weddding ceremony takes place after Panigrahan. However when a man and a woman marry with each others consent but may not have the consent of their family or are unable to involve them due to geographical reasons, then this wedding is called Gandharva Vivah. Here we describe the procedures for Prajapati Vivah only.

The role of dharma and culture in our life is the same as the role of the foundation in a building. The higher the building the deeper must be the foundation. But instead of building higher and higher buildings of bricks and mortar which block the Sun and hinder the path of migrating birds, we should try and build a higher level of spirituality and life style by developing a deeper understanding of our dharma and our culture.

As a first step we are starting a page called Swayamvar for people to meet who are interested in the Hindu pratha and wish to continue in that tradition by finding appropriate life partners of similar interst. After that we describe the wedding ceremony of Ram and Sita from the *Ramcharitmanas.*

Other auspicous times are Godhuli (the time of the cow dust when Krishna came back with the cows) or at dusk. For the correct time for all days consult the table. Basically one should take care to see that the main ceremony when marriage vows are taken is completed within the selected lagna. Generally the tithi of Purnima or the day there is a full moon is considered auspicous for all activities.

WEDDING CEREMONY

The Ramcharitmanas written by Tulsidas describes the wedding of Rama and Sita after their Swayamvar which was conducted according to the local rites of Janakapur which is now in Bihar but was part of ancient Mithila. After Sita had made her selection, Raja Janak invited King Dasratha to come to the wedding festivals. King Dasratha went to Janakpur with his two other sons and a lot of people, horses and elephants etc. They were put up in a guest house arranged by Raja Janak. Customarily the bridegroom's mother did not attend his wedding and there is not mention of the three Queens of Dasratha in this journey.

A barat or a wedding party is organized which travels with great fan fare to the home of the bride. There the bride's mother and her friends receive the Bridegroom by performing an Arati or showing lamps to his face. After this the first ceremony is Ashirvad which is the blessing of the bridegroom as well as the bride in separate rooms by well wishers and elders. The next ceremony is Panigrahan or Kanya dan when the bride and bridegroom sit with their hands tied together and the bridegroom receives the bride from the bride's father as the priest recites wedding mantras. In the case of Ram and Sita's wedding the ceremony included the wedding of all four brothers Ram, Lakshman, Bharat and Shatrughana to the daughters of the King of Janakpur. But in normal wedding this is done as make believe and the bridegroom is accompanied by a boy similarly and the bride is also accompanied similarly with a small girl dressed like the bride. They are called secondary bridegroom and secondary bride respectively.

After this the ceremony of Sindur dan and phera are conducted. As the priest recites the wedding vows the bridegroom applies vermilion to the forehead of the bride. After this they perform their turns of seven times clockwise around a fire and throw some fluffed corn into the fire together as witness of their wedding. The bride and bridegroom spend the night with the friends of the bride together and a lot of stories are told or songs are sung. This part of the ceremony may take place the same night or next day when the bridegroom tries to take home the bride. At this stage the bride's friends make fun of the bridegroom and his background telling ribald jokes. The bridegroom and his party make replies. After this the bride takes leave of her childhood friends and relatives as she plans to move to her husband's home.

This is a sad occasion and the Ram Charit Manas describes how Sita says goodbye to her mother's pet Parrot who calls her name every morning saying: Where is Sita, Where is Sita. (Note: This phrase will be repeated by Ramchandra when Sita is abducted by Ravana from the forest.) After this the husband and wife go back to their home with all the nice gifts that were given to the bride. Ramchandra's mother receives Sita at home and a few other ceremonies are held there. One of the ceremonies involves the sharing of food between the bride and bridegroom when they feed each other which signify taking care of each other. Finally a great feast is held at the husband's home to culminate the wedding. On this night the bride and bridegroom retire for their first night alone together and it is called Suhagrat. In Bengal it is called Phulsajja or the bed of flowers. In all cases the bed is decorated with flower where the bride and bridegroom go to sleep alone. There are some other ceremonies after this sometimes of going to a temple and performing Puja.

The term "Hindu" in post-independence Hindu law governing marriage, divorce, adoption, maintenance, guardianship and succession, describes not only persons who are Hindu by religion, but also those who are Sikh, Buddhist, and Jain. Roughly speaking, the term "Hindu" encompasses those Indians who are not Christian, Parsi, Muslim, or Jewish for the purposes of the law. What is a proper or valid Hindu marriage? Since in India various communities have different customs and ceremonies, the law says that a marriage can be performed or "solemnised" according to the customary rituals and ceremonies of the community to which either the bride or the groom belongs. It is very important to understand that the rituals and ceremonies carried out must be recognised and accepted by the community concerned as being the proper ones for formalising a marriage. For example, the law makes it very clear that in a Hindu marriage, where the ceremony includes the saptpadi, the ritual of circling the sacred fire seven times, the ceremony becomes complete and the marriage binding when the seventh round is completed.

Hindus can opt for a civil marriage, often incorrectly referred to as a "court marriage," under the Special Marriage Act, 1954. Provisions in the Act govern civil marriages and require no religious ritual or ceremony of any kind. The necessary requirement is that the persons intending to marry inform the marriage officer of the district in which at least one of them lives. The marriage officer then posts the information on a public notice board and keeps it up for 30 days. During those 30 days, any person can object to the marriage on grounds such as the intended bride is under age or that she is too closely related to the bridegroom or that she has been married before. If no valid objections are received, the couple signs a declaration in the marriage office in the presence of three witnesses. The marriage officer then issues a certificate of marriage to the couple as proof of the marriage. The Special Marriage Act, in S.21-A clearly states that if a special or civil marriage takes place between two persons both of whom are Hindus, Buddhist, Sikh or Jain, such persons continue to be governed by other aspects of Hindu personal law, such as the law relating to succession.

Neither bride nor groom should already be married or have a living husband or wife. A divorced person, a widow or widower is free to remarry; Both should have reached the minimum age for marriage: 18 years in case of the bride and 21 in case of the groom; Apart from being able to give their voluntary consent to the marriage, both must also be free of any mental disorder which could make them unfit for marriage; The bride and groom should not be within the "prohibited degrees of relationship" nor should they be "sapindas" of each other (these expressions are explained in detail in s.3 (f) and 3(g) of the Hindu Marriage Act). This rule does not apply if it can be established that a custom or usage is applicable to each permitting marriage between the two. Significantly, the rule does apply when the relationship is based on adoption.

In three situations such a marriage is said to be void, which means that it is invalid, as if it never took place: If one of the parties to the marriage has a living husband or wife; or If the parties are within the prohibited degrees of relationship; or If they are sapindas of each other. If the conditions regarding valid consent have not been fulfilled, the resulting marriage is void. That means that the party wishing to challenge it can approach the court for a decree of nullity. Once such a decree is passed, the marriage would have no legal force whatsoever. For example, if after the solemnization of the marriage it is found that the groom could not have given his valid consent because of the unsoundness of his mind, the woman can get the marriage nullified through the court. Naturally, the court must be satisfied with the proof of mental disorder and unsoundness of mind claim. If voidable marriages are not challenged in court, they remain valid for all legal purposes.

A woman whose marriage was performed when she was under 15 years of age can reject the marriage, or "repudiate" it and get a divorce on that ground alone. She can only take the step after turning 15, but before turning 18. However, by doing so she loses the right to maintenance or alimony which a divorced woman can claim legally. Such marriages are voidable. If the consent of the complaining party has been obtained by force or by fraud relating to the nature of the ceremony performed or to any significant fact or circumstance concerning the opposing party, the marriage can be voided. However, a petition for annulment in such a case must be presented within one year after the force ceased to operate or the fraud has been discovered. Most important of all, the petitioner or complaining party should not have lived willingly with the other after the end of the force or after discovering the fraud. A marriage is also voidable if it can be proven that the wife was pregnant at the time of marriage by another man. In this situation the husband must file his petition within one year of the date of the marriage.

A woman can seek the help of the police to help her stop her marriage if she is being forced to marry against her will. However, given the level of mistrust that prevails in our society vis-à-vis the police, such an intervention can boomerang on the woman and may lead to more trouble. In such situations, social pressure applied judiciously might work better on her parents as opposed to legal interventions. A young woman being forced to marry against her will by her parents should first try to identify and approach influential people within her own community or extended family who have the moral clout to influence her parent's decision. Alternatively, sympathetic teachers or respected social workers in the area could also be approached for help. However, these social interventions are outside the realm of legal rights and in extreme cases where social pressure does not work, police help may be sought.

The registration of Hindu marriages is not compulsory. However, registration of one's marriage provides proof of it for legal purposes and therefore we highly recommend it for women as a safety measure. A Hindu marriage register is found in the Office of the Registrar of Marriages, usually located in District or Divisional court compounds. The Registrar is normally some type of magistrate. A Hindu marriage can also be registered under the Special Marriage Act, 1954 if both parties so desire. If that is done, the marriage is treated as a civil marriage governed by that Act from the date of registration.

Marrying again during the lifetime of one's wife or husband is known as bigamy. It is a criminal offence, punishable with imprisonment and fine. A bigamous marriage is void, a complete nullity. If a woman has prima facie evidence that she is lawfully married to a man who is about to or has remarried, she can register a criminal complaint and the police are expected to stop him from getting remarried. If a wife learns that her husband is going to marry again she can get an injunction from the court forbidding the marriage before it occurs. After it has taken place, a wife can ask the court for a "declaration" that the second or bigamous marriage is null and void. Proving bigamy, however, is not easy. The complainant wife has to prove that both the marriages, her own as well as the second bigamous one, have been performed properly according to the appropriate ceremonies. Most prosecutions for bigamy fail because the complainant does not have the proof of the bigamous marriage. The accused husband can usually successfully claim against all efforts to prove the contrary that essential parts of the ceremony were never carried out and escape punishment.

If the couple wishes to have a religious marriage governed by Hindu law, then the non-Hindu partner must convert to Hinduism. If the non-Hindu partner is a Christian then it is also possible for the couple to marry according to Christian rites under the Indian Christian Marriage Act, 1872. Christian Personal Law then governs the marriage. The third option, in some ways the simplest, is to have a civil marriage under the Special Marriage Act which facilitates marriages between any two people, including members of any two religious communities. It does not involve conversion and also permits people to avoid various complications that arise from marriages under various religion-based personal laws. Such a child is considered legitimate regardless of the status of the parent's marriage, if the marriage was performed according to Hindu rites under the Hindu Marriage Act, 1955 or was a civil marriage under the Special Marriage Act, 1954. Such a child may inherit the property of his parents. However, he/she does not acquire rights in relation to joint family or ancestral property.

Vivaha refers to marriage within the Hindu tradition. Because of the great importance attached to married couples and their roles within society, vivaha is considered the most important samskara (life cycle rite) undertaken by individuals. Marriage and the ensuing ghrastha (householder) stage are deemed crucial within Hindu society for a variety of reasons. During their marriage the couple is expected to cultivate three of the four goals of life. The first goal is dharma (duty), and is achieved through their joint performance of sacrificial offerings to the gods. The art of love, pleasure, and fulfillment of sexual desire is known as *Kama* and facilitates procreation. This enables the couple to repay their debt to the ancestors.

Finally, as householders they participate in the greater social order by pursuing artha (the pursuit of wealth and material possessions).

Importance & Symbolism of Marriage: In many ways, marriage symbolizes the beginning of social life for both women and men. For women, it also enables their participation in religious matters. The vivaha samskara is akin to the upanayana (sacred thread) ceremony undergone by males during the sisya (student) stage. Thus, after marriage, a woman may fulfill her religious duties.

The importance of marriage for women is paralleled in Hindu literature. Unmarried goddesses are often portrayed as dangerous and uncontrollable (as in the case of Mariyamman - the fever goddess), reinforcing beliefs surrounding the inauspiciousness of unmarried, divorced, or widowed women. Comparatively, in the epic, Ramayana, the hero Rama and his wife Sita represent an idealization of marriage that is upheld for Hindu couples to aspire to.

Marriage is of near equal importance for men. Within the social realm, vivaha is especially important for males of lower class varnas. It may be one of the few samskaras performed for lower class males or combined with several other life cycle rites to reduce the associated costs. With few exceptions, males cannot perform sacrificial offerings without a wife and marriage is seen as necessary to live in accordance with dharma. This importance is likewise symbolized within Hindu religious mythology and unmarried gods may be depicted as powerless. For example, in one of the representations, the god Siva is a corpse until his marriage to Sakti animates him. Hence, vivaha serves both religious and societal functions within Hinduism that are mirrored within the religious literature itself.

Betrothal: In India, arranged marriages are still the norm. Within the upper varnas (classes), it is traditionally the bride's family who initiates the search for an appropriate partner. Interclass marriage (unions between different varnas) is generally not tolerated. However, hypergamy, or marrying up for women within one's own *varna* is usually the goal of the bride's family. The Hindu Marriage Act of 1955 made dowry (payment to the groom's family by the bride's family) illegal in India. Nevertheless, expensive gifts or other financial arrangements are still made. Polygamy and caste restrictions in India were also abolished by the Hindu Marriage Act, along with child marriages and restrictions on divorce for a more detailed discussion of the Hindu Marriage Act].

Despite these legal amendments, many of these traditions are still observed in rural areas. Parental consent to marriage is important within Hindu society as marriage links not only individuals, but lineages as well. There are eight types of marriages recognized within the influential Dharma Sastras: brahma, daiva, arsa, prajapatya, asura, gandharva, raksasa, and paisaca. The first four are arranged with the approval of the bride's family and are considered the most desirable. To illustrate, the marriage category of brahma is an arrangement where a father gives his daughter to a man who has studied the sacred literature.

Typically, this type of marriage is the most highly regarded and would be preferable for individuals within the brahmana (priestly) class. Within the remaining four types where consent is not always issued, raksasa refers to the abduction of a bride against her will and is considered suitable for ksatriyas (warrior classes), whereas gandharva describes a love match between the bride and groom and is generally thought to be inauspicious. Auspiciousness is of great concern in Hindu society and marriages are no exception. Before a marriage can be arranged, the families involved must consult the astrological charts of both the bride and groom to determine the auspiciousness of the match, as well as to determine the best time for the ceremony to take place. Great care is taken in determining auspiciousness and a union considered inauspicious is abandoned. Once a suitable partner and time is found, preparations can be made for the ceremony itself. Ceremony & Associated Rituals: Weddings are lavish affairs, meant to display the families' social status within the community. The rituals associated with vivaha may carry on as long as twelve days, however, the wedding ceremony alone generally lasts only a few hours and traditionally should be performed at night. A great canopy is set up where the rituals and ceremony will take place and the canopy is elaborately decorated with lights and other ornaments. Weddings are considered a time of great ritual purity. Persons deemed inauspicious or polluted (such as widows) are forbidden to attend.

During this time the bride and groom are treated as if they were deities and are thought to be living embodiments of gods and goddesses. Their status is elevated to such a point it is said the couple receives the right of way over individuals who normally carry a higher status than themselves.

The bride and groom are ritually bathed and anointed with oils. The bride will be dressed in her finest jewels and sari and will have her hands and feet colored with henna. A Brahmin priest is contracted to preside over the rituals. The actual wedding ceremony varies considerably from place to place; however, Sharma (1985) outlines six rites commonly observed.

The first is madhuparka in which the groom and his party arrive at the bride's house, traditionally on horseback. They are received by the bride's family and the groom is honored as a deity. The second element is that of kanyadana. This is where the father gives his daughter to the groom and the couple lights a fire in the sacrificial pit. During panigrahana, the groom takes the bride by the hand and presents her with a mangalasutra, or pendant, that is tied around her neck (73-5) following the ritual of panigrahana, the bride steps on the north stone by the sacrificial fire.

This is known as *asmarohana* and symbolizes the couple's strength against their enemies. During asmorahana, the bride throws three oblations of rice into the fire (*lajahoma*). The final rite during the wedding ceremony is considered the most important and is what legally seals the marriage. Referred to as saptapadi, the bride and groom circle the sacred fire seven times with corners of their garments tied together.

Also known as the seven steps, each step symbolizes a different aspect of the marriage such as friendship, wealth, and fertility. By taking the seventh and final step, the marriage is made official.

After completion of the ceremonies, there is typically a celebration held that includes dancing, singing, and feasting. Varagrhaprasthana marks the bride's departure from her family's home to her husband's, where she will remain during the course of her marriage under her in-laws care. Consummation of the marriage does not take place until 3 days after the marriage ceremony and is known as caturthikarma.

3

The Ritual Wife

Hindu wedding ceremonies are traditionally conducted at least partially in Sanskrit, the language in which most holy Hindu ceremonies are conducted. The local language of the people involved is also used since most Hindus cannot understand Sanskrit. They have many rituals that have evolved since traditional times and differ in many ways from the modern western wedding ceremony and also among the different regions, families, and castes such as Rajput weddings and Iyer weddings. The Hindus attach a lot of importance to marriages and the ceremonies are very colorful and extend for several days. In India, where most Hindus live, the laws relating to marriage differ by religion. By the Hindu Marriage Act of 1955 passed by the Union Parliament of India, for all legal purposes, all Hindus of any caste, creed or sect, Sikh, Buddhists and Jains are considered as Hindus for the sake of the Hindu marriage Act -and can hence intermarry. By the Special Marriage Act, 1954, a Hindu can marry a non-Hindu employing any ceremony provided certain legal conditions are fulfilled.

The pre-wedding ceremonies include engagement (involving vagdana or oral agreement and lagna-patra written declaration), and arrival of the groom's party at the bride's residence, often in the form of a formal procession. The post-wedding ceremonies involve welcoming the bride to her new home. Just as Hinduism is hard to grasp and contrast against the newer, book-defined, structured religions such as Christianity and Islam, India's prevalent wedding traditions are also hard to categorize purely on a religious basis. They have a closer similarity to ancient cultures such as Greek, Roman, Egyptian and Chinese. An important thing to note is that despite the fact that the modern Hinduism is largely based on the puja form of the worship of *devas* as enshrined in the Puranas, a Hindu wedding ceremony at its core is essentially a Vedic yajna (a fire-sacrifice), in which the Aryan deities are invoked in the Indo-Aryan style.

It has a deep origin in the ancient ceremony of cementing the bonds of friendship/alliance (even among people of the same sex or people of different species in mythological contexts), although today, it only survives in the context of weddings. The primary witness of a Hindu marriage is the fire-deity (or the Sacred Fire) *Agni*, and by law and tradition, no Hindu marriage is deemed complete unless in the presence of the Sacred Fire, seven encirclements have been made around it by the bride and the groom together.

Ancient system of Hindu-Vedic-marriages was fully scientific. It did not differentiate between male and female as is being done presently.

- The basis for a fulfilling and happy life

Te santu jard- istayah sampriyau royisnu sumansyamanau |

Pasyema sharadah shatam jivema sharadah shatam shrunuyam shardah shatam | |

"We should be able to live a graceful life that is full of mutual love and warmth. Our sentiments should be auspicious. We should be able to see for a hundred years, live a healthy life of a hundred years and listen the music of spring for a hundred years."

The sage of the above mentioned Vedic -aca has emphasized that the basis of happy and fulfilling married life is the sense of unity, intimacy and love between husband and wife. Therefore they should have sex, marriage is not for self-indulgence but it should be considered a life long social and spiritual responsibility. Married life is an opportunity for two persons to grow from life partners into soul mates.

THE MAIN RITUALS

All of the rituals vary based on family traditions. The names of the rituals also vary.

PRIOR TO MARRIAGE

Ceremony conducted at the homes of the parents of the bride and the groom.

Engagement

A decision made by the parents in front of the community members to have the marriage, sometimes using a document.

Barni Bandhwana

Approximately 15 days prior to the actual wedding, on an auspicious day, the pundit will perform a puja to Lord Ganesh (the remover of obstacles). During this puja, a piece of mauli (thread) is tied to the hands of the groom, and his parents. This puja is done to make a humble request to Lord Ganesh that the wedding happens without any problems, beside the occasional mishap e.g. tripping over. After that day, the family performs a puja to Lord Ganesh every day until after the wedding is complete.

Mamara

The mamaraTemplate: Mama-maternal uncle is an important ceremony, common to both the bride and the groom's families. This ceremony is performed by the maternal uncle of the groom/bride, who, along with his wife and family, arrives with much fanfare, and is received by the bride/groom's mother with the traditional welcome. The clothes that the uncle gives are then worn by the family during the wedding.

Sangeet Sandhya

The sangeet sandhya is an evening of musical entertainment. The bride's family puts on a show for the groom and bride included as part of this event is an introduction of all the family members for the bride.

Tilak Ceremony

Tilak is a mark of auspiciousness. It is put on the forehead using Kumkum, a red turmeric powder. The male members of the bride's family, like her father, brother, uncles place a tilak on the forehead of the groom. This is typically followed by giving some gifts to the groom and the groom's accompanying family members requesting them to take care of the bride later.

Another name for "Vivah" is "hath pila karna" or simply translated, making hands yellow. Mehendi (henna) is applied to the bride's hands and feet. In the right hand, a round spot is left open for Hathlewa.

DURING MARRIAGE FESTIVITIES

Barat Nikasi

The groom, leaves for the wedding venue riding a decorated horse or elephant. This is a very colorful and grand ceremony. The groom is dressed in a sherwani (long jacket) and 'churidars' (fitted trousers). On his head he wears a 'sehra' (turban) with a 'kalgi' (brooch) pinned onto it. The turban usually has flowers extending from it to keep the grooms face covered during the wedding ceremony. Before he departs, his relatives apply the ceremonial 'tilak' on his forehead and his sister feeds the horse or elephant sweetened grain. The 'barat' (consisting of the groom seated on the horse or elephant, and relatives and friends of the groom) is headed by the dancing of the congregated folks. Accompanied by the rhythm of the north Indian dholak, the barat reaches the place of the wedding. Upon arriving at the venue of the wedding, the groom is welcomed by a welcome song. This is called "talota". Then the groom knocks on the door with his sword and enters.

Var Mala / Jay Mala

The groom is led to a small stage where he is greeted and "showered" by the bride's family with flowers. The maternal uncle, brother or brides' best friends bring the bride to the stage. The bride and the groom are handed the garlands while the priest is chanting the religious hymns. Following this, the groom and bride exchange garlands, which are the *var mala* or *jay mala,* signifying their acceptance of each other as husband and wife. Then, the groom's mother-in-law measures the groom's chest, and pokes and prods him to make sure he is tough enough to defend her daughter. She then puts *kajal* on the groom to ward off evil spirits.

Arti

The 'baratis' (groom's party) are received by the bride's family and at the entrance to the wedding venue. The bride's mother welcomes the groom by performing the 'arti' (traditional Indian welcome ritual with a lamp or 'diya' placed on a platter or 'thali') to welcome her son-in-law and placing a tilak on his forehead.

Basi-Jawari

This event takes place the day of the wedding. The bride's sisters hide the groom's shoes and ask for money if he (groom) wants them back and are able to go home with the bride.

Kanya Dan

Kanya Dan which means gifting away a virgin has been derived from the Sanskrit words Kanya which mean a virgin and Dan which mean donation. Kanya Dan is a very significant ritual performed by the father of the bride in presence of a large gathering that is invited to witness the wedding. The father pours out libation of sacred water symbolizing the giving away of his virgin daughter to the bride groom, who is a form of god. The groom recites Vedic hymns to Kama, the god of love, for pure love and blessings.

As a condition for offering his daughter for marriage, the father of the bride requests a promise from the groom for assisting the bride in realizing the three ends:

- Dharma,
- Artha, and
- Kama.

The groom makes the promise by repeating three times that he will not fail the bride in realizing *dharma, artha* and *Kama*. This ritual is performed early on before Phere. Ideally, the parents of the bride place the right hand of the bride over the right hand of the groom and place their own left hands at the bottom and the right hands (the two of them) on top, securing the Conch with gold, betel nut, flowers and a little fruit (in it) placed in bride's hand. It is at this point that the purpose of the Kanyadan is clearly stated per scripture (kamo data..., etc) and the names of the parents and forefathers are stated from both sides. Wedding can not legally proceed without this Kanyadan step in which parents of the bride agree to the wedding.

This must be remembered that in Hindu Wedding, the bride and groom marry each other and the priest only assists with the Mantra. He can not declare them married as no authority is vested in him to do so. Agni, gods and the invited members of the family and friends are the witness. Also, Kanyadan must not be treated like a Godan in which the cow/calf is given away with the rope with no subsequent rights on the objects gifted away.

Kanyadan still leaves parents with certain rights on their daughter. It is in recognition of that residual right that the daughter can and does perform a partial shraddh on their demise just like the son does - only a more elaborate one. Feminism feels the Kanya Dan is a male dominated ritual which shows women like objects. But in fact, Kanya Dan ritual makes a husband to consider that his wife is the most precious gift given to him by the god. In Hindu Marriages, Woman who marries for the second time is not eligible for Kanya Dan ritual.

Panigrahana Hathlewa

After being led to the wedding mandup, the bride and groom have their hands tied together. The priest does a puja to Lord Ganesh and then puts a coin and mehendi on the bride's right hand where the round empty spot is (where no mehendi was put) and ties his hand with the brides. This puja is done schedule in advance based on an auspicious time and date.

Gathabandhan

In this ritual, priest tying a knot using the ends of the clothing worn by the bride and groom. The priest ties the end of the groom's dhoti or the kurta; whichever he is wearing, with that of the bride's saree, the knot signifying the sacred wedlock.

Laja Homa and circumambulation

The ritual connotes the actual core wedding ceremony, for the very meaning of the word "vivah" is-marriage. The groom and the bride then circle the holy fire seven times, making seven promises to be fulfilled in the married life, after which they are considered to be 'married' to each other. This ritual is called "phere". Traditionally, there were three pheras. But now this has been mixed with saptapadi and now seven pheras are done for each "vachan".

Saptapadi

The bridegroom gets up from his seat holding his bride's right hand. He then goes around the Holy Fire (Agni) from the right side, by lifting his bride's right foot at each step. This is done for seven steps. With each step, he recites a mantra addressed to the bride with the following meaning.

- To provide for food always.
- To give you excellent health and energy.
- Todained in Vedas, during your life time.
- To give you happiness in life.
- To make your cows and good animals to grow in strength and in numbers. (Animals such as horse can now be substituted with "Car")
- To make all the seasons be beneficial to you.
- To make the homams (sacrifices to be done in Holy Fire) to be performed by you in your life as ordained in Vedas, successful and free from hindrances.

The idea behind this is to pray to Lord Vishnu, the protector of life, for his blessings in marital life. The groom then recites a mantra to convey the following meaning:

After crossing seven steps with me thus, you should become my friend. I too have become your friend now. I will never discard this friendship and you should also not do that. Let us be together always. Let us resolve to do things in life in the same manner and tread the same path. Let us lead a life by liking and loving each other, having good hearts and thoughts, and enjoying the food and our strong points together. Let us have undivided opinions. We will perform the vrithas united. Let us have same and joint desires. I will be Sama (one of the vedas); you will be Rig (another Veda). Let me be the Heaven; you are the Earth. Let me be the Shukla (Moon) and you be its wearer. Let me be the mind and you its spokesman (Vak). With these qualities, you be my follower. You the sweet tongued, come to me to get good children and wealth.

Blessings

Blessings by the parents, acharya and elders for the new couple and it may be preceded by a talk on practicing their grahastha-dharma, coundut as a married couple.

Vidai

This is considered to be the most emotional ritual, when the bride leaves her parents' home and makes her way to her husband's. Family and friends, who also shower her with blessings and gifts, give her a tearful farewell. The male members of the bride's family bid farewell to the groom by applying the traditional 'tilak' (vermilion) on his forehead and shower him with gifts. In earlier times the bride use to leave in a palanquin. These days the couple leaves in a decorated car.

AT THEIR NEW HOME

Darshan

After Vidai, the couple first visits a temple, preferably that of Lord Rama and Sita, to seek their blessing from where they move towards Groom' house.

Dwar-Rokai

After leaving the groom's father-in-law's house, the couple comes home. They are stopped at the entrance of the house by either the groom's sister or his father's sister. There, in an earthen vessel, the sister/aunt uses a mixture of salt and water to ward off evil spirits from the groom. After this, the pot is thrown on the ground and destroyed. After this, the couple enters the house.

Griha Pravesh

When the bride arrives at her new home, her mother-in-law welcomes her with the traditional 'Arti'. At the entrance, she puts her right foot onto a tray of vermilion powder mixed in water or milk, symbolizing the arrival of good fortune and purity. With both her feet now covered in the red powder paste, she kicks over a vessel filled with rice and coins to denote the arrival of fertility and wealth in her marital home.

Mooh Dikhai

The family now indulges in a series of games and post-wedding rituals, amidst much laughter to make the new member feel comfortable. One such ritual is the Mooh dikhai. Literally translated, Mooh Dikhai means 'show your face', but this is a ritual, which helps to introduce the newly wed to members of her husband's family! Each member of the groom's family comes in turn to make an acquaintance with the new bride.

MODERN HINDU WEDDINGS

Modern Hindu weddings are often much shorter and do not involve all of the rituals of the traditional ceremony which sometimes went on for five days. Instead certain ceremonies are picked by the families of the bride and the groom depending on their family tradition, caste, jâti etc. Hence the ceremonies vary among the various ethnic groups that practice Hinduism. The wedding is normally conducted under a wedding mandap, a canopy traditionally with four pillars, and an important component of the ceremony is the sacred fire (Agni) that is witness to the ceremony. Sometimes, the bride comes to her husband's house in a doli which a palanquin is traditionally made of wood and decorated with jewels.

Before the wedding party departs to the Hindu temple, the priest will sometimes place a coconut under the tire. In the old days a horse-drawn carriage was used to carry the bride and groom, and the breaking of the coconut demonstrated the road-worthiness of the horse-drawn carriage. The joy and pride of marriage is obvious and that is the fundamental reasoning behind the united family where husband, wife and children live together in harmony. This marriage is the supporting pillar for the Indian nation's culture. In the Indian culture, life together for a man and woman as husband and wife begins only after the wedding. Marriage has been defined since the Vedic period and rigorously followed ever since.

Wedding function is considered as the biggest occasion in one's life. To make the occasion very memorable, the wedding is normally celebrated on a grand scale. For a man and woman, marriage is the stepping stone to start sharing their lives with each other. Therefore, marriage is an important milestone in one's life. Though marriage is the beginning of the life together for a man and woman, this is a sudden turning point in the life of the girl. In order to create much enthusiasm in the girl's mind, and to make the transition in her life easy, marriage is celebrated on a grand scale, like a festival.

Wedding function consists of a series of rituals. Instead of making the wedding function as a routine ritual performance, they have made it more colorful and enjoyable for both the bride and the groom. The function includes i) exchange of garlands, ii) pidi sutrudhal (throwing colorful rice balls after taking them around the couple three times - symbolic gesture to ward off any evil eye on the beautiful bride and the groom), iii) nalangu (a fun filled evening for the bride and the groom, in which both of them play with each other like kids, joking at each other etc). This is mainly to reduce the inhibition between the groom and the bride. This incidentally provides an opportunity for the audience, invitees to the wedding, to make fun of the groom and the bride.

Nalangu function is done in different fashion depending on the family and geographical tradition.

In the western countries, marriage is considered for satisfying sensuous pleasures (Chitrinbam). But in India, marriage is considered as the first step towards attaining Perinbam. [Perinbam -reaching the feet of The Lord or liberation from the worldly bondage- is the ultimate aim of every soul.] A happy marriage is a fresh start of life with all sorts of good things for the man and the woman. Vedas define wife as a good friend (Pathnihi (wife) sarvasya mithram). Vedas say that among the couple, there should be mutual trust, give and take attitude (adjusting to each other), and loyalty. These are the three essentials for a happy married life. A man's life is said to be divided into four asramas (stages). They are 1. Brahmacharyam, 2. Grahastham, 3. Vanaprastham and 4. Sanyasam

Gauthama Maharishi (the great sage Gauthama) says, "Yadha Nadhi Thadha Sarve Sagareyanthi Samsthitham hathraivasramanas Sarve Grahastham Yanthi Samsthitham"

This verse says that whichever direction the river or a tributary flows, it should finally end up in the ocean. Similarly, the people in various stages (asramas) of life depend on the grhasthan (a married man) for their sustenance. That is because a brahmachari and a sanyasi should eat only through alms offered by a grahasthan. They should not light a fire for cooking.

When you do yaga or yagna, you offer the havirbagam (offerings) in the fire for the devas. Even this havirbagam can be given only by the grahasthan. This means that even devas depend on the grahasthan for their havirbagam. Such is the merit of the married life. In ancient times, marriages were not arranged by the elders. A man and a woman fall in love, like in the modern society, they start living together in harmony, trust and loyalty. They vow to stay together for the rest of their lives.

It was just an agreement between the two of them and nobody else knows about it. As one can expect, in some unfortunate instances, the man leaves the woman after some time contrary to his promise. Since there were no witnesses for their sacred union, there is none to question or reprimand the culprit. This sort of behavior from men eventually increased the burden on the society. That is the start of celebration of the marriage on a grand scale in the presence of friends and relatives, who potentially become witnesses to the occasion. Poet Tholkappier says,

"Poyyum Vazhuvum Thonriyapin

Aiyer yaththanar Karanam Enba"

Just to stop the injustices mentioned above they started to perform the marriage functions publicly in the presence of a large gathering of friends and relatives. Rig Veda says that there are eight types of marriages. They are:

1. *Brahmam*: The parents chose the right spouse for their daughter and give away the daughter in a wedding function e.g., Sri Padmavathi Kalyanam.
2. *Prajapathyam*: Groom wants to marry to become a grahasthan for doing dharma e.g. Sri Rama marrying Sita.
3. *Arusham*: A man realizing that he cannot function by himself without a wife approaches the girl's father to give away the daughter to him. In the own crude way, the man offers two cows in exchange. (What a bartering system?)- Thank goodness! There was no women's lib then or probably that was the time when women's lib movement started!
4. *Daiveekam*: When yagna is done, kings offer their daughters as Dakshinai (fees for the conductor of the yagna for the services rendered) to the rishis who conduct the yagna e.g., Maharajah Romapada offered his daughter to sage Rishyasringar.
5. *Asuram*: Give a lot of money or other forms of wealth either to the girl or her parents and marry e.g., Maharajah Chandanu married a fisherman's daughter, Machagandhi; by promising to give his kingdom to her would be born son.
6. *Gandharvam*: A man and a woman falling in love out of

lust and then getting married e.g., King Dushyantha marrying Sakuntala.

7. *Rakshasam*: Abducting the girl and getting married e.g., Lord Krishna marrying Rukmani.
8. *Paisasam:* Getting married to a girl when she is sleeping or unaware of what is going on (like under the influence of drug or intoxication).

Though there are different marriages as mentioned above, the way the marriages are celebrated in modern days follows a procedure described in Rig Veda's tenth Mandalam and 85th Sooktham. This 85th Sooktham mentions how a man called Soman invited Aswini Devas when he married Suryai. Many manthras (chantings) in a marriage used at the present time are seen in Rig Veda. Therefore, the wedding of Soman and Suryai is the basis of all our wedding rituals. These rituals differ depending on the family and caste traditions. However, majority of the modern marriages follow most of the routines, as narrated here.

The main events of a modern day marriage in Tamil Nadu consists of

1. Jana Vasam (inviting the groom),
2. Kasi Yathrai (Pilgrimage to Varanasi/Banaras),
3. Exchanging garlands,
4. Swing (Oonjal),
5. Mangalya Dharanam (Key Event),
6. Panikgrahanam,
7. Homam or Havan,
8. Sapthapadhi,
9. Looking at stars Dhruva and Arundhadhi, and
10. Mangala Arathi.

Jana Vasam

This is celebrated on the evening of the day before the marriage. It is the formal reception of the groom to the bride's place. In Tamil the groom is called a Mappillai. The function is called Mappillai Azhaippu (inviting the groom). In Hindi, the place where the groom stays (during marriage) is called

Jan Vasa. Thus in due course the whole function is named Jana Vasam.

Kasi Yathrai

This is symbolic in that the groom from the brahmacharya asramam moves into grahasthasramam. Many things restricted to brahamcharis are allowed in grahasthasramam, like wearing footwear, use of an umbrella, using cosmetics (like eye liners, fragrances, etc.). So, during Kasi Yathrai, the groom is allowed to use all the things that are not allowed during brahmacharyam. Tsssssssshis is also called "Samavarthanam".

Exchanging Garlands (Malai Matral)

Normally, wearing the garland (lei) worn by some one else is not allowed. But, in a wedding, the man and the woman exchange their garlands - symbolic of that they have two bodies with one life from now on. The fragrance associated with the garlands symbolizes the inner fragrance of the groom and bride (vasanas) for which both have to adjust with each other. They exchange the garlands three times for emphasizing their symbolic gesture.

Oonjal (Swing)

The chains that support the swing, coming down from the ceiling, represent symbolically that this human body we have got is due to our Karma in previous births. Similarly, the swing's motion forward and backward tells the couple that they have to be strong together in life at times of both upward and downward movement in life.

Mangalya Dharanam

Mangalyam is called as Thali in Tamil. Thali is made of two syllables. The first syllable Tha and the second syllable Ni represent that than veru Nee Veru Alla (i.e., you and I are not separate. We are in this together). This Thani in colloquial usage became Thali. When the Thali is tied around the neck of the bride, they normally put three knots. The three knots symbolizes Brahma, Vishnu and Rudhra. Thali is of two types.

The first type has saw tooth at the bottom and the second one has a semi-spherical shape. The second one is called a "Pottu". They also call it as Tortoise Thali, since it has a shape of the back of a tortoise.

Panikgrahanam

Before the practice of Mangalya Dharanam, Panikgrahanam used to be the main event of the wedding. In this the groom and the bride hold their hands in public. By holding the hands in public, they indicate to the world that their hearts are set to live together in harmony.

Homam

A particular sect of people performs Agni Hothram and Oupasanam daily. Since these people do their daily ritual with the fire, homam (which is also done with the help of fire) also became part of the wedding rituals. They considered the fire (Agni) as one of the witnesses for the marriage. Generally, fire as the witness symbolizes the heat in our body. As long as that body fire (heat) is alive, we should not separate from each other and the body heat is the witness for our vow. This is the whole idea of the homam. Fire as a witness was adopted by Tamilians at a very latter date.

Sapthapadhi

Sapthapadhi means taking seven steps together. This is considered to be the most important in a wedding function. Some consider this as more important than Mangalya Dharanam. If one follows seven steps with another person, it is considered as a confirmation of their eternal friendship. [In olden times, when they give a send off to somebody undertaking a pilgrimage, they use to follow the vehicle (horse or bullock drawn) for seven feet.] Proclaiming to the world that the groom and the bride will keep up their friendship for life and also partake equally in both good and bad times in life is the whole idea behind Sapthapathi. The meaning of the manthras chanted during Sapthapadhi is summarized below.

1. Let the first step you take be with full of emotions.
2. Let the second step be with full of valor and strength.
3. Let the third step be for disciplined and controlled life.
4. Let the life together be a comfortable one.
5. Let the life be full of desirable wealth.
6. Let the seasons (nature) be good to you.
7. The seventh step symbolizes that the couple declare that they aspire for all the above for a happy, married life together

They further vow that if you are Rig Veda, let me be the Sama Veda. If you are Booloka (earth), let me be the heaven. If I am bright, you wear the rays from my brilliance. If I am the mind, you are the word. So, please come and join me. Let us give a very good progeny to this world. This declaration is the whole theme behind Sapthapadhi.

Looking at Dhruva and Arundhadhi Stars

In the middle of the Milky Way (Saptha Rishi Mandalam), Arundhadhi is a subtle star. At the bottom of the Milky Way, the brightest star called Dhruva is located. In English, it is called the Pole Star. The Pole Star remains stationary at the same place irrespective of the earth's movement. The saptha rishis representing the Milky Way are 1. Kasyapa 2. Athri 3. Bharadwaja 4. Viswamitra 5. Gauthama 6. Jamathagni and 7.Vasishta. The wives of saptha rishis are known as Krithika. The other six krithika consider Arundhadhi as the Pathivratha Sironmani.thus by seeing the Arundhadhi star, it is believed that the bride will be as chaste as Arundhadhi. So, the groom is supposed to show the Star to the bride.

Mangala Arthi

At the conclusion of the marriage function, they take Mangala Arthi for the wedded couple. In this they mix lime and turmeric powder in water and take it around the couple three times. This is supposed to ward off any evil cast on the couple. This concludes the brief description of marriage rituals according to Vedas under Brahmam system.

Tamil Nadu Weddings according to Manu Dharma Shasthra

1. Kasi Yathrai, 2. Kannikadhanam (giving away the bride), 3. Mangalya Dharanam, 4. Malai Matrudhal (exchanging garlands), 5. Sapthapadhi and 6. Poriyidal (offering of puffed rice in the homam) are all the part of our marriage function, according to Manu Dharma Shasthras) with certain changes in the Vedic manthras.

The function is normally conducted in a big Pandhal (an open air tent). For erecting this Pandhal, they install four bamboo poles at four corners of the Pandhal. Four Vedas are symbolized in these four bamboo poles. The main priest who conducts the whole proceedings of the marriage rituals and formalities symbolizes Brahma, the creator. The various stages/steps in a wedding in Tamil Nadu are given briefly in the following paragraphs.

- Sri Vigneswara Pooja - On any auspicious occasion, it is customary to pray Lord Ganesa (Vigneswara, Maha Ganapathi, Vinayaka are the other names by which Lord Ganesa is called) for a smooth and uninterrupted proceedings of the function.
- Punyahavachanam - Prayer to Lord Varuna to purify the water and other materials we use during the marriage celebration.
- Arasanikkal Nadal - Five elderly married ladies offer prayer to a branch of the Arasu (Holy Fig tree) tree, and tie sacred raksha (protection from all evils) to the bride and the groom. The groom and the bride are also given new clothes to wear.
- Kasi Yathrai - As described earlier. Some people prefer to pray Lord Vinayaka instead of Kasi Yathrai.
- Mana Pongal - Offering Pongal (rice pudding) in five plantain (banana) leaves - In South India it is customary to eat on a banana leaf. In modern days, these leaves are substituted by the dinner plates.
- Pooja to Sacred Waters - Five beautifully designed earthen ware pots are filled with water. The water in these pots

are symbolic of the waters from the holy rivers in India. Prayer is offered to these waters.

- Upaveetha Dharanam (wearing the sacred thread)- The groom and the father of the bride are inducted into wearing the sacred thread. Any one who is doing an auspicious thing must wear the sacred thread first, irrespective of the caste. Then only they are entitled to partake in the rituals. Some follow the tradition of wearing a raksha (kappu) after the upaveetha dharanam.
- Kannikadhanam (Giving away the bride) - The person giving the bride away introduces the bride with a brief introduction of her genealogy (of three generations). Similarly, the person accepting the bride introduces the groom with his side of genealogy (of three generations). Then the father or the person giving the bride away hands over the bride (with three drops of water) to the groom. The water drops are symbolic of the transfer of total responsibility of the bride to the groom.
- Pada Pooja - The groom does prayer at the feet of his parents (pranams) to get their blessings for a happy and prosperous married life.
- Kappu Kattudhal (Raksha Bhandan) - The groom ties a Kappu (Raksha - a sacred yellow thread) on the left hand of the bride. This is for the protection of the bride from all evils.
- Mangalya Pooja - The Mangalyam is considered sequel to Goddess Lakshmi (Goddess of wealth). The Mangalyam is worshipped first with a small pooja and shown to the audience individually to get their blessings.
- Mangalya Dharanam - As described earlier.
- Homam - Described earlier
- Sapthapadhi - described earlier
- Poriyidal - offering of puffed rice in the homam.
- Asirvatham - People who are older than the groom sprinkle Akshadai (rice mixed with turmeric powder) on the couple and give their blessings.

- The priest unties the Kappu from the groom's hand and the groom unties from the bride's hand.
- Mangala Arthi - described earlier.

MARRIAGE AS DONE IN ANDHRA PRADESH

- The parents of the groom do the Vigneswara Pooja and punyahavachanam first. Then they tie the raksha to the groom and do the Samavarthanam. The groom gets ready for Kasi Yathrai.
- The bride does Sri Gowri pooja and gets ready to come to the altar.
- The groom goes for Kasi Yathrai. The bride's brother requests the groom to take the hands of his sister in marriage and settle in life, instead of going to Kasi (Banaras or Varanasi). Sweet (or jaggery) is then given to the groom.
- The groom is then invited to come to the altar.
- At the altar, a screen is placed in front of the groom and the bride is brought on the other side of the altar.
- A small portion of a powdered mixture of cumin seeds and jaggery on a small leaf is placed on the heads of the bride and the groom. The priest recites a manthra called "Choornikai" and removes the screen between the couple.
- Kannikadhanam - giving the bride away. (as described earlier)
- Madhubarkham - The bride is given the Muhurtha Saree (the wedding dress).
- Mangalya Dharanam - When the bride comes back in the wedding dress (muhurtha saree), mangalya dharanam is done.
- Sapthapadhi - as described earlier
- Akshadaropanam - The couple are seated facing each other and a bowl of rice (uncooked) is placed between them. The groom puts some rice on the bride's head three times reciting three manthras. Then the couple alternately put the rice on each other's head till the bowl is empty.

- A small game - The couple are seated facing each other as before and a bowl of water is placed between them. A ring or a conch is put in the water. The couple is then asked to take out the object. This is played three times. Some believe that if the ring/conch is picked up by the bride first, then the couple's first baby will be a girl. If it is picked up by the groom first then their first born will be a boy.
- Arundhadhi seeing - as described earlier.
- Mangala Arthi

SIGNIFICANCE OF RITUALS PERFORMED IN A HINDU MARRIAGE

A Hindu Wedding is not simply an exchange of vows and rings. It includes a number of religious rites before and during the nuptials, which are performed in the presence of family deities. These represent the importance of the bond between a husband and wife. A Hindu marriage or «Vivaha» is incomplete without the blessings of a spiritual or divine element.

MISRI (RING CEREMONY)

All prayers in Hindu ceremonies start by invoking the blessings of Lord Ganesha (Lord Ganesha unlike all the other Hindu deities has an elephant head as a result of the unfortunate conditions explaining Lord Ganesh's elephant head – his own father axed off his son's head and then replaced it with that of the first animal he saw – the Hindu devout shows his lack of preference between the Lords by making his preliminary prayers to Lords, Ganesha). Seven married ladies (portraying 7 forms of God for each day of the week) use red power to make a Ganesh sign (clockwise swastika) on a pot of misri (crystalline sugar) asking him to bless the couple and make the ceremony run well.

The ladies also sew designs on a white piece of cloth to ward of any Nazar (evil eyes cast) that may come upon the happy occasion. This cloth is worn by the couple on the wedding day. (Note some couples leave the preparation of the white cloth until the Ghari puja.) A puja is done by the couple and their parents welcoming God in different forms and asking for his blessings.

They pray to Lord Ganesha, Varun Devta, Laxmi & Narayan, the Gods on governing the 9 planets, and Om (i.e. Triumverate Brahma, Vishnu and Shiva). Garlands are exchanged by the couple in order to welcome each other into their lives. This part of the ceremony is known as the Varmala.

As gold lasts for ever, rings made of gold are exchanged by the couple in order to represent a long married life. It is believed that the fourth finger of the hand has a vein leading directly to the heart. Hence the groom wears the ring on the fourth finger of his right hand and the bride wears hers on the fourth finger of her left hand in order to form a complete heart. The groom's family places a basket of fruits, clothes, cosmetics or ornaments on the girl's lap (in her jholi) to represent their acceptance into her family and bestowing her with happiness and prosperity. The groom's family gives a verbal promise of marriage and feeds misri (crystalline sugar) to the girl's family to confirm the engagement. The eating of sweet is considered auspicious by the Hindus and thus is eaten on all happy occasions.

MEHNDI (HENNA - PAINTING OF HANDS AND FEET)

This festive occasion, originally of Muslim origin, is usually held in the late afternoon. This is primarily a ladies tea-party; however the male relatives are allowed to be present. On the mehndi, the future bride has her hands and feet intricately patterned with a paste which is a recipe of henna, oil, lemon juice and some water tinted with tea. The application of mehndi or henna takes about four hours to complete. Ideally, the bride-to-be should not wash her hands until the paste has completely dried. Invitees at the party also design each others hands with mehndi. Mehndi signifies the strength of love in a marriage and darker the mehndi, the stronger the love.

SANGEET PARTY (MUSICAL PARTY)

Music is the soul of any wedding ceremony, regardless of faith or origin. Without music & festivity, the wedding lacks sparkle. On the Sangeet night, entertainment is provided with the help of professional singers who sing popular Hindi film songs. Family and friends eat, drink and dance the night away.

SAGRI (ACQUAINTANCE)

The sisters and female relatives of the groom visit the bride-to-be in her home. They bring with them perfume, cosmetics and flowers that are strung together in the form of earrings, bangles, hairpieces and garlands. The sisters adorn their sister-in-law to be with the flowers, suggesting their affection for her. The purpose of this ceremony is to increase familiarity between the bride and her new family, creating an atmosphere that is fragrant and beautiful.

NAV-GRAHA PUJA (WORSHIP TO THE NINE PLANETS)

This is the prayer to the nine planets of our Solar System. Ancient Indian studies indicate that various celestial bodies have tremendous influence on the destiny of every individual, and among them the effect of the nine planets is "supposed" to be the most profound. During this puja, the Gods associated with these planets are asked to bless the couple and their families.

GHARI PUJA

This is the final and most important religious custom that is performed on the eve of the wedding day. Ghari Puja is carried out in the respective homes of the couple. The priest performs the prayers with rice, coconut, wheat grains, oil, betel nuts, turmeric and a number of other spices. Married ladies grind wheat on a small old fashioned grinder symbolising that the home will always be prosperous. The groom offers a handful of grains to the priest indicating that although he is changing his lifestyle, he will always give to charity and look after those less fortunate than himself.

The mothers of both the bride and groom dress up in their bridal finery. Carrying an earthen pot of water on their heads, they walk to the threshold of their homes. The son-in-law of the respective families cut the water with a knife to ward off any evil spirits. The parents are adorned with garlands of flowers and money by their friends and relatives. The bride and groom wear old clothes that are torn off by their friends and family members amidst merriment, illustrating the end of their old life.

SWAGATAM (WELCOME)

After the bride dresses up in her wedding ensemble, her sisters or female relatives escort the groom to the bride's house. At the entrance, the groom places his right foot on the top of the brides foot, signifying that he should be the dominating strength in their life together. After the groom enters the house, the bride's parents rinse his feet with milk and water. It is believed that due to all the prayers that have preceded this moment, the groom is an embodiment of Lord Vishnu on this wedding day.

HATHIALO (JOINING OF THE HANDS)

In this ceremony, the corner of the bride's sari is tied to a scarf which is worn by the groom. The right hands of the couple are tied with a thread that has been blessed with religious incantations. The typing of the hands signifies an eternal bond that will join them forever. The couple then prays to the Gods to give them strength and bless their union.

THE WEDDING CEREMONY

The wedding ceremony is performed by the priest in the presence of family and friends. The bride and groom are seated in front of a holy fire and the priest recites various religious sayings from the Holy Scriptures. According to the Hindu religion, fire is considered the sustainer of life. It is believed that the Gods and Goddesses sit around this auspicious fire. The priest directs various family members to give offerings into the holy fire.

The couple walks around the fire four times exchanging vows of duty and love, fidelity, respect and a fruitful union. The groom then places the brides hand on his forehead, to denote that he accepts her as his wife for better of for worse, in health or in sickness and that it his destiny to marry her. The couples heads are held together implying that although they are separate individuals, from this day onwards, they are one in body, mind and spirit.

KANYA DAN (ENTRUSTING OF THE DAUGHTER)

The bride's parents entrust their daughter in the safe keeping of the groom and his family.

ASHIRWAD (BLESSING)

The priest explains to the couples their responsibilities to each other and then gives them his holy blessings. This completes the marriage ceremony.

DATAR (SALT CEREMONY)

After friends and family have greeted the couple, they leave for the groom's house. At the entrance of their new home, the bride's feet are rinsed by the groom's parents. A cover is placed over her head as she sprinkles milk in all corners of the house. This signifies that she will maintain the respect of the family and that if there are any misunderstandings within the family, she is supposed to help solve or "cool" them. Surrounded by her new family, the bride picks up a handful of salt and places it in the hands of her husband. He passes it back into her hands without spilling any salt. This is done three times. Similarly, the datar is carried out with all members of the groom's family. Exchanging salt symbolises that just as salt blends in and gives taste to food, so must the bride blend in and become a part of her new family.

THE WOMAN IN THE VEDIC SRAUTA RITUAL

The role and importance of women in earlier Vedic literature is much more apparent, and observable than it is today. The participation of women was vital, and much more significant in previous centuries, during Vedic srauta [an extensive body of sacrifices performed on specific occasions] ritual. Two myths that are said to be the main cause of women's restrictions in sacred Vedic ritual are Varuna's noose and Indra's curse. Indra's curse is said to be the mythic catalyst that led to restrictive rituals that must be adhered to when a woman is participating in religious sacrifice. The Taittariya Samhita reveals that when Indra (God of lightning and thunder) killed Visvarupa, he transferred one third of the "stain" of murdering a Brahmin to women.

The "stain" that was transferred to women comes in the form of menstrual blood, and is seen as dangerous and impure. It is regarded in this way because the menstrual blood is literally Indra's curse. Therefore when a woman is menstruating she is not able to perform her religious duty; a ritual must be postponed or a substitution is made in her place. The Taittariya Brahmana states that half the ritual dies if it is performed while the wife is menstruating (3.7.1.9) and for this reason she is prohibited from entering the sacrificial area. Varuna's noose is the other mythic tale that has given authority to the types of restriction that women must endure.

Although the notion of Varuna's noose is to restrain the power of women, it also represents the many aspects of femininity that are crucial for worship and religious sacrifices. The wife of the sacrificer is bound with a species of grass called munja, which occurs once the wife enters the sacrificial area. She is bound while sitting because it is said that she becomes virile while in this type of position. The binding of the waist is a symbolic representation of Varuna's noose, which he uses to ensure that the propagation of the created world occurs within the bounds of a properly conceived cosmic order.

Women are an important aspect because they contain a certain kind of power that is attributed exclusively to females, and is expressed primarily through their sexuality and reproductive capacity. Leslie has found support for this notion in the Taittiriya Brahmana, declaring that a sacrifice without the wife is no sacrifice at all; her presence in the ritual assures effective cosmic reproduction which coincides with human reproduction (1992:24). The tying of the "noose" symbolically ties the wife to her husband, and brings her into a meaningful relationship with the gods.

The Taittiriya Brahmana concludes that through this working relationship with the gods the wife causes the sacrifice to copulate with her; bringing the sacrifice within her thereby intensifies and expands her feminine creative power. Since many Vedic sacrifices include the element of reproduction, the woman is an essential participant. It is through her feminine creative power and the symbolic tying of the rope, which promotes proper or controlled human procreation. The asvamedha (horse-sacrifice) is one of the most well known Vedic rituals and has been in existence since the time of the Rg Veda.

Athough this ritual has not been performed for centuries; it exemplifies the importance that the wife plays in relation to its concerns with reproduction. Historically the asvamedha is performed by a king partly to gain offspring and gain royal glory. At one point in the beginning of the ritual the king lies between the thighs of the wife who is named vavata (who is the beloved one). This physical action between husband and wife is a symbolic act, to bring fertility to the wife; it also mimics the action that the queen performs with the horse after one year. At the end of the year, with the finishing of the ritual, the king's queens perform a short ritual after the horse has been exterminated, which infuses the horse with vital breath, and brings fertility.

As Dange has briefly explained, the three wives circle the horse clockwise and then counter-clockwise, repeating this three times on both sides for a total of nine times. While they are circling the horse they are also fanning it which is said to instil vital breath within themselves and the horse. After this is completed the mahisi (chief queen) lies near the horse, is covered with a large cloth, and performs a mock copulation. This mock copulation is supposed to infuse the queen with the symbolic seed of her husband in hopes that she will produce children. The ability to produce offspring is very important in Vedic tradition, especially in terms of producing a male heir. The need for the presence of the wife is undeniable; without the female power, ritual reproduction would not be possible. The Rg Veda, Sama Veda, and Atharva Veda are the earliest known texts of Indian religion that mention the involvement of women.

Although women are present during sacrifice and play a role in the ritual, they are not able to offer sacrifice. This restriction placed upon women is reinforced by The Laws of Manu. It is stated that sacrifice performed by a woman is displeasing to the gods and inauspicious for men. In orthodox Hindu tradition, women are not educated in Vedic verse or ritual; therefore they are not able to perform sacrifice due to lack of experience and understanding.

A wife attempting to make a sacrificial offering on her own could bring on a multitude of negative effects to herself and those around her, especially her husband, because of her inexperience. While a woman is not "traditionally" able to perform sacrifice on her own, her presence is essential for her husband to properly perform the ritual.

Julia Leslie has found that although the Laws of Manu prohibits women from performing the role of sacrificer, the laws insist that a wife is ordained to take part in joint religious rituals (1989:109). The epics and puranas also have textual evidence that enforces the role of the wife as the individual who shares in her husband's religious duties. The magnitude of the woman's presence is compounded by the fact that a man has no authority to act alone.

A man cannot fulfil his religious duties to gods, ancestors and guests without a wife: for the wife shares the sacrifice, bears the children and prepares the food. The relationship between husband and wife may seem unequal in the orthodox tradition of Vedic rituals, but it is a shared partnership; one may not act without the other.

4

Dance and the Hindu Woman

Bharatanatyam Re-ritualized

It was once generally believed that in the matter of culture and civilisation, South India was largely if not exclusively indebted to the North. A critical study of the cultural history of Ancient India would however show that the advent of the Aryans into India and their subsequent vic-torious progress ultimately resulted not so much in the Aryanisation of India as in the Indianisation of the Aryans. The excavations at Mohenjodaro and Harappa have revealed that there existed in this country a very rich and perfect civilisation even before the advent of the Aryans. "It became evident that long before the arrival of the horse-riding Northerners, there were highly organised and splendidly built brick cities in a vast area of India in which a pre-Aryan people of remarkable skill and knowledge lived.

That they were some kind of Dravidian people, predecessors of the present inhabitants of South India cannot be proved with certainty, but the cumulative evidence is so strong that a few serious scholars now doubt the Dravidian character of the pre-Aryan city dwellers of Western India. After all, there is a good deal of reference to their cities in the most ancient writing of the Aryans the Rig Veda." The so called Aryanisation of South India was in several respects quite unlike the Aryanisation of North India. For, the most tangible result of it was the acceptance by the South Indians not of Aryan theology but of Hindu sociology as reflected in the caste system. Secondly, this movement does not seem to have evoked much opposition. On the contrary, there is evidence to show that the changes brought by it were welcomed by the Dravidians with alacrity. And, thirdly the incursions from the North were not so violent as to root out the languages and the peculiar religious culture of the South. The Aryanisation of South India may be said to have begun round about 1000 B.C. and been completed before the time of Ashoka.

The movement of Aryanis*ati*on was of the nature of Hindui*sati*on rather than of Aryanis*ati*on. In this movement between the North and the South, there was more of give rather than of take on the side of the Dravidians. The greatest gift of South India to Hinduism is God Siva. The word Siva in proto-Dravidian meant 'red'.

There is ample evidence to show that long before the advent of the Aryans, the cult of Siva had spread far and wide in this country - different aspects of this religion being emphasised in different regions. Four gods which may be mentioned as peculiarly Tamil Gods are Siva, Balarama, Krishna and Murugan.

The contribution of South India to the totality of Indian culture is great and has a special significance. This is due to the fact that the South did not suffer from foreign invasions to the extent that the other parts of the country did.

DATE OF CILAPATHIKARAM

The history of dance reveals that from the earliest times, dancing has been intimately associated with religion. The Tamil country or Tamilakam can boast of an antique and original culture. The geographical limits of Tamilakam have been defined in an old work as 'Venkatam', in the North, 'Kumari' in the South and the Sea to the East and West. It is well known that long before the beginning of the Christian era, the Tamil language had built for itself a great literature and moulded it according to the genius of its people as is seen in the Sangam works of the Tamils.

The Sangam epoch has been assigned to the period commencing with the 5th Century B.C. and ending with the 4th Century A.D. The Sangam age in Tamil Literature was a period of great literary glory never to be surpassed in the history of any literature whatsoever. It was the production of a colossal volume of Tamil poetry in its pristine purity. The age was a period of national awakening when the arts and the sciences flourished alike, when the peo-ple obtained all social amenities and when far flung trade and commerce secured to the Tamils prosperity and power. The second century of the Christian era is called the 'Golden Age' in Tamil letters.

Cilapathikaram and Manimêkhalai, 2 of the 5 major epics are believed to have been written during this Golden Age. They are the Iliad and Odyssey of Tamil poetry and it is impossible to exaggerate their importance. Silappadikãram, classified under the category of totar-nilaicceyyal amazes us, by its perfect sense of form, its harmonised blending of (iyal) poetry, isai (music) and natakam (drama), its gorgeous and picturesque descriptions, epic dignity civili*sati*on in which the theatre, music, dancing, poetry, architecture, painting and seasonal feasts celebrated with enchanting fantasy formed part of the daily life of every class and occupation.

Cilapathikaram is not only one of the world's greatest literary masterpieces, but it is also a vast storehouse of information on the arts of music, dancing, building and other activities of the Ancient Tamils. Wood carving, stone cutting, clay modelling, bronze casting are all phases of the sculptural art, and the Tamils attained a high degree of proficiency and perfection in all these forms of art at a very early period. In fact, the earliest literary reference to the art of image-making in South India is found in Cilapathikaram. A perfect South Indian bronze is one of the highest achievements in the plastic arts, as it combines in a remarkable manner deep spiritual vision, technical skill and an age-old tradition.

South Indian bronzes have won worldwide reputation for their intrinsic beauty and artistic merit. What is so extra-ordinary in the images of Siva Nataraja whose five functions are creation, preservation, destruction, purification and grace is the tremendous display of energy revealed in transcendental calm. On a critical study of the dances and music mentioned in the Cilapathikaram, it is clear that the ancient Tamils had developed a very high standard of technique in dance and music, which probably formed the basis for the Aryans to develop and write a highly systematised and perfect technique on the art of dancing and dramaturgy like Bharata's Natya Sastra and Nandikeswara's Abihinaya Darpana.

DATE OF NATYA SASTRA

The Natya Sastra is the most important and authoritative treatise on Sanskrit dramaturgy dealing exhaustively on poetics, metre, music and drama as they affect the composition and representation of the drama. Nandikeswara's Abhinaya Darpana on the other hand, deals exhaustively on the art of Bharatanatyam only. Nothing definite can be said about the date of the Natya Sastra. It has been assigned by different scholars to various dates between the 2nd century B.C. to 3rd century AD. In fact, the date of the *Natya Sastra*, according to some, is placed in the 3rd century A.D., i.e. a 100 years after the date of Silappadikãram.

The prakrits recognised by the Natya Sastra are later than those of Asvagosha. It recognises the use of the Ardha-Magadi which is not found in the dramas other than those of Asvagosha and Bhasa. On the other hand, it ignores the Maharashtri which it freely used in the later classical dramas. The fact that Bhasa violates some of the rules of Bharata suggests that in his days, the Natya Sastra had not obtained sufficient sanctity. All this evidence goes to suggest the 3rd century AD, as a probable date of this work.

DANCE AND MUSIC IN CILAPATHIKARAM

As mentioned already, Silappadikãram gives a fund of information about the music and dance of the ancient Tamils 2000 years back. While giving the necessary qualifications of the ideal dance master in 'Arang-eru Kadai', Silappadikãra;m mentions that an ideal master must have thorough knowledge of the characteristics of the 2 broad divisions of Ahakkoothu and Purakkoothu. When conducting the 2 general varieties of dance Ahakkoothu and Purakkoothu that include the songs, the tales and their combinations, he should have an eye upon the movements with the single and double hands, beauty hands and expressive hands known as Pindi and Pinayal, Ezhirkai and Thozhirkai respectively.

The Ahakkoothu and Purakkoothu referred to by Ilango Adigal are only the Nritta and Nritya aspects of Bharatanatyam which are the 2 major aspects of this great art. Purakkoothu or Nritta is pure dance which consists of movements of the body and limbs which are performed to create beauty and decorative effect and not to convey any specific meaning or idea to the beholder. Ahakkoothu or Nritya on the other hand is dance with facial expressions. i.e. a dance which is performed specifically to convey the meaning or import of a theme or an idea to the beholder. This Nritya is accomplished through the use of suggestive facial expressions and codified gestures of the hands.

The Pindi and Pinayal mentioned here are the single handed gestures or Asamyuta Hastas and double handed gestures or Samyuta Hastas. The Pindi or single handed gestures are 28 in number and they are: -Pataka, Tripataka, Ardha-Pataka, Kartari-Mukha, Mayura, Ardha-chandra, Arala, Sukatunda, Mushti, Sikjara, Kapittha, Kataka-Mukha, Suci, Chandra-kala, Padma-kosa, Sarpa-sirsa, Mrga-sirsha, Simha-Mukha, Kangula, Sola-padma, Chatura, Bhramara, Hamsasya, Hamsapaksha, Samdamsa, Mukula, Tamrachuda and Trisula. The Pinayal or double-handed gestures which are 24 in number are Anjali Kapotha, Karkata, Swastika, Dolahasta, Pushpa puta, Utsanga, Sivalinga, Katakavardhana, Kartari-Swastika, Sakata, Sanku, Chakra, Samouta, Pasa, Kilaka, Matsya, Kurrna, Veraha, Garuda, Nagabanda, Khadva, Berunda, and Avhitdin.

Of these 28 and 24 hand gestures only some are used while performing the pure dance or Purakkodoothu. Such of those hand gestures that are used in Pure Dance as ornamental adjuncts are called 'Ezhirkai' (hand used to create beauty) and all those that are employed for expressing some idea or meaning are called 'Thozhirkai' as they serve the purpose of conveying an idea. Thus, while the 'Thozhirkai' are 28 plus 24 52 in number, used in the Nritya aspect of Bharatanatyam, 'Ezhirkai' are comparatively less in number i.e. 13 in number as they serve only as ornamental adjuncts.

The dance master should see that pure dance does not get mixed up with dance with expressions and vice versa, and he should not mix-up the foot movements of the Kuravaikkoothu with those of Varikkoothu. On the other hand, a dancer had to undergo rigorous training for 7 years starting from her 5th year in music and dance. She was expected to be able to sing songs composed in foreign languages as well as play on the Yal, flute and drum. This compares well with the verse in the Abhinava Darpana'.

'Kantena lambayeth geetham
Has-the nartham pradarsayeth
Chakshurbhyam darsayeth bhavam
Padabhyam talamachareth.'

The dancer must sing producing music from the throat, bring out the meaning of the song by appropriate gestures of the hand, her eyes must speak out the bhava or expression and feet must keep perfect time.

'Yatho hasthas tha tho drushtir
Yatho drushtis tha tho manaha
Yatho manas tha tho bhavo
Yatho bhavastha tho rasaha.'

Eyes should follow the hand, mind should follow the eye where the mind goes there is expression and where there is bhava or expression there is rasa. The dance master must be able to choreograph harmoniously the various kinds of Purakkoothu with the 14 types of vilakku or songs. Besides, he should have thorough mastery over the eleven types of dances from Alliyam to Kodu-kotti. These eleven types are:- Alliyam, Kodu-kotti, Kudaj, Kudam, Pedi, Kadayam, Pandarangam, Mal, Tudi, Marak-kal and Pavai. The dances referred to are that of Siva, Muruga, Kama, Durga, Krishna, Lakshmi and Indrani. While the Cilapathikaram gives slight descriptions of the context and occasion for these dances, they do not throw much light as to how they were danced - the technique and manner of presentation.

Alliyam: Sri Krishna and his brother Balarama had to pass through many a peril when they were brought to Mathura, the capital of King Kamsa to be slain. One such was the royal elephant Kuvalaya-peeda which was driven furiously on them. On that occasion, it is said that Krishna dances a wonderful dance when he pulled out the tusks of the maddened beast and struck it dead. Kodu-Kotti is ascribed to Lord Siva. The 3 invincible Asura brothers who ruled the 3 cities made of gold, silver and iron could be slain only when they came together once in many thousands of years for a second and that, too, with a single arrow only.

Only Lord Siva could undertake that mighty task. Slaying them and standing on the battle field where lay the ashes of the burnt cities, he danced a fierce dance of triumph and victory clapping his hands in glee while his consort Bhairavi was alone left to keep time to his weird measures known as Kodu-kotti.

Kudai: In the great battle between the Asuras and Devas, the Divine Boy, Skanda, the leader of the Divine Armies, lowered his great umbrella and using it as a side curtain danced a dance of disdain and merriment (Kudai-umbrella).

Kudam: Usha, daughter of Bana, the Asura king of Shontapura fell in love with Anirudda, son of Kama and grandson of Sri Krishna. Bana on coming to know if it was enraged and put Anirudda in jail after a hard fight. Then, Sri Krishna who went in disguise to the city of Bana to see his grandson danced a strange dance with a pot in his hands (made of clay and five metals) that was always kept moving to keep time to his evolutions (Kudam -pot).

Pedi: The dance of Kama along the streets of the city of Shonta-puram to effect the release of his son held in captivity changing himself into a combination of man and woman (Pedi -Eunuch).

Kadayam was the dance performed by Indrani in the same city of doom. She is said to have danced the last of the dances (Kadai -last).

Pandarangam is also another dance of Lord Siva white with the ashes of the vast crematorium, on the battle field after the burning of the Tripura.

Mal: The dance of Govinda disguised as a wrestler when he challenged and crushed Bana. the Asura in fair fight. The evolutions during the bout are given the name of a dance, because it was so simple and merry a feat to the Lord.

Tudi: The dance of victory of Lord Skanda keeping time on the Tudi on one hand, over Sura Padma the mighty Asura who took refuge on top of the waves in mid-ocean.

Marakkal: Mahadevi sister of Vishnu was enraged when the Asuras took refuge by changing themselves into poisonous snakes and scorpions. The Devi, with legs of wood danced, crushing the life out of the poisonous brood (Marakkal - wooden leg).

Pavai: Lakshmi assumed a wondrous form that melted the hearts of the Asuras and put chaos into their brains, and they ran after her madly. The beautiful gait and charming movements of Lakshmi are known as Pavai.

These eleven dances with their appropriate songs and tales and the sentiments underlying each, should be part of the equipment of the teacher and the pupil in dance.

The mention of 2 types of Koothu has been interpreted in various ways as:

Shanthikkoothu as against Vinodakkoothu

Kuravaikkoothu as against Varikkoothu

Vasaikkoothu as against Varisanthikkoothu

Tamil as against Aryan

Desi as against Margi.

From the standard works on music and dance used as references by Adiyarkunallar in his commentary on Cilapathikaram, Shanthikkoothu may be taken to mean the classical dance or Bharatanatya and Vinodakkoothu the folk dances. As under Shanthikkoothu mention is made of Chokkam or Pure Dance consisting of 108 Karanas. Mai is divided into Desi, Vadugu and Singala. Abhiriaya is the interpretation of a song with facial expressions and Nataka is dance with the dramatic element. Under the Vinodakkoothu comes the Kuravai in which 7, 8 or 9 persons take part. Love and conquest form the subject.

The songs are composed in the metre Kuravai.

Kalinatam -acrobatics of professional gymnasts and tumblers.

Kudam -is a dance with water pots on the head.

Nokku -marked by stateliness, afility and seductiveness.

Tholpavai -is the dance of the puppets or Tholubommalatham with figures of leather and an illuminated curtain as the back ground.

Vasai -also called Vinodakkoothu related to sentiments of merriment and laughter admitting of 2 divisions -one before the kings -Vettiyal and the other before the common people - Poduviyal.

Cilapathikaram gives the legendary origin of dancing. Once in the Sabha of Indra, Indra's son Jayantha is said to have lost his balance in his behaviour towards the celestial dancer Urvasi, which enraged Sage Agastya who cursed him to be born as a Bamboo stick in the Vindhya Hills and Urvasi a Courtesan on the earth. Urvasi was to be freed from the curse on being presented with the 'Talaikkol' which was symbolical of Jayantha on her Arangetral day. The talaikkol was usually the central shaft of a white umbrella captured in the battlefield from monarchs of great repute and symbolical of Jayantha.

Thus Jayantha is celebrated in the ceremony and worship of 'Talaikkol'.

This ancient ceremony of Talaikkol finds a parallel in the ceremony of 'Thandiam Pidithal' practised by the Devadasis of more recent times. The Devadasis as the name implies were professional temple dancers attached to the temples and they preserved the highest traditions of Bharatanatya in their original grandeur and pristine purity. The young daughters of the Devadasis started learning dancing at the age of five, first by watching the elder student dancers and practising by themselves. In about the 7th year when they were initiated for practice, the ceremony 'Thandiam Pidithal' (holding the pole) is held.

On an auspicious day and hour, a quantity of paddy is spread in the centre of the Silambakkoodam in a square or rectangular form and a pole or stick is held across the centre by 2 elderly Devadasis firmly at both sides. The girl commencing her practice has to hold the middle of the stick with both her hands and begin to dance the first movements, with her feet over the paddy as the teacher beats the timing with his stick (Thattu.kazhi). The seed of Bharathanatyam is thus sown in her. Thus after 7 years of rigorous training in dancing the Arangetral or the first appearance on the stage is made as did Madavi of Cilapathikaram 2000 years ago. The mention that Madavi danced both the Desi and Margi styles of dance may well mean the indigenous style developed by the ancient Tamils as against the alien style of the Aryans though essentially the technique of Bharatnatya was the same.

Thus, Cilapathikaram gives ample evidence to a high state of evolution in the art of dancing. We also find that the instruments used by the ancient Tamils were the yal, kuzhal and maddalam. The qualifications of the songster, drummer, flutist and the vina player are also elaborately given. The detailed and technical description of the musical instruments and players clearly indicate that the ancient Tamils had a highly developed musical system and used a scale of 22 srutis -that is the scale of just intonation. Apart from the fund of information that we get about classical dancing and music in the Arangerukadai of Cilapathikaram, we also come across the various ritual and folk dances that were popular in those ancient days.

The ancient Tamils believed in invoking the blessing of Gods during times of great distress and calamity and this they did by singing, dancing, fasting and feasting. The chief gods invoked by them were Murugan, Mayon, Siva, Korravai or the Goddess of Victory, Balarama, Varuna, Indra etc. Among the ritual dances, we come across Vettuvavari in honour of Korravai which was often performed by the Maravar tribe. The ritual dance Kuravaikkoothu was performed by the women of the community in honour of Lord Krishna who married the cowherdess Pinnai. The Kuravaikkoothu, we are told, was performed by Madari and her daughter in order to invoke the blessing of Lord Krishna as a number of ill-omens indicated some disaster to the city and its people. So in order to avert the impending danger, the Kuravaik-koothu was arranged.

In concluding the chapter, we can draw the inference:

The ancient Tamils had developed a unique and original culture long before the beginning of the Christian era when literature and fine arts flourished. But, by the time of the Cilapathikaram, that is the 2nd century AD, Aryanisation had already started which had its effect in influencing all phases of life including the arts and literature. It is probable that soon after the early Aryans penetrated the South, many Sanskrit or Prakrit words gained general currency.

This was before the Christian era, and may have extended over a period of some centuries. The influence of Aryan culture is clearly seen in the life described in the Cilapathikaram. That is the reason; we find the introduction of a number of Aryan gods, and Sanskrit beliefs in the work. But, this need not lead one to believe that all fine arts were borrowed from the Aryans and that Sansskrit alone gave the key to the whole of Indian culture. It may be assumed that the style of dancing and music developed by the ancient Tamils were studied and perfected by the early Aryans who wrote such great treatises like the 'Natya Sastra' and 'Abhinaya Darpana'.

It may also be argued that the very fact that only the Tamil country has been able to preserve through the ages the Bharatanatyam in its original grandeur and pristine purity points to the fact that this was the dance that had been handed down by the age old ancestors of the present Tamils which later was perfected by the early Aryans. The Tamil country especially Tanjore, has always been the seat and centre of learning and culture. It was the famous quartet of Chinnayya, Ponniah, Sivanandam and Vadivelu of the Tanjore Court during King Saraboji's time (1798- 1824) which made a rich contribution to music and Bharatanatyam and also completed the process of re-editing the Bharathanatyam programme into its present shape with its various forms like the Alarippu, Jathiswaram, Sabdham, Varnam, Tillana etc.

The descendants of these 4 brothers formed the original stock of Nattuvanars or dance teachers of Bharatanatyam in Tanjore. Originally, they formed a community by themselves and most of them were Saivite non-brahmins, their mother tongue being Tamil. Probably they were the direct descendants of the ancient Tamils who tried to preserve the age-old traditions of dance and music passed on by their ancestors. Though Bharatnatyam is over 2000 years old, it has always been a growing art.

Its basic principles and ideals have remained practically unchanged although its repertoire and forms of presentation have been changing from time to time to suit changing conditions and concepts of artistry. Thus the arts of India, especially music and dance are a revela-tion of many thousands of years of culture and civilisation.

Avanthi Meduri speaks from experience; she is a Bharatanatyam dancer and choreographer. She is also a soul-searching female scholar who raises significant questions regarding the place of Bharatanatyam as danced by a modern-day woman. The above quote represents a feminist investigation within a contemporary dance framework, yet the potency and persistence of such queries are timeless for any female dancer. When India's Bharatanatyam revival and reform movements gained momentum in the 1920s and 30s, dialectical tensions arose between the separate camps, their ideologies, and their activities; for the "perverted" dance of the devadasi was reconstructed as a nationalist emblem while the devadasi, herself, was legislatively barred from her religious profession.

Interrogating this potent time period, many feminists have deconstructed the development of contemporary Bharatanatyam. They use material theory to point to the dancer's exploitation, commodification, and marginalization as the temple dance became secularized and the dancer became objectified, inscribed within patriarchal or Orientalist paradigms as a gendered, emblematic, or sociopolitical Other. These constrictions and inscriptions have also influenced modern choreographers as they tried to reclaim and empower the dance form by further reconstituting it, absorbing its "formal" technique and corporeal vocabulary into their own choreographic theory and dance compositions.

But, where does God fit into these arguments and strategies? Especially critical is an acknowledgement of both the devotional, spiritual journey which constitutes the art of Bharatanatyam and, more generally, the transcendental power of dance. This is where a divine tension lies which can empower the dancing, female body. Significantly, when the dance is disconnected from its divine potential, it may sit as an inanimate object, ready for commodification and control. Further, when the dancing body is discussed separately from the spirit, it can be positioned as a material site of exploration and deconstruction by theorists. Yet, in Bharatanatyam, such concepts of dualism are nowhere to be found. Its dance journey is both religious sacrament and divine conduit, resulting in a realization of the oneness of self and the cosmos.

In this same vein, the erotic/sexual (*shringara*) element of Bharatanatyam represents synthesis between opposites by which a new empowered entity can arise, exceeding each isolated binary unit. When genders maintain separate, fundamental essences, the energetic movement through multiple significations may result in a complex composition of wholeness. In this chapter, the dialogical engagement with feminists who have critically examined the material significations of Bharatanatyam in its contemporary configuration and the aspects of their critiques fall short when they ignore the metaphysical power of the devotional dance. For a woman may progress through stages of Bharatanatyam; and in a sublime, performative moment-a moment that has been achieved by "gendered" agency-she may rise to the level of the superior being. In order to combine with Shiva, she meets him on the same plane.

According to Hindu belief, dance on earth would not have happened without the woman. As recounted in the *Natya Shastra* (100 BCE - 200 AD), Brahma, the Supreme One, created the fifth *Veda* (the scripture of drama) and presented it to Bharata who then composed the first drama and sought "the help of Shiva for the steps of the dance. Shiva taught the steps to his disciple Tandu and to Parvati [Goddess and consort/ wife] and the harmony of the masculine and feminine in the dance was blended symbolically." Thus is suggested a gender synthesis which underpins all dance; however, the female is not completely sublimated within this phenomenon.

According to many legends, dance exists in its earthly incarnation thanks, in great part, to Parvati who "was the first teacher of dancing who brought the art down from the heavens to teach it to the people of the earth." Dance, therefore, embodies harmony countered with gendered interplay and tension-the force of which obliterates the ego while realizing divine wholeness. In her article "Feminist Perspectives on Classical Indian Dance," Judith Lynne Hanna writes: "With pleasure he [Shiva] exuberantly dances out the creation of the universe. [...] Shiva's frenzied Tandava (virile, manly) dance causes chaos and represents the destruction of the world. For his creative dance, his consort Parvati's (tender, womanly) dance is imperative."

Although legends such as these may suggest an essentialist reading regarding the "feminine" aspect of dance, another Goddess manifestation of Parvati- Kali- is the very antithesis of "tender, womanly" qualities. Goddess Kali is a powerful, destructive force which allows creation to occur. She is the ego destroyed-a ground-scorching pathway to divinity. Dancer and scholar Kapila Vatsyayan speaks of the ideal Indian dancer who "rides the body" with the "fire of experience" in a quest toward obliteration of self toward "spiritual transcendence." This concept is beautifully conveyed in the hymn to Kali recounted by Ananda K. Coomaraswamy: "Because thou lovest the Burning-ground, I have made a Burning-ground of my heart-that Thou, Dark One, haunter of the Burning-ground, mayest dance Thy eternal dance." Thus, Indian dance is inextricably connected to a multifaceted, female image of divine power.

This mythic and spiritual connection can also speak to material strategies by feminists who wish to address the dance in its sociocultural context. Hanna writes:

Female images of the divine may empower some women both spiritually and socially to take control of their lives. Perhaps, as in other cultures with rituals of rebellion, powerful goddesses serve to present complementarities, compensation and alternatives to the male dominance models as well as to remind men not to exceed acceptable limits in their behavior towards women. As stated above, sociocultural perspectives cannot be ignored when addressing feminism and dance in India. Specifically, a critical scholar must address and engage the Indian context in which Bharatanatyam was born and with which it is most often identified. Yet, this exploration can sometimes prove daunting and depressing for women.

For, if Goddesses figure powerfully in the ancient Hindu scripture of India, their earthly counterparts do not fare as well. Scholar Wendy O'Flaherty looks at the scripture-sanctioned devaluing of women in the *Vedas* and major Indian epics and legends which were authored or controlled by high-caste males and are kinetically visualized by dance. She states that the image of a woman in the texts is that of an "insignificant receptacle for the unilaterally effective male fluid a thing to be possessed." Further, Hanna cites ancient Indian law which specifies that "in childhood, a woman must be subject to her father, in youth to her husband and, when her lord is dead, to her sons. A woman must never be independent." In 1989, Vanaja Dhruvarajan stated that "while Indians have high regard for women as mothers, they devalue them as persons. The female principle is worshipped; yet in flesh and blood, females are humiliated, depersonalized, and dominated."

The material realities of many Indian women today-many of which may be learning, teaching, and/or dancing Bharatanatyam-do not often bespeak power, agency, or freedom from gender-scripted confines:

Indian women are routinely sold into marriage, and brothers are almost invariably favored over sisters. Successful and affluent women are sometimes unaware of the problems of the terrorism of drunken husbands, brutal landlords, or the starkness of poverty. Suman Krishan Kant's Women's Grievances Group organization receives complaints and directs investigations of attacks on women, many of them involving burning and scalding of brides by in-laws who feel they were short-changed on dowries.

Yet, a specific female model from India's past suggests the possibility of sociocultural prestige and spiritual empowerment for the dancing woman. This model is the devadasi; with her lineage traced to India's classical or Sanskrit period, she is oft said to represent a 2,000-year-old tradition of temple or devotional dance. Historically attributed to the Tamil region, the devadasi danced a form of Bharatanatyam under the original moniker of *sadir nac*, *sadir attam*, or *dasi attam*. Dedicated to God through temple ceremonies, the devadasis became constituents of the temple as brides and devotional servants to the deity.

Hanna writes that although a daughter might be given to the temple by her family to fulfil a vow or for financial reasons, a woman could also "offer herself out of devotion, for the prosperity of her family, or out of weariness of her husband or her widowhood." Thus, even though the devadasis came from and belonged to a hereditary community of temple dancers, musicians, and teachers (*isai vellala*), life as a devadasi could sometimes be a matter of choice for the woman. Hanna also details specific freedoms and modes of empowerment accorded the devadasis; they "learned to read and write, an opportunity denied other women. Furthermore, some dancers acquired wealth through gifts from admirers, owned land, and made large donations to temples."

Within this economical system, the devadasi also wielded power in her household where she was the primary wage earner, materially supporting her family. Furthermore, her public sphere reflected her private sphere; for in contrast to greater Indian society, the *isai vellala* was, by and large, a matriarchal community. Included in this fiscal/material paradigm of authority and agency was the devadasi's oft employed career strategy of inviting the solicitation of patrons (e.g., Brahmins or rulers-never an Untouchable) who could provide additional assets in return for sexual or consort relations. Dangerous is the contemporary interpretation of this arrangement as prostitution with its connotation of victimization and powerlessness, however. For even more crucial than material wealth was the psychological security accorded the devadasi by her respected status in society. Scholar Amrit Srinivasan historicizes the place of the devadasi as follows:

> As a woman with the protection of a living husband-the deity and lord of the temple corporation-the devadasi was provided with the excuse to enter secular society and improve her artistic skills. As a picture of good luck, beauty, and fame, the devadasi was welcome in all rich men's homes on happy occasions of celebration and honor i.e., an adjunct to conservative domestic society, not its ravager.

Yet, Srinivasan is also careful to point out the flip side of such a "revered," potent place in a society of men who had the power to revert icons to objects in order to proprietarily "own" a degree of sanctity. The following quote is lengthy but paints a vivid picture of the commodification of the devadasi by a patriarchal society, sanctioned by a patriarchal religion.

Here, a devadasi's proclaimed freedom and empowerment may have been trumped by her conversion to pawn by the male powerbrokers with whom she necessarily dealt:

> The fascination of a "wife-of-the-god" may be mythic just as the fascination for a bed in which Napoleon slept or a saint's relic. It converts itself into exchange value when the socialite-client, collector or believer wishes to own the commodity in question or touch it for him. Intimacy with a devadasi consequently demonstrated public success which visibly marked a man apart from his peers. Seen in this light, the devadasi represented a badge of fortune, a form of honor managed for civil society by the temple. The temple for its own part was no disinterested participant-the patronage extended to the devadasi was by no means passive. It recognized that her art and physical charms attracted connoisseurs (in the garb of devotees) to the temple. She invited "investment," economic, political, and emotional in the deity.

The conception and evolution of "devadasi as prostitute" became even more pervasive and problematic under British rule where "the imperialist hold economically weakened the Indian rulers who patronized the dancers." Further, the constitutive philosophy of temple dance (*sadir*), "wherein sexual ecstasy is a path to spirituality was an anathema to the British." By the turn of the 19th century, the devadasi subsisted, as Avanthi Meduri writes, within an "uneasy political atmosphere with her former generous patronage vanishing;" thus, she was "forced to choose between economic necessity and man-made [British] rules of decorum." Significantly, Meduri lauds this "female professional" who, in the face of a changing political and social climate, became less discriminate in patron relations, choosing to "live on her own moral terms."

Unfortunately, such individual, gendered "moral terms" were ignored, obfuscated, or translated by the "moral authorities" (read "male moral authorities") of the day. In 1927 (at which time, there were still 200,000 temple dancers in the Madras Presidency alone), reform-supporter Mohandas Gandi wrote: "There are, I am sorry to say, many temples in our midst in this country which are no better than brothels." Thus was provided the ultimate patriarchal, authoritarian declaration of devadasi decay and spiritual bankruptcy.

Indeed, male authority had often inscribed and dictated the traditional role of the devadasi, compromising the agency or power she may have believed herself to have. Hanna goes so far as to describe the hereditary devadasi community as a "reproduction of patriarchy ensconced in religious sanctification." She writes: "Male Brahmins, the priestly caste, initially 'choreographed' the dance (received from the gods) which male professionals, non-Brahmins who came from hereditary families of teachers and musicians (nattuvanaras or gurus) then taught to the devadasis."

Was the devadasi simply fooling her, believing to possess spiritual and secular authority that was all the time allotted, controlled, and measured by her male patrons, conductors, teachers, and authors? Are we fooled today as we idealize her social, sexual, spiritual power? Did this woman even exist? Srinivasan cites the power of the traditionally male guru who "exercised control over the dancer" while the dasis "feared and respected" them as "teachers and artists and informal religious leaders of the community whose curse could ruin a girl's career and prospects." Furthermore, returning to the "commodification" argument, power over the dasi often seemed to equate money and/or acquisition of property for men.

Srinivasan describes the dasi as the "proverbial goose that laid the golden egg" for male teacher/conductors, for if "handled properly," she could yield "dividends over the years in the shape of fees and gifts." This relationship, in many ways, persists today and must be reconciled with the "empowered" devadasi legacy claimed by the contemporary Bharatanatyam dancer. Hanna writes that a modern-day guru still "expects respect and credit for a piece he has taught a dancer. He tends to be jealous if one studies with another teacher or creates her own dances. If a dancer wishes to be creative, she breaks the dependency mold. Then the dancer has to find another [teacher]."

This gendered social tension between male authority and dasi recognition could also be seen within her hereditary community as male members became increasingly frustrated by their lack of complete dominance over their women. "The privileged access of women artists to rich patrons and their wealth underscored more sharply their absolute non-availability to their own men. The antagonism felt was in recognition consequently of the power and influence the devadasis had as women and as artists." The debate over the role of the devadasi in society reached a boiling point in the 1920s and 30s as she was denounced by British colonizers as a seedy symbol of a perverse and backward Indian culture.

Yet, what is more complex and troubling is her appropriation by Indian nationalists in their fervor to declare an independent state replete with ancient, holy traditions. As factions were formed, the "reformist" (or "anti-nautch") group squared off against the "revivalist" movement in a "religious" war. Reformists proclaimed the devadasi to be a "prostitute" who must be removed, and revivalists claimed her to be a "nun" who must be reconstituted and re-presented to a "respectable" Indian public. To both, however, the "sociohistoric complexity of the structure that enabled the devadasi to devote herself to perfecting her art was ignored." Each side maintained a "conviction that somewhere a pure custom had been polluted and must be cleansed."

Although there were women involved in the debate (famously, Rukmini Devi), many men were also invested in the struggle; they figuratively pulled at the arms of the devadasi, restricting her dance while claiming her as a means to accomplish their own political agendas. Brahmin priests decried the regulatory measures taken by the government to outlaw temple dedications as infringements on their own religious freedoms (not to mention the wealth and power brought to the temple through the dasi). Indicative of this is an account by Rustom Bharucha who describes the opposition to reform by S. Sathyamurthy in the Madras Congress as motivated by "no real concern for the devadasis themselves" but as a "concealed attempt to preserve a Brahmanic hegemony in matters of religion and culture." Bharucha asserts that Sathyamurthy represented other upper-caste men who feared the abolition of devadasis would serve to precipitate a non-Brahmin demand for "the abolition of temple priests, who were Brahmins. He was merely safeguarding his community's [Mayruam] vested interests sanctified through religion."

Not all men were working against reform measures, however. Uttara Asha Coorlawala details the diverse male demographic siding with the reform movement:

> The non-Brahmin Backward Classes, disgruntled by the educational and professional advantages gained by the pro-nautch Brahmins, and the Untouchables/Depressed classes under British legislation which deliberately fostered casteism, joined the anti-nautch campaign to gain support for their own political ends. This comprehensive group included male members within the devadasi community, who participated in performances as musicians and teachers and felt that their own artistic contributions were slighted.

In any case, the devadasi seemingly lost a battle in which she was ironically relegated to the sidelines. In 1930, Bill No. 5 was passed by which devadasis were absolved of their services to the temples; their material interests were then converted to land grants or deeds (*pattas*) to be administered by the government. Devadasis had previously been allotted temple land shares as part of their dedication and service. In that men could not previously inherit these shares (as could the dedicated sisters), "the process of converting traditional usufructury rights to public land (attached to office) into private taxable property favored the men over their womenfolk" as men controlled the marketplace and could purchase the previously unavailable land.

Furthermore, as part of this "liberating" process, the "freed" devadasi was often forced to convert her remaining wealth into a dowry in order to attract a husband and, thereby, acquire social respectability. In 1947, the Congress Ministry dealt a final death blow to the devadasi, passing the Madras

Devadasis Act which officially abolished all temple dedications. In the politically charged period surrounding the 1930 and 1947 legislative acts, the revivalists also scored critical victories which must be taken into account in any analysis of Bharatanatyam as it exists today. As the revivalists worked to return the dance to its "pre-prostitution" glory, their restoration became a zealous project of redefinition, reconstitution, and re-population.

They renamed the dance Bharatanatyam to remove any nominal vestiges of the devadasi who was inextricably linked to the old moniker, *sadir*. The revivalists led by female pioneers such as Brahmin Rukmini Devi-worked to make the art "respectable" for a new caste of dancers. The Madras Music Academy-a new academy formed by the revivalists (and still recognized as a prominent Bharatanatyam academy today)- passed a 1937 resolution dictating that "in order to make dancing respectable, it is necessary to encourage public performances thereof before respectable people." With this sweeping declaration, the revivalists moved the dance out of the temple and into the public forum while claiming the dance as property of the upper classes. As Srinivasan points out, however, the "dance technique remained unchanged and was learnt from the original *nattuvanars* [conductors] and performers."

Therefore, the movement needed to be underpinned by an incorruptible philosophy and, in a sense, protected from it so that it could not degenerate again as in the past. Rukmini Devi publicly danced Bharatanatyam in concert form and wrote treatise upon treatise as to its purely devotional function (sans "devadasi" sexuality). As more Brahmin women followed suit, Bharatanatyam was re-presented as "art" and danced by a new caste of women positioning themselves as the dance's authoritative guardians of respectability. The dancers and scholars were also intent on "purifying" the tradition by asserting an unquestionably sacred linkage to the *Natya Shastra* and other classical epics; the revivalist camp turned to text as an authoritative means by which to reinvent the dance and its lineage. Srinivasan notes:

Ancient dance-dramas were revived by Sanskrit scholars and introduced into the female genre. The more erotic and bawdy songs of the devadasi's repertoire were excluded. The low-key approach to *shringara* or the artistic convention of love between man and woman in the dance mimetic sequence was justified as a means of reducing its overt eroticism and replacing it with an "inward essence."

In *A Dictionary of Theatre Anthropology,* Eugenio Barba and Nicola Savarese refer to the revivalists' research and reconstruction process as a "restoration of behavior" which, in some ways, negates the hereditary power often cited by the contemporary Bharatanatyam dancer as part of her sacred history. As Bharatanatyam was codified according to ancient texts, the "new" dance became the definer of the "old" or ancient form of *sadir;* meanwhile, the current form of *sadir* was claimed to be a "faded, distorted remnant of some ancient classical dance" and denied its place as a dance in its own right. Regarding the "smoke and mirror" strategy to reinvent *sadir* as a legitimate Bharatanatyam progenitor, Barba and Savarese write, "The ancient classical dance is a projection backward in time. A dance is created in the past in order to be restored for the present and future."

Regardless of whether or not ancient lineage can be proven, the contemporary Bharatanatyam, as danced by a woman, cannot be disassociated from its 20th century lineage and revivalist context. Here, I suggest that the revivalist project may be viewed in two different feminist lights:

1. In terms of material feminism, the powerful Brahmin women may represent a socioeconomic group who disenfranchised and marginalized their "sisters"-who reinscribed the patriarchal order by negating a possible subversion of the norm by disempowering and dismantling the "matriarchal" society of the devadasi.
2. The movement may, however, suggest female empowerment as the Brahmin women claimed a "public victory," saving a spiritual art denoted as "feminine" and raising it to a place of prestige in a secular, male-

dominated society. In either case, ownership, authorship, and translation became defining aspects of the dance.

Coorlawala writes:

> What was achieved by the bill (1947) was to clear the way for nondevadasi women from respectable families to study dance. The reconstruction of the *sadir* dance was undertaken by Westernized and Sanskritized Brahmins. *Sadir* was reclaimed as Bharatanatyam, the purest and most "authentic" traditional dance of the *Natya Shastra*. As the above quote refers to the "Westernized" reconstruction of *sadir*, an astute observer might also find inherent in Bharatanatyam the dangerous (and often gendered) phenomenon of Orientalism. In Edward Said's terms, Orientalism is a "Western style for dominating, restructuring, and having authority over the Orient. The Orient cannot represent itself."

When a woman dances, Orientalism becomes another strategy of gendered authority and control. Further, when Bharatanatyam is danced or presented by a female Westerner, the resulting Orientalist paradigm can "reaffirm the West's superiority, as it takes a Western woman to understand and represent the essence of the East." Although this interpretation may read somewhat essentialist, limiting, and paranoid *(Only Asian women can authoritatively claim the dance?)*, there is historical precedence of Orientalism in the revival of Bharatanatyam, its spiritual appropriation by Westerners, and, consequently, its contemporary configuration. In 1926, American modern dancer Ruth St. Denis, having previously gained notoriety for her "nautch" dances, toured India and created a sensation on the concert stage with these sanctioned-yet, blatantly inauthentic-works. (St. Denis' earliest "nautch" dances were choreographed and performed throughout the 1910s and into the early 1920s-years before she actually visited India and witnessed its nautch dancers.)

Curiously, she was lauded by the upper, educated classes in India for her respectful and artistic treatment of "Indian" dance. In Orientalist fashion, she stated with religious fervor: "I am beginning to see that I already possessed the soul of

India. I see that I was sent to the Orient to give a truth as well as receive one." Although St. Denis was influential, the 20th century revival movement is more often associated with Western ballet dancer Anna Pavlova who toured India in 1929 and famously asked Brahmin scholars and politicians: "Where is your dance?" This same woman asserted her power as a dance prophet, sent to incite the rebirth of Indian dance through Western dance authority.

She stated: "The East had always fascinated me. One of the greatest ambitions remaining to me was to subjugate the Orient to my art, proving its power over people of any race or color." Indeed, Pavlova is inseparable from the resurrection mythos of Bharatanatyam; revivalist dancer Rukmini Devi credited Pavlova "with a pivotal contribution to India's rediscovery of its own dance forms." Through the "Pavlova" connection, the Western influence and authorship runs deep and was fully realized through the political efforts and dance of Devi, herself:

She [Pavlova] apparently met Rukmini Devi Arundale socially on a luxury liner somewhere between Australia and London, and urged her to study Indian dance. So it came about that Rukmini Devi studied *sadir,* which she later renamed Bharatanatyam and performed in public. This Brahmin lady-married to the British head of the Theosophical Society, Lord Arundale-founded the institution of dance called Kalakshetra in Madras. Western influence, ideology, and appropriation seemingly foreground much of Bharatanatyam. But is this situation as dire as insinuated by some scholars and theoreticians? A slap on the wrists for "intrusive" Westerners like St. Denis and Pavlova seems much too simplistic.

These were women who loved dance and, seemingly, loved Indian dance. I believe their motives were pure and their work allowed a powerful art form to reach audiences that might have otherwise ignored its presence and complacently allowed its demise. And at the risk of Orientalist blasphemy, I wonder whether Bharatanatyam would have been allowed to die, buried alive by its "rightful owners," without the

Western intervention? Dangerous territory to travel, yes, but an invested female dancer has a responsibility to pose such troubling questions, to unearth the complex paradigms, and, thereby, travel risky terrain. Once potentially constrictive and subjugating influences, ideologies, and hegemonies of Orientalism are exposed and explored, the female dancer can acknowledge, negotiate, and then exceed the confinements and inscriptions while progressing along a temporal path toward spiritual transcendence.

She is not bound by this paradigm. Further, as a negotiating strategy, the female dancer can recognize the currently employed modes of ownership that may be shaping and controlling a dance so often assumed to be a liberating, empowering force for a woman.

Only then can she break through its barriers, confound the East/West binary, and claim the dance as her own to perform without boundaries.

In addition to her sensitivity toward these bordered significances, she must also be aware of gender inscriptions and restrictions within the art form itself. Judith Lynne Hanna has written at length regarding the gender coding and potential gender rebellion provided by dance:

Dance may be understood as a medium through which choreographers, directors and producers manipulate, interpret, legitimate and reproduce the patterns of gender cooperation and conflict that order their social world. Dance images may lead to the reinforcing of ongoing models, the acquiring of new responses, the weakening or strengthening of inhibitions over fully elaborated patterns in a person's repertoire, and the facilitating of performance of previously learned behavior that was encumbered by restraints. Distanced from the everyday, a dance performance also permits exploration of dangerous challenges to the status quo, without the penalties of the everyday life situation.

More specifically, dance sends gendered messages through reoccurring tales and themes. Here, Hanna takes Bharatanatyam somewhat to task. She states that its dancers, mostly female, send the following messages (both religious and secular) to men and women:

1. Women should "accept men's lustful, quasi-divine or symbolically one-with-the-universe freedom to wander outside of marriage;"
2. Women have a "duty to be faithful, giving, and forgiving;" and
3. Women should "serve their husbands as subordinates and bear children."

The canonical depiction of femininity in Bharatanatyam is somewhat dictated by its source text/bible, the *Natya Shastra*, whereby eight heroines are codified as "male-defined ideal women." In the resultant repertory, the woman's plight consists of "longing, hesitation, sorrow, loneliness, anxiety, fear, parting, yearning, pleading, forgiveness, faithfulness, despondency, envy, self-disparagement, depression, derangement, madness, shame, grief, and being rebuked, insulted and mocked by one's family and deceived by one's lover."

In addition, dancers may reinforce these "feminine" inscriptions in their physical interpretations of *padam* song verses. The *padam* is one of the most demanding and creative midsections of the Bharatanatyam recital. It is all expression (*abinaya*), containing devotional, narrative songs by which the dancer enacts stories of the Supreme Being and his lovers. The section's gendered themes become embodied by the female dancer as she mimetically expresses exemplary submissive sentiments such as the following: "You alone I desire, you are my protector always. Quickly come to me! I am endowed with virtues. With deep desire in my heart, I await you. Oh, compassionate one, do not slight me now, but come!"

Themes such as this one are deeply seeded culturally in India through Bharatanatyam. Further, even the "poster goddess" of feminist dancers-Kali-can be inhibited and defeated by the gender-coding inherent in dance. For example, following is a legendary account of Shiva, Kali, and their dancing dynamic:

Legends say Shiva and his counterpart, the goddess Kali, compete in dance contests [...]. Shiva performed many dances that Kali was able to imitate perfectly. Out of frustration, Shiva exploited her sense of modesty and raised his right foot to the level of his crown and danced in that pose. Kali could have emulated this pose, but feminine modesty led her to withdraw from the contest. Kali lost not because she was an inferior dancer, but because she is a woman and affirmed her subservience in this role.

Thus, the encoding by the Bharatanatyam repertory and its tales of love for and liaisons with the Divine-does not stop at the parameters of the performance space but creeps into the cultural, collective consciousness. Amateur dance student Shakuntala voices her desire to embody and emulate Bharata Natyam's "ideal Indian woman." She states, "The dance allows me to act the pleading, teasing, coquettish movements, and they imply female subjugation. The subjugation or deference lies at the very root of the Indian family tradition. So although I couldn't be the person in the dance, I can experience it through the dance."

Although this statement may read like a "feminist nightmare," closer study also suggests female power and agency. Indeed, Shakuntala may interpret her dance as one of subjugation, but she nonetheless chooses to dance this interpretation. With the fluidity of interpretation under her control, she may just as easily choose to dance another "meaning." For implicit in Bharatanatyam performance and repertory is a dancer's agency as she embodies the text. Furthermore, in a performative paradigm, female audience members may also employ agency as they translate the dance messages. Hanna admits that many of the Bharatanatyam themes and tales are open to feminist reinterpretation as they "may evoke erotic fantasy, provide avenues for repressed and suppressed energies, and allow women temporary escape from human toil (and, a feminist perspective might add from male dominance) through identification with the prestige and freedom of the devadasi."

Furthermore, "women may imagine themselves as *Gopis* (milkmaids) who sport with the deity in wild carnal love." In addition, *padams* may also include tales "of women who are not so resigned, and who vent their anger on the wayward man by taunting him and by denigrating their rivals." A crucial feminist strategy when negotiating the Bharatanatyam repertoire is the engagement of multiple meanings, especially in the thematic context of divine love and longing. The reoccurring theme of the woman overwhelmed and confined by longing for her lover is just one earthly or temporal translation of what is actually "an expression of the love and longing of the human soul for union with the divine spirit."

Even more important is the allowance within the *padam* for "an exhaustive exploration of every possible meaning of a phrase which is repeated several times in order that the dancer may interpret every shade of meaning." Through expression of theme, action, or emotion in Indian dance (*abinaya*), the dancer is no longer limited by the text but is freed and spiritually empowered through her own creative control and interpretative choices. Dancer Kalanidhi Narayanan describes *abhinaya* in Bharatanatyam as "true emotion"-a phenomenon in which one "lives the situation" on stage.

She affirms the freeing power of *abhinaya* which is "like catching the horizon. You have to go on and on." And dancer/teacher Priya Govind declares that the freedom of the divine journey begins with the control, technique, and, therefore, power of a dancer who has discovered her "inside energy" and who has learned "to pause, to 'throw' with effect, to understate, and to use the grammar of dance" to reach divinity. The female control and agency displayed through a Bharatanatyam performance has slowly found larger representation in the social setting of contemporary India.

During the revivalist movement of the 20s and 30s, women started moving into the formerly male domain of teaching as the devadasis began instructing the new Brahmin dancers. And today, "women are beginning to participate in national political life, become priests, assume guru roles, and choreograph and teach their own dances." Furthermore, Bharatanatyam may be viewed as a vital component of the socialization of many Indian girls by which they also take a public role in a nationalist project of cultural identity. Contemporary dancer and choreographer Shobana Jeyasingh (now living in the United States) recounts her parents' insistence that she take classes as a young girl: "The idea was that by doing that [taking class], we kept faith with something ancient and precious about Indian culture."

Yet, some material feminists would argue that a patriarchal socioeconomic structure currently exists which limits this "personal and political" potential for many women. Meduri writes:

Dance now needs money, which trusts and various arts associations are providing to ensure its continuity. Who has the money in the present system? In a traditional patriarchal society such as India, men have always been invested with power and they have always made the rules. The female dancer, then, by returning to this system, is actually returning to man.

Whereas dance once provided an affirmation of community and a means of professional achievement for the devadasi, the contemporary dance scene seems to impart the impression of a community that is competitive and somewhat fractured. India "cannot provide solo concerts for all of its dancers as the number of dancers outweighs the number of performance slots;" thus, women are forced to negotiate the world marketplace, marginalizing those without economic means to compete on this scale.

Meduri laments the "schizophrenic" modern Bharatanatyam dancer who must dance stories of gods on stage while competing in a "ruthless secular world" offstage. Scholars continually debate whether female freedom and spiritual agency actually exists for classical Indian dancers today. Specifically, Anne-Marie Gaston explores the still prevalent male control over the female Bharatanatyam dancer:

In some ways, the husband (or even the father) of the contemporary dancer can be said to serve the same function as the patron of the devadasi; his influence, and sometimes his financial backing, help to secure performances for his wife (or daughter). For while teaching Bharatanatyam has become a lucrative profession, there are few dancers who can support themselves as performers alone. Further, Hanna states that "few married women are permitted to pursue public performance," while Meduri deploy the all-important weapon of the feminist when decrying her object position at the hands of the male spectator: that is, the "male gaze." She writes, however, from a personal and potent perspective:

I have had critics review me as a dancer with a "graceful figure" and "a lot of glamour." I disdained this reduced position intellectually, but I actually reinforced it in my own action, attitude, and manner. Who was I dressing for, and why? In fact, I was taught to dance, to gesticulate, and even to feel by male dance teachers. Although there are some female dance teachers today, most contemporary women dancers are taught by men. Thus, the dancer, in the most impressionable period of her life, is taught to interpret herself and her art through the male filter.

Here, I must again intercede as I feel the shackles of objectification imposed by the "gaze" do not need to be resignedly accepted by the dancer, nor does she have to see herself complicit in this male-orchestrated strategy to sexualize and objectify her. I repeat, Bharatanatyam invites assertion of agency by the female dancer. Famous dancer-choreographer Mrinalini Sarabhai recounts in *Creations* her "rebellion" against a male guru, asserting her own physical/spiritual claim to the dance and its transcendent power:

A particular step he taught me, my body refused to do. My mind also rejected the *adavu*. I requested him to change it, which he did. "You are a dancer from your last birth," he said. "That *adavu* was not for you. I took it from a film I saw. It is not really Bharatanatyam."

Sarabhai represents legions of Bharatanatyam dancers who have used the dance to negotiate or negate the "gaze;" they acknowledge the mechanism and return its "stare" by examining and performing a more personal, female experience which they own-*it is their tale to tell*. In one of her dances, Sarabhai depicts a young girl who dances the traditional form of Bharatanatyam; however, once the girl "is snatched away in the midst of her games and play, to be married," Sarabhai incorporates less orthodox movement. She explains: "The *sollukathus* of Bharatanatyam (the rhythmic syllables) became alive for I infused them with expressiveness and stressed the powerful rhythm of each beat. The hatred, the greed, the jealousy are brought out in forceful movement and desperation and sorrow in the accented syllables."

Other contemporary dancer-choreographers have become more radical in their use (or nonuse) of traditional Bharatanatyam elements, prompting dance critic Leela Venkataraman to plead with modern choreographers in an interview with journalist Molly McQuade: "You can bring Bharatanatyam forward and do new things with it, but please do not change it beyond recognition." Many of these dancers are critical of the lack of physical freedom they find inherent in the dance. Jeyasingh feels the body is too "constrained" in Bharatanatyam and uses modern dance in her choreographic reconfigurations. She recounts: "I wanted to make the dancers roll on the floor and embrace it in a much looser way than doing Bharatanatyam footwork."

Choreographer Parijat Desat (based in Los Angeles) uses some of Bharata Natyam's external techniques but "resists" most traditional aspects of the dance which she feels reinscribe female subjugation: "What draws me to Bharatanatyam is the linear clarity, from the edge of your fingertips through the whole body-but I feel constrained by the position of the body in Bharatanatyam." Probably the most renowned Indian dancer-choreographer, who incorporates Bharata Natyam's technique, while engaging in a critical dialogue with many other aspects of the dance, is Chandralekha.

Often cited as a feminist, Chandralekha takes issue with the repertoire and themes of Bharatanatyam; she "questions the appropriateness of as basic a convention as the yearning of a female dancer for her male lover, her master, her God." Therefore, she prefers "abstract themes" conveyed through modern dance and vestiges of Bharata Natyam's basic vocabulary. Her themes often address gender roles in society. For example, "she performs a duet during which she straddles a male dancer whose head appears from between her legs. The role reversal she expresses comes from the concept of Shakti as an active female force."

The resistance and arguments by these dancers pose significant problems for me, however. When using a "gendered" paradigm to claim power through their dance, they are also reinscribing said paradigm which may have subjugated them in the first place. Although I applaud the celebration of female presence, I believe the dance should also be recognized as having the potential to exceed the gendered body-to move dancer and audience beyond these binary, earthly parameters. "Indians say, 'Without Shakti, Shiva is nothing.'" And it must be noted that the Bharatanatyam dancer does not solely become the woman depicted in the songs and tales of the *padams* and *varnams*. She also embodies Krishna and other male deities as she travels a gendered path to divine unity. Hanna notes that "female dancers see themselves empowered as they play both goddesses and gods. In role reversal, there is momentary sharing in power."

Furthermore, as the dancer moves between genders, she becomes powerful enough to rise above them, creating a new form of spiritual energy which is no longer defined by biology or gender. Barba and Savarese cites dancer Sanjukta Panigrahi who refers to the energy as "Shakti which is neither masculine nor feminine. A performer of either sex is always Shakti, energy which creates." This complicates and somewhat challenges Chandralekha's choreographic suggestion that Shakti is an energy of only one gender-that is, female. With both genders present, I believe the energy for the dancer and audience (female and male) becomes more inclusive, multifaceted, tensioned and, therefore, more powerful and unrestricted by material/physical realities.

The Indian concepts of *lasya* and *tandava* also speak to this paradigm. "These terms do not refer to women and men or to masculine or feminine qualities, but to softness and vigor as aspects of energy interaction between opposites which brings to mind the poles of a magnetic field or the tension between body and shadow. It would be arbitrary to particularize them sexually." This phenomenon is potently illustrated by Ardhanarishvara who is a manifestation of Shiva as "Lord who is half woman," i.e., Parvata. Significantly, the halves of this dancing, divine incarnation are gendered as the following song lyrics to the dance *Shiva Ardhanarishwara* illustrate: "Two gods in one. The female half jingles with golden arm bracelets; the male half is adorned with bracelets of serpents. The female half is capable of all creation; the male half is capable of all destruction."

But what divine, exceedant power may be manifest through this interplay of gendered energy! Within this image, one may find "expression of the reciprocal action of the male and female elements in the cosmos. The first dance created by Shiva Ardhanarishvara was crude and wild (*tandava*) while the dance created by his Parvati half [...] was delicate and gentle (*lasya*)." Again, more than gender, the energies reflect cosmic opposition and tension-a colliding, combustible dialectic by which a new entity is created which is free and open, enabling its mergence with said cosmos.

The above paradigm suggests incredible potential for any Bharatanatyam dancer and seems to render moot most gender arguments. For me, the critical feminist question when interrogating Bharatanatyam is as follows: What defines freedom and power for a woman in this dance? I would argue that the release from self as one realizes divine unity with the universe is an ultimate realization of freedom and power. Heinrich Zimmer writes that in Bharatanatyam, "The dancer becomes amplified into a being endowed with supra-normal powers. The dance induces trance, ecstasy, the experience of the divine, the realization of one's own secret nature and, finally, mergence into the divine essence."

Bharatanatyam is situated within Hindu philosophy (as is all classical Indian dance), providing a pathway to enlightenment for performers and audience alike. The art can invoke *rasa* which is defined by Abhinavagupta (11th century scholar and authoritative interpreter of *Natya Shastra*) as "a state of union with the universal spirit which both artist and spectator achieve by transcending the pain and pleasure of everyday life." Within this dynamic, "the duality of subject and object disappear through intense introversion and, ultimately, a state is evoked unlike any empirical experience. This state is a transcendental one." Yet, one does not have to ascribe to the Hindu faith to achieve this state through dance. Theorist Sondra Horton Fraleigh asserts that all dance performance, whether intentionally devotional or not, becomes transcendental; dance cannot help but be a spiritual, communal conduit due to its innate intersubjectivity:

Because the material of dance is lived within an intersubjective field as the self escapes its boundaries toward the other, the dancer and the audience both transcend self-limitations in the dance, the dancer in the performance of the dance and the audience in the perceptual enactment of the dance. The dancer and audience come together for just this purpose. They seek a common ground of understanding and display a desire for communion, a communion that is tacitly undertaken and lived instantly through the body. In one sense, they share bodily lived limitations, those of being body; likewise, they share transcendent possibilities because of the self-transcendent nature of the body.

This is not to suggest that all dancers embrace Bharata Natyam's spiritual power. As previously noted, there is a female faction of the Bharatanatyam community who criticizes and resist what they view as restrictive aspects of the dance. Curiously, many of these critics refer to it in purely physical terms, e.g., the contemporary choreographers Jeyasingh and

Desat cited earlier in this article. Furthermore, some take issue with the revivalists who placed the dance strictly within the realm of the devotional when reconstituting the dance in the 20s and 30s. In her revivalist fervor, Rukmini Devi stated: "Like the *Vedas*, the *Upanishads*, the *Bhagavad Gita*, *Dhmmapada*, and other scriptures, Bharatanatyam is a method of spiritual learning for human ends. Therefore, it is not to be expected to reflect modern life and its ways."

To this, feminist dancer Meduri retorts, "Indian dance today functions in a secular reality-in the gap between philosophic vision and every day reality. Today's Bharatanatyam, with its danced stories of God evoked in a secular world, is analogous to a human being walking forward with his face turned backwards."

The spiritual debate is typified by the differing views held by many in the dance community over the presence of the Nataraja (holy figure of dancing Shiva) on the stage during performance. Devi felt that its presence was necessary to reinforce the spiritual, devotional purpose of the dance. Early Brahmin dancer Nirmala Ramachandran does not advocate having the Nataraja on stage, citing the philosophy of Bharatanatyam pioneer Balasaraswati (a hereditary dancer of devidasi lineage) who never brought the Nataraja to the stage, declaring the temple to be "in the mind."

Critic Shanta Sherbeet Singh recently wrote: "Worshipping Nataraja should be private and should not be part of the show. The presence of Nataraja shows the confused state of mind of the dancers." Yet, do these arguments and criticisms negate the power of Bharatanatyam-a power that may be accessed by a woman and shared with her audience? I submit that these arguments actually fuel the cosmos.

Recognized and channeled, the tensions energize and translate the mortal dance, enabling the woman to exceed earthly limitations. Further inciting the tensions, arguments have also ensued over the sex and eroticism component of Bharatanatyam. Wenndy O-Flaherty posits that excessive energy "endangers the universe;" yet, she submits that dance, using a corporeal means (i.e., a sexual body), can facilitate spiritual engagement, control, and expansion.

"Like yoga, dance channels violent but useful forces; and, like yoga, it both heightens sexual powers and internalizes them through the use of techniques of elaborately pinpointed physical control and deep concentration." Therefore, Bharatanatyam would seemingly be robbed of power if denied its *shringara* (eroticism); this element "interweaves dance with sex to convey messages of love for God and find analogy in the bliss of sexual congress, a phase of the soul's migration, akin to mystery, potential danger, heaven and ecstasy." *Padams* are often centered on erotic content concerning of the desirous women and incarnations of God. Through the dance, however, sexuality becomes spirituality, thus negating the possibility of objectification or commodification of the female dancer by the male viewer. Projesh Banerji writes in *Erotica in Indian Dance*: "No iota of sensual vulgarity or indecency is attached to the doings of the heavenly creatures. Sex is regarded as divine, with complete negation of human lust."

And although Devi and other revivalists tried to minimize the erotic component of Bharatanatyam, other dancers stressed its importance. Hereditary dancer Balasaraswati disparaged the "cleansing efforts" by the revivalists as follows: "*Shringara*, which is considered to be the greatest obstacle to spiritual realization, is itself an instrument for uniting the dancer with Divinity. Therefore the question of 'purifying' *shringara* becomes a redundancy, if not impertinence." Interestingly, even the spiritual component of Bharatanatyam has been criticized by some feminists as an impossible ideal which enslaves women as they futility attempt to attain *rasa* or translation through the dance. For example, Meduri writes:

> The twentieth-century performing artist, living in a secular reality, struggles to embrace, emotionally and intellectually, the theoretical ideal that has been set up. If she cannot personally achieve the ideal, she repeats the theory. So theoretician and artist trace the same circle, the figure eight,

in which both are held mutually captive. As stated above, the spiritual quandary seems unanswerable and unsolvable for the female dancer. But, who can measure and define such an intangible and highly personal phenomenon as spiritual translation, wholeness, and enlightenment? I believe one must simply have faith in the possibility, power, and resultant liberation of the transcendent experience.

Also empowering for women are the testimonies offered by lifelong dancers who have experienced Bharata Natyam's mystical, divine unity. Balawaraswati likened Bharatanatyam to a sacred temple, with the dancer moving through great halls toward its inner sanctum where "the drum beats die down to the simple and solemn chanting of sacred verses in the closeness of God. The devotee takes to his heart the god he has so far glorified outside." Sarabhai writes that the dance "becomes so personal and intimates an expression that the one who sees often becomes one with the one who seeks. Even a moment of forgetfulness is the beginning of awareness. Art, at its greatest, liberates the spirit."

And although Meduri posits that "this theatre is an expression of just one religious world view," other teachers, choreographers, and dancers would describe the spiritual component and power of Bharatanatyam as knowing no one specific religion, God, or world view.

Guru Indira Rajan declares that "any god can be there." For a Christian student's recital, Rajan "composed a *varnam* for her on Jesus." Echoing these universal and inclusive sentiments, Mulk Raj Anand states that Bharatanatyam incites "intense awareness in those who can read behind the symbols of any faith the meaning of their own individual spiritual struggles."

As evidenced by these affirmations of the spiritual power inherent in the dance, women should embrace the metaphysical possibilities that refute objectification. Without Hindu ascription, the dance phenomenon alone still suggests an obliteration of the ego which facilitates a synthesis of a higher order. Fraleigh entitles this phenomenon "I-thou:"

The I- thou relation describes simple wholeness, the dissolution of objectivity. It is difficult to conceive as relation, because there is no thing-it has disappeared. I do not live myself toward the dance when I am unified in it because I am not aware of it as a thing, I am its unfolding, with no thought about it. As one attains her purposes in dance, the vibrant life of her dance appears. In mystical thought and art, present centeredness is valued as participation in the essence of God.

In the concept of the "I-thou," I find great inspiration, hope, and empowerment for female dancers. In Bharatanatyam, I find living evidence of the "I-thou" as testified by its practitioners. It is here I rest my argument, for if I am looking for female power and freedom through dance as my rebuttal to feminist criticism, I have found it in this paradigm, i.e., in the transcendent possibilities of Bharatanatyam.

On mid-thirties that E. Krishna Iyer the freedom fighter, first coined the term 'Bharatanatyam' for the then Sadir dance. It is the most widely practised of Indian classical dances in South India, and has its origin in Tamil Nadu. It is the most ancient of all the classical dance forms in India, which are based on Natya Shastra, the Bible of the classical Indian dance. The term "Bharathanatyam" was introduced in the mid-thirties by E. Krishna Iyer and later spread by Rukminidevi Arundale, and is thought to derive from the four syllables, BHAva (expression) RAga (music)TAla(rhythm) NATYAM(dramatic art).

It is highly probable that E. Krishna Iyer was inspired by Subrahmanya Bharathi's poem written before 1929, wherein he writes, Bharatanatya Kuttidvire in the context of wishing Indians to become accomplished in every art, science and craft. However, the social taboo was considerably removed from Sadir by E.Krishna Iyer's re christening that dance form as Bharatanatyam. This dance has now come to stay as the classical dance that originated in Tamilnadu. But this again has no relevance today, for it has become deeply rooted in various states of India. Dance teachers have enormously contributed to national harmony by starting institutions all over the country.

The legend says thay Gods and Godesses pleaded with Lord Brahma for another Veda to be created that would be simple for the common man to understand, which is particularly important in Kali Yuga. Granting their wish, Lord Brahma created the Panchamaveda, the Fifth Veda, or NatyaVeda, a quintessence of the main four Vedas. Brahma took pathya (words) form the Rigveda, abhinaya (communicative elements of the body movements, cf. mime) from the Yajurveda, geeth (music and chant) from Samaveda, and rasa (vital sentiment and emotional element) from Atharvaveda to form the fifth Veda, NatyaVeda. After creating this Veda, Lord Brahma handed it to sage Bharata and asked him to propagate it on earth. Obeying the fiat of Lord Brahma, sage Bharata wrote down Natyashastra. Bharata together with groups of the Gandharavas and Apsaras performed natya, nrtta and nrtya before Siva.

It became the most authoritative text on the artistic technique of classical Indian dances, especially Bharathanatyam and Odissi. It is also possible that the term "Bharathanatyam" partly owes its name to sage Bharata's. The Natya Shastra reads, "When the world had become steeped in greed and desire, in jealousy and anger, in pleasure and pain, the Supreme One (Brahma) was asked by the people to create an entertainment which could be seen and heard by all, for the scriptures were not enjoyed by the masses, being too learned and ambiguous." "This art is not merely for your pleasure, but exhibits cosmic expression (bhava) for all the worlds.

This art has been created following the movements of the world in work and play, profit, peace, laughter, battle and slaughter, yielding the fruit of righteousness to those who follow the moral law, a restraint for the unruly, and a discipline for the followers of the rule; to create wisdom in the ignorant, learning in scholars, afford sport to kings, and endurance to the sorrow-stricken; it is replete with the diverse moods, informed with varying passions of the soul, and linked to the deeds of mankind -the best, the middling and the low - affording excellent counsel pastime and all else." Another version of the origin of Bharathanatyam is that Goddess

Parvathi taught this dance art to Usha, daughter of demon Banasura. Usha handed it down to the Gopikas of the city of Dwaraka, Lord Krishna's birth place. Lord Shiva is himself the Supreme Dancer, and the whole Universe is His Divine Dance. Goddess Parvathi dances with Him.

One can imagine that the Gods and the Goddesses, being dancers themselves, have been passing the art of the heavenly dance through many other human channels, whose aptitude, understanding, and personal idiosyncrasies naturally varied from person to person, and created a number of styles ranging from Odissi to Bharathanatyam. Bharathanatyam has been undergoing a lot of change over the centuries. It used to be and is still mostly performed by women dancers. Centuries ago the Hindu temples in South India had dancers-priestesses called devadasis who would sing, dance Dasi Attam (old version of Bharathanatyam), and play many musical instruments. They were well-versed in Sanskrit and other languages as they had to adapt compositions to suit the audience.

The devadasi tradition gradually degraded. Initially, devadasis lead a very strict and celibate life and were not allowed to have a family. As the dance entered the royal courts, the dancers were called Rajanartakis, who performed in the royal courts and gradually became royal concubines. The British colonial rule has completely corrupted the devadasi tradition. In the first half of the 19th century Bharathanatyam was revitalized and redefined by the contributions of four talented brothers known today as the Tanjore Quartet: Chinniah, Sivanandam, Ponniah and Vadivelu. Styles of Bharathanatyam were preserved in practice mostly by the guru's and performers of the Isai Velalar community of Tamil Nadu. The Tanjore Quartet organized all the basic Bharathanatyam movements of pure dance into a progressive series, adavus.

Each adavu is a basic unit taught in systematic order and then combined with others to produce choreographed Bharathanatyam sequences based upon the rhythmic pattern of a musical composition. The brothers composed new music specifically for Bharathanatyam, and introduced a different sequence of items which integrated various aspects of dance and music into a carefully coordinated, aesthetically sound progression. This infusion of creative energy marks the early 19th century as one of the most innovative periods in the history of Bharathanatyam. In the 20th century, the social status and image of Bharathanatyam was restored by Rukminidevi Arundale, the founder of Kalakshetra.

Bharathanatyam has undergone much change but is still deeply rooted in the spiritual Hindu heritage. Contemporary classical Indian dancers are both male and female artists. While most learn it as a hobby, very few make it their career and a lifestyle, as it is extremely demanding and complex in terms of dedication and daily practise. Most of the contemporary choreographers and dancers may use the formal Bharathanatyam technique or its elements to stage ballets presenting various themes such as nationalism, unity of religions, the sanctity of the environment, the animal rights activism, the greatness of a king or a political party, or even the delightfulness of Coca-Cola.

In Vande Mataram, a dance festival organised under the auspices of Natyarangam, a project of Narada Gana Sabha in 1997 in Chennai, there was a host of topics: evils of the current education system, the caste and reservation systems, threat of nuclear weapons, AIDS, the population explosion, corruption in politics, bribery, religious fanaticism, secularism, the greed for riches, the Chinese aggression, the Dandi March, literacy, agriculture, mechanisation, industrialisation. Most recently, some dancers manage to draw their divine inspiration even from Condom Songs. The true Bharathanatyam, it has to be stated clearly, is not a vulgar form of entertainment but a sacred ritual that is supposed to bring the rasanubhava (catharsis, or spiritual upliftment) to the rasika (audience) and the dancer.

5

Sati
Victim or Victor

The role of women in Hinduism is often disputed, and positions range from quite fair to intolerant. Hinduism is based on numerous texts, some of which date back to 2000 BCE or earlier. They are varied in authority, authenticity, content and theme, with the most authoritative being the Vedas. The position of women in Hinduism is widely dependent on the specific text and the context. Positive references are made to the ideal woman in texts such as the Ramayana and the *Mahabharata*, while some texts such as the Manu Smriti advocate a restriction of women's rights. In modern times the Hindu wife has traditionally been regarded as someone who must at all costs remain chaste or pure.

This is in contrast with the very different traditions that have prevailed at earlier times in 'Hindu' kingdoms, which included highly respected professional courtesans (such as Amrapali of Vesali) sacred devadasis, mathematicians and female magicians (the *basavis*, the Tantric *kulikas*). Some European scholars observed in the nineteenth century Hindu women were "naturally chaste" and "more virtuous" than other women, although what exactly they meant by that is open to dispute. In any case, as male foreigners they would have been denied access to the secret and sacred spaces that woman often inhabited.

There is a wide variety of viewpoints within the different schools and sects of Hinduism concerning the exact nature and gender (where applicable) of the Supreme person or being; there are even sects that are sceptical about the existence of such a being. Shaktism, for example, focuses worship on the goddess Devi as the supreme embodiment of power, or Shakti (feminine strength; a female form of God). Vaishnavism and Shaivism both worship Lakshmi with Vishnu and Parvati with Shiva respectively as beings on an equal level of magnitude (the male and female aspects of God). In some instances such as with Gaudiya Vaishnavism, specific emphasis is placed on the worship of God's female aspect (Radharani) even above that of her paramour Krishna. Thus it could be said that Hinduism considers God to have both male and female aspects, as the original source of both.

Male deities (such as Shiva and Indra) are believed, in some traditions, to themselves offer worship to the Goddess, Durga:

"O Parameshwari, (The supreme Goddess) who is praised by the husband of the daughter of Himalayas (Shri Shiva)..." "O Parameshwari, who is worshipped with true feelings by the husband of Indrani (Indra) please give us the spiritual personality, the victory, the glory and destroy our enemies."

Elsewhere Shiva and Vishnu are also described as possessing feminine qualities represented through their Ardhanarishvara and Mohini forms respectively. There have also been male devotees who have claimed to be incarnations of goddesses, such as Narayani Peedam and Bangaru Adigalar of Melmaruvathur, Tamilnadu who claim to be forms or avataras of the goddess Narayani. Hindu feminists such as Phoolan Devi have also used the goddess Durga as their icon. Traditions which follow the advaita philosophy consider that ultimately the Supreme Being is formless without any particular gender, or is transcendental to such considerations.

Arthashastra and *Manusamhita* are sources about the woman's right to property or 'Stridhan', (literally meaning, property of wife). It is of two types: maintenance (in money or land given by the husband), and anything else like ornaments given to her by her family, husband, in-laws and the friends of her husband. Manu further subdivides this into six types - the property given by parents at marriage, given by the parental family when she is going to her husband's house, given by her husband out of affection (not maintenance which he is bound to give), and property given separately by brother, mother and father [Manu IX 194]. Pre-nuptial contracts are also mentioned where the groom would agree to give a set amount of brideprice to both parents and the bride. Such property belonged to the wife alone and was not to be touched by the groom or her parents except in emergencies (in sickness, in famine, threated by robbers, or for performing holy deeds). At the same time, the Manu Smriti contradicts itself by declaring that a wife has no property and the wealth earned is for the husband.

Daughters and sons equally inherited their mother's property; but some scriptures insist that a mother's property belongs solely to the daughters [Manu IX 131], in order of preference: unmarried daughters, married but poor daughters, married and rich daughters. When a father died, unmarried daughters had to be given a share in their father's property, equal to one-fourth from every brother's share [since it is assumed that the married daughter had been given her share at marriage] [Manu IX. 118]. If the family has no sons, the (appointed) daughter is the sole inheritor of the property [Manu IX 127]. Several women sages and seers are mentioned in the Upanishads, the philosophical part of the Vedas, notable among them being Gargi and Maitreyi. The Sanskrit word for female teachers as Acharyâ (as opposed to Acharya for teacher and Acharyini for teacher's wife) reveal that women were also given a place as Gurus.

The Harita Dharmasutra (of the Maitrayaniya school of Yayurveda) declares that there are two kinds of women: Sadhyavadhu who marry, and the Brahmavadini who are inclined to religion, they can wear the sacred thread, perform rituals like the agnihotra and read the Vedas. Bhavabhuti's Uttararamacharita 2.3 says that Atreyi went to Southern India where she studied the Vedas and Indian philosophy. Shankara debated with the female philosopher Ubhaya Bharati, and

Madhava's Shankaradigvijaya (9.63) mentions that she was well versed in the Vedas. Tirukkoneri Dasyai (15th century) wrote a commentary on Nammalvar's Tiruvayamoli, with reference to Vedic texts like the Taittiriya Yajurveda.

The Bhagavata Purana states that the *Mahabharata* was written specifically for women and also men who were not in the priestly Brahmin caste:

"Out of compassion, the great sage thought it wise that this would enable men to achieve the ultimate goal of life. Thus he compiled the great historical narration called the *Mahabharata* for women, laborers and friends of the twice-born."

In several schools for Vedic priests, many graduates are women. The most sacred part of the wedding ceremony involves circumambulating the sacred fire in seven steps to a Vedic mantra where the groom addresses his wife. In the Manu Smriti, on the other hand, 8 types of marriage are specified; two involve bedecking the bride with costly garments and ornaments before giving her away, two involve the groom's family giving a gift to the bride's and the other four do not involve an exchange of gifts. The Manusmriti enjoins 'Let mutual fidelity continue until death,' this may be considered as the summary of the highest law for husband and wife. [Manu IX 101]

Rigvedic verses suggest that the women married at a mature age and were probably free to select their husband. The wedding hymn in the Rigveda (RV 10.85.37-38) speaks of "husbands" (plural) for a single wife, but this may have a mythological character.

DOWRY

The practice of dowry is not endorsed by orthodox Hinduism and "may be a perversion of Sanskritic marriage prescriptions". Dowry is linked to caste status: among higher castes a dowry is expected from the girl's family, among lower ones the dowry is paid to the girl's family. As a result the prevalence of dowry increases with the process known as "Sanskriti*sati*on" and urbanization; abuse of the system has thus increased in recent years.

DIVORCE

Hinduism in general is abhorrent to divorce. A divorced woman has, in a typical Hindu society, been forced to live as a widow. However in theological areas both *Manusamhita* and *Arthashastra* say that, if the husband is impotent, a traitor, evil-liver, has become an ascetic or an outcast or is missing for a prescribed number of years, then the wife can leave him without blame and marry again. Arthashastra also declares that in other circumstances, divorce can take place only by mutual consent. Manu discusses situations where the wife wishes to return to her first husband whether she has simply deserted him or had married another.

In traditional families, widows were, and in some cases are, required to wear white sarees, and give up their ornaments, including the bindi, which signified auspiciousness; their presence at religious rites was considered inauspicious, and they were supposed to devote their lives to an austere pursuit of religion. These restrictions were traditionally strongest in the highest castes, in which the head was frequently shaved as well, and which had the severest restrictions on remarriage. These restrictions are now strictly observed only by a small minority of widows, though some degree of ritual inauspiciousness remains.

In NAsmR 12.45-48, there are three types of *punarbhu*, or remarried widow: The virgin widow, the woman who abandons her husband to take up with another man and then returns to her husband, and the woman who has no brothers-in-law who can give her offspring. Although this list is not exhaustive, it makes it clear that a punarbhu was not just any widow; she may not have been a widow at all (the second case). In the other two cases, she is a childless widow, which is an important distinction that should not be ignored. It is important to mention that although many texts do seem to admit to the existence of the remarriage of widows and sometimes allow it, it is not considered an ideal situation. A punarbhu would not be given the same rights as a woman who was married only once. I think you must also mention that the son of a punarbhu, a punarbhava, is often listed as one who is unfit to invite to a sacrifice, as is the husband of a remarried woman. The punarbhava also did not inherit as would a 'natural son'.

As of 2007, 3 per cent of the population of India consists of widows. Most of the widows are left to survive on charity; many are reduced to begging on the streets. Some surveys show that steeped in their religious beliefs and fearful of violating social customs they were brought up to believe in, many widows themselves do not want to remarry. Satî was a funeral practice among some Hindu communities in which a recently-widowed woman would either voluntarily or by use of force and coercion immolate herself on her husband's funeral pyre. This practice is now very rare and outlawed in modern India.

The term is derived from the original name of the goddess *Sati*, also known as Dakshayani, who self-immolated because she was unable to bear her father Daksha's humiliation of her (living) husband Shiva. The term may also be used to refer the widow herself. The term *sati* is now sometimes interpreted as "chaste woman." Few reliable records exist of the practice before the time of the Gupta Empire, approximately 400AD. After about this time, instances of *sati* began to be marked by inscribed memorial stones. The earliest of these are found in Sagar, Madhya Pradesh, though the largest collections date from several centuries later, and are found in Rajasthan. These stones, called *devli*, or *sati*-stones, became shrines to the dead woman, who was treated as an object of reverence and worship. They are most common in western India.

By about the 10th century *sati*, as understood today, was known across much of the subcontinent. It continued to occur, usually at a low frequency and with regional variations, until the early 19th century. Some instances of voluntary self-immolation by both women and men that may be regarded as at least partly historical accounts are included in the *Mahabharata* and other works. However, large portions of these works are relatively late interpolations into an original story, rendering difficult their use for reliable dating.

Also, neither immolation nor the desire for self-immolation is regarded as a custom in the *Mahabharata*. Use of the term *'sati'* to describe the custom of self-immolation never occurs in the Mahabarata, unlike other customs such as the Rajasuya yagna. Rather, the self-immolations are viewed as an expression of extreme grief at the loss of a beloved one. The ritual has prehistoric roots, and many parallels from other cultures are known. Compare for example the ship burial of the Rus' described by Ibn Fadlan, where a female slave is burned with her master. Aristobulus of Cassandreia, a Greek historian who traveled to India with the expedition of Alexander the Great, recorded the practice of *sati* at the city of Taxila.

A later instance of voluntary co-cremation appears in an account of an Indian soldier in the army of Eumenes of Cardia, whose two wives vied to die on his funeral pyre, in 316 BC. The Greeks believed that the practice had been instituted to discourage wives from poisoning their husbands. Voluntary death at funerals has been described in northern India before the Gupta Empire.

The original practices were called *anumarana,* and were uncommon. Anumarana was not comparable to later understandings of *sati,* since the practices were not restricted to widows -rather, anyone, male or female, with personal loyalty to the deceased could commit suicide at a loved one's funeral. These included the deceased's relatives, servants, followers, or friends. Sometimes these deaths stemmed from vows of loyalty, and bear a slight resemblance to the later tradition of seppuku in Japan.

PRACTICE

The Commission of *Sati* (Prevention) Act of 1987 Part I, Section 2(c) defines *Sati* as:

The burning or burying alive of:

i. Any widow along with the body of her deceased husband or any other relative or with any article, object or thing associated with the husband or such relative; or

ii. Any woman along with the body of any of her relatives, irrespective of whether such burning or burying is claimed to be voluntary on the part of the widow or the women or other-wise.

The act of *sati* is said to exist voluntarily; from the existing accounts, many of these acts do indeed occur voluntarily. The act may have been expected of widows in some communities, and the extent to which social pressures or expectations constitute compulsion has been much debated in modern times. However, there were also instances where the wish of the widow to commit *sati* was not welcomed by others, and where efforts were made to prevent the death. Traditionally, a person's funeral would have occurred within a day of the death, requiring decisions about *sati* to be made by that time.

When the husband died elsewhere, the widow might still die by immolation at a later date. *Sati* often emphasized the marriage between the widow and her deceased husband. For instance, rather than mourning clothes, the to-be *sati* was often dressed in marriage robes or other finery. In the preliminaries of the related act of Jauhar, both the husbands and wives have been known to dress in their marriage clothes and re-enact their wedding ritual, before going to their separate deaths.

Accounts describe numerous variants in the *sati* ritual. The majority of accounts describe the woman seated or lying down on the funeral pyre beside her dead husband. Many other accounts describe women walking or jumping into the flames after the fire had been lit, and some describe women seating themselves on the funeral pyre and then lighting it themselves. Some written instructions for the ritual exist. For instance, the *Yallajeeyam* provides detailed instructions about who may commit *sati*, cleansing for the *sati*, positioning, attire, and other ritual aspects.

COMPULSION

Sati was supposed to be voluntary, but it is known that it has often been forced. Setting aside the issue of social pressures, many accounts exist of women being physically forced to their deaths. Pictorial and narrative accounts often describe the widow being seated on the unlit pyre, and then tied or otherwise restrained to keep her from fleeing after the fire was lit. Some accounts state that the woman was drugged. One account describes men using long poles to prevent a woman from fleeing the flames.

ROYAL FUNERALS

Royal funerals sometimes have included the deaths of many wives and concubines. A number of examples of these occur in the history of Rajasthan. Maharani Raj Rajeshwari Devi of Nepal became regent in 1799 in the name of her son, after the abdication of her husband, who became a sanyasi. Her husband returned and took power again in 1804. In 1806 he was assassinated by his brother, and ten days later on 5 May 1806, his widow was forced to commit *sati*.

SYMBOLIC SATI

There have been accounts of symbolic *sati* in some Hindu communities. A widow lies down next to her dead husband, and certain parts of both the marriage ceremony and the funeral ceremonies are enacted, but without her death.

JAUHAR

The Rajput practice of Jauhar, known from Rajasthan and Madhya Pradesh was the collective suicide of a community facing certain defeat in war. It consisted of the mass immolation of women, children, the elderly and the sick, at the same time that their fighting men died in battle.

BURIALS

In some Hindu communities, it is conventional to bury the dead. Deaths of widows have been known to occur in these communities, with the widow being buried alive beside her husband, in ceremonies that are largely the same as those performed in immolation.

PREVALENCE

Records of *sati* exist across most of the subcontinent. However, there seem to have been major differences historically, in different regions, and among different communities.

NUMBERS

There are no reliable figures for the numbers who died by *sati* across the country. A local indication of the numbers is given in the records kept by the Bengal Presidency of the British East India Company. The total figure of known occurrences for the period 1813 to 1828 is 8,135,; another source gives a comparable number of 7,941 from 1815 to 1828, thus giving an average of about 507 to 567 documented incidents per year in that period. Raja Ram Mohan Roy estimated that there were ten times as many cases of *Sati* in Bengal compared to the rest of the country. Bentinck, in his 1829 report, states that 420 occurrences took place in one (unspecified) year in the 'Lower Provinces' of Bengal, Bihar and Orissa, and 44 in the 'Upper Provinces' (the upper Gangetic plain).

COMMUNITIES

It is said by some authorities that the practice was more common among the higher castes, and among those who considered themselves to be rising in social status. It was little known or unknown in most of the population of India and the tribal groups, and little known or unknown in the lowest castes. According to at least one source, it was very rare for anyone in the later Mughal Empire except royal wives to be burnt. However, it has been said elsewhere that it was unusual in higher caste women in the south.

REGIONAL VARIATIONS

It was known in Rajasthan from the earliest (6th century) to the present. About half the known *sati* stones in India are in

Rajasthan. However, the extent to which individual instances of deaths resulted in veneration (glorification) implies that was not very common. It is known to have occurred in the south from the 9th century through the period of the Vijayanagara Empire. Madhavacharya, who is probably the best known of those historical figures who justified the practice, was originally a minister of the court of this empire. The practice continued to occur after the collapse of the empire, though apparently at a fairly low frequency. In one instance more than fifty women committed *Sati* in Hampi after the war of Talikot.

In the North-Western Karnataka about fifteen *sati* stones brought from Vijayanagara can be found. The actual immolation of widows might have taken place elsewhere. The relatives of *Sati* when they migrated took *Sati* stones along with them and resurrected at their new abodes. A record exists of a minister of the kingdom of Mysore giving permission for a widow to commit *sati* in 1805. In the Upper Gangetic plain, while it occurred, there is no indication that it was especially widespread. The earliest known attempt by a government to stop the practice took place here, that of Muhammad Tughlaq, in the Sultanate of Delhi in the 14th century.

In the Lower Gangetic plain, the practice may have reached a high level fairly late in history. Based on available evidence and the existing reports of the occurrences of it, the greatest incidence of *sati* in any region and period, in terms of total numbers, occurred in Bengal and Bihar in the late 18th and early 19th centuries. This was during the earlier period of British rule, and before its formal abolition. The Bengal Presidency kept records from 1813 to 1829.

The frequency increased in periods of hardship and famine. Ram Mohan Roy suggested that it was more prevalent in Bengal than in the rest of the subcontinent. An unusually large number of the surviving reports for this period are from Bengal, also suggesting that it was most common there. In modern times, *sati* has been largely confined to Rajasthan, mostly in or near Shekhawati, with a few instances in the Gangetic plain.

CURRENT INCIDENCE

Sati still occurs, albeit rarely, in the rural areas. A well documented case from 1987 was that of 18-year old Roop Kanwar. In response to this incident, some more recent legislation against the practice was passed, first by the state government of Rajasthan, then by the central government of India. On 18 May 2006, Vidyawati, a 35-year-old woman allegedly committed *sati* by jumping into the blazing funeral pyre of her husband in Rari-Bujurg Village, Fatehpur district in the State of Uttar Pradesh. On 21 August 2006, Janakrani, a 40-year-old woman, burnt to death on the funeral pyre of her husband Prem Narayan in Sagar district.

JUSTIFICATIONS AND CRITICISMS

Brahmin scholars of the second millennium justified the practice, and gave reasonings as to how the scriptures could be said to justify them. Among them were Vijnanesvara, of the Chalukya court, and later Madhavacharya, theologian and minister of the court of the Vijayanagara Empire, according to Shastri, who quotes their reasoning. It was lauded by them as required conduct in righteous women, and it was explained that this was considered not to be suicide (suicide was otherwise variously banned or discouraged in the scriptures). It was deemed an act of peerless piety, and was said to purge the couple of all accumulated sin, guarantee their salvation and ensure their reunion in the afterlife.

LAW BOOKS

These are relatively late works. Justifications for the practice are given in the *Vishnu Smriti*. Now the duties of a woman (are)... After the death of her husband, to preserve her chastity, or to ascend the pile after him. There is also justification in the later work of the *Brihaspati Smriti* (25-11). Both this and the *Vishnu Smriti* date from the first millennium. The *Manu Smriti* is often regarded as the culmination of classical Hindu law, and hence its position is important. It does not mention or sanction *sati* though it does prescribe life-long asceticism for most widows.

SCRIPTURES

Although the myth of the goddess *Sati* is that of a wife who dies by her own volition on a fire, this is not a case of the practice of *sati*. The goddess was not widowed, and the myth is quite unconnected with the justifications for the practice. The Puranas have examples of women who commit *sati* and there are suggestions in them that this was considered desirable or praiseworthy: A wife who dies in the company of her husband shall remain in heaven as many years as there are hairs on his person. (Garuda Purana 1.107.29) According to 2.4.93 she stays with her husband in heaven during the rule of 14 Indras, i.e. a kalpa.

In the *Ramayana,* Tara, in her grief at the death of husband Vali, wished to commit *sati*. Hanuman, Rama, and the dying Vali dissuade her and she finally does not immolate herself. In the *Mahabharata*, Madri, the second wife of Pandu, immolates herself. She holds herself responsible for the death of her husband, who had been cursed with death if he ever had intercourse.

He died while performing the forbidden act with Madri, who blamed herself for not having rejected his advances, although she was well aware of the curse. However it must be noted that this may be a much later addition to the *Mahabharata* as the entire epic as it exists now was not written and modified over millenia. Passages in the Atharva Veda, including 13.3.1, offer advice to the widow on mourning and her life after widowhood, including her remarriage.

ARGUMENT THAT THE RIG VEDA SANCTIONS SATI

It is often claimed that this most ancient text sanctions or prescribes *sati*. This is based on verse 10.18.7, part of the verses to be used at funerals. Whether they even describe *sati* or something else entirely, is disputed, the hymn is about funeral by burial, and not by cremation. There are differing translations of the passage. The translation below is one of those said to prescribe it.

Let these women, whose husbands are worthy and are living, enter the house with ghee (applied) as collyrium (to their eyes). Let these wives first step into the pyre, tearless without any affliction and well adorned.

The text does not mention widowhood, and other translations differ in their translation of the word here rendered as 'pyre' (*yoni*, literally "seat, abode"; Griffith has "first let the dames go up to where he lieth"). In addition, the following verse, which is unambiguously about widows, then contradicts any suggestion of the woman's death; it explicitly states that the widow should return to her house.

Rise, come unto the world of life, O woman - come, he is lifeless by whose side thou liest. Wifehood with this thy husband was thy portion, who took thy hand and wooed thee as a lover.

A reason given for the discrepancy in translation and interpretation of verse 10.18.7, is that one consonant in a word that meant house, *yonim agree* "foremost to the *yoni*", was deliberately changed by those who wished claim scriptural justification, to a word that meant fire, *yomiagne*.

COUNTER-ARGUMENTS WITHIN HINDUISM

No early descriptions or criticisms of the practice within Hinduism, (or in the other native religions of Buddhism or Jainism), are known before the Gupta period, as the practice was little known at that time. Explicit criticisms later in the first millennium included that of Medhatithi, a commentator on various theological works. He considered it suicide, which was forbidden by the Vedas,

One shall not die before the span of one's life is run out,

Another critic was Bana, who wrote during the reign of Harsha. Bana condemned it both as suicide, and as a pointless and futile act. Reform and bhakti movements within Hinduism tended to be anti-caste, favoured egalitarian societies, and in line with the tenor of these beliefs, they generally condemned the practice, sometimes explicitly. The Alvars condemned *sati*, in the 8th century. The Virashaiva movement in the 12th and 13th centuries also condemned it. In the early 19th century, Ram Mohan Roy wrote and disseminated arguments that the practice was not part of Hinduism, as part of his campaign to ban the practice.

NON-HINDU VIEWS AND CRITICISMS

The Sikh religion explicitly proscribed the practice since Sikhism's origin. The principal early foreign visitors to the subcontinent, who left records of the practice, were from Western Asia, mostly Muslim, and later on, Europeans. Both groups were fascinated by the practice, and they sometimes described it as horrific, but they also often described it as an incomparable act of devotion. Ibn Battuta described an instance, but said that he collapsed or fainted and had to be carried away from the scene. European artists in the eighteenth century produced many images for their own native markets, showing the widows as heroic women, and moral exemplars.

As Islam established itself in the subcontinent, opinions about *sati* changed and it was increasingly regarded as a barbaric practice. The earliest known governmental efforts to halt the practice were undertaken by Muslim rulers, including Muhammad Tughlaq. Europeans also showed a change in their attitudes regarding local customs as their home countries became dominant local powers. The earliest Europeans to establish themselves were the Portuguese in Goa. They tried early on to override local customs and practices, including *sati*, as they attempted to spread Christianity throughout the territories in their control. The British entered India as a trading body, and in the earlier periods of their rule, they were largely indifferent to local practices.

The practice of *sati* and its later legal abolition by the British (along with the suppression of the thuggee) went on to become one of the standard justifications for British rule. British attitudes in their later history in India are usually given in the following much repeated quote, usually ascribed to General Napier –

You say that it is your custom to burn widows. Very well. We also have a custom: when men burn a woman alive, we tie a rope around their necks and we hang them. Build your funeral pyre; beside it, my carpenters will build a gallows. You may follow your custom. And then we will follow ours.

In her article "Can the Subaltern Speak?" Gayatri Spivak, then an English professor at Columbia University, discusses whether *sati* can be a form of self-expression by women who cannot demonstrate their independence in any other manner.

SUPPRESSION

MUGHAL PERIOD

Humayun issued a royal fiat against *sati*, which he later withdrew. Akbar required that permission be granted by his officials, and these officials were instructed to delay the woman's decision for as long as possible. The reasoning was that she was less likely to choose to die once the emotions of the moment had passed. In the reign of Shah Jahan, widows with children were not allowed to burn under any circumstances. In other cases, governors did not readily give permission, but could be bribed to do so.

Later on in the Mughal period, pensions, gifts and rehabilitative help were offered to the potential *sati* to wean her away from committing the act. Children were strictly forbidden from following the practice. The later Moghul rulers continued to put obstacles in the way but the practice still persisted in areas outside their capitals. Guru Nanak, the first Guru of the Sikhs spoke out against the practice of *sati*. The strongest attempts to control it were made by Aurangzeb. In 1663, he "issued an order that in all lands under Mughal control, never again should the officials allow a woman to be burnt". Despite such attempts however, the practice continued, especially during periods of war and upheaval.

BRITISH AND OTHER EUROPEAN TERRITORIES

By the end of the 18th century, the practice had been banned in territories held by some European powers. The

Portuguese banned the practice in Goa by about 1515, though it is not believed to have been especially prevalent there. The Dutch and the French also banned it in Chinsurah and Pondicherry. The British who by then ruled much of the subcontinent, and the Danes, who held the small territories of Tranquebar and Serampore, permitted it until the 19th century.

Attempts to limit or ban the practice had been made by individual British officers in the 18th century, but without the backing of the British East India Company. The first formal British ban was imposed in 1798, in the city of Calcutta only. The practice continued in surrounding regions. Toward the end of the 18th century, the evangelical church in Britain and its members in India started campaigns against *sati*. Leaders of these campaigns included William Carey and William Wilberforce, and both appeared to be motivated partly by a desire to convert Indians to Christianity. These movements put pressure on the company to ban the act, and the Bengal Presidency started collecting figures on the practice in 1813.

From about 1812, the Bengali reformer Raja Rammohan Roy started his own campaign against the practice. He was motivated by the experience of seeing his own sister-in-law commit *sati*. Among his actions, he visited Calcutta cremation grounds to persuade widows not to so die, formed watch groups to do the same, and wrote and disseminated articles to show that it was not required by scripture. On 4 December 1829, the practice was formally banned in the Bengal Presidency lands, by the then governor, Lord William Bentinck. The ban was challenged in the courts, and the matter went to the Privy Council in London, but was upheld in 1832. Other company territories also banned it shortly after.

Although the original ban in Bengal was fairly uncompromising, later in the century British laws include provisions that provided mitigation for murder when "the person whose death is caused, being above the age of 18 years, suffers death or takes the risk of death with his own consent". *Sati* remained legal in some princely states for a time after it had been abolished in lands under British control. Jaipur banned the practice in 1846. Nepal continued to practice *Sati* well into the 20th century. On the Indonesian island of Bali, *sati* was practised by the aristocracy as late as 1905, until Dutch colonial rule pushed for its termination.

MODERN TIMES

Following outcries after each instance, there have been various fresh measures passed against the practice, which now effectively make it illegal to be a bystander at an event of *sati*. The law now makes no distinction between passive observers to the act, and active promoters of the event; all are supposed to be held equally culpable. Other measures include efforts to stop the 'glorification' of the dead women. Glorification includes the erection of shrines to the dead, the encouragement of pilgrimages to the site of the pyre, and the derivation of any income from such sites and pilgrims. Another instance of systematic *Sati* happened in 1973, when Savitri Soni sacrificed her life with her husband in Kotadi village of Sikar District in Rajasthan. Thousands of people saw this incident.

Following the outcry after the *Sati* of Roop Kanwar, the Indian Government enacted the Rajasthan *Sati* Prevention Ordinance, 1987 on October 1, 1987 and later passed the Commission of *Sati* (Prevention) Act, 1987. The *Prevention of Sati Act* makes it illegal to abet, glorify or attempt to commit *Sati*. Abetment of *Sati*, including coercing or forcing someone to commit *Sati* can be punished by death sentence or life imprisonment, while glorifying *Sati* is punishable with 1-7 years in prison. However, enforcement of these measures is not always consistent. The National Council for Women (NCW) has suggested amendments to the law to remove some of these flaws. Prohibitions of certain practices, such as worship at ancient shrines, are a matter of controversy.

On October 11, 2008, a 75-year-old woman committed '*sati*' by jumping into her 80-year-old husband's funeral pyre at Checher in the Kasdol block of Chhattisgarh's Raipur district. Though *sati*is considered a Hindu custom, the women, known as *Sati* in Hindu religious literature, did not commit suicide on their dead husband's pyre. The first woman known as *Sati* was the consort of Lord Shiva. She burnt herself in fire as protest against her father who did not give her consort Shiva the respect she thought he deserved, while burning herself she prayed to reborn again as the new consort of Shiva, which she became and her name in the new incarnation was Parvati.

Other famous woman in Hindu literature titled *Sati* was Savitri. When Savitri's husband Satyavan died, the Lord of death, Yama arrived to take his soul. Savitri begged Yama to restore Satyavan and take her life instead, which he could not do. So Savitri followed Lord Yama a long way. After a long way in which Yama noticed that Savitri was losing strength but was still following him and her dead husband, Yama offered Savitri a boon, anything other than her husband's life. Savitri asked to have children from Satyavan. In order to give Savitri her boon, Lord Yama had no choice but to restore Satyavan to life and so Savitri gained her husband back.

These two women along with other women in Hindu mythology who were exceptionally devoted to their husbands symbolized the truthful Indian wife who would do everything for their husband and they were named *Sati*. The meaning of the word *sati* is righteous. But as written earlier the women named *Sati*, in Hindu religious literature, did not commit suicide on their dead husband's pyre. Therefore the custom of burning the widow on her dead husband's pyre probably did not evolve from religious background but from social background. There are different theories about the origins of *Sati*.

One theory says that *Sati* was introduced to prevent wives from poisoning their wealthy husbands and marry their real lovers. Other theory says that *Sati* began with a jealous queen who heard that dead kings were welcomed in heaven by hundreds of beautiful women, called Apsaras. And therefore when her husband died, she demanded to be burnt on her dead husband's pyre and so to arrive with him to heaven and this way to prevent the Apsaras from consorting with her husband. There are also other theories about the origins of *Sati*. Even though *Sati* is considered an Indian custom or a Hindu custom it was not practiced all over India by all Hindus but only among certain communities of India. On the other hand, sacrificing the widow in her dead husband's funeral or pyre was not unique only to India. In many ancient communities it was an acceptable feature.

This custom was prevalent among Egyptians, Greek, Goths, Scythians and others. Among these communities it was a custom to bury the dead king with his mistresses or wives, servants and other things so that they could continue to serve him in the next world. Another theory claims that *Sati* was probably brought to India by the Scythians invaders of India. When these Scythians arrived in India, they adopted the Indian system of funeral, which was cremating the dead. And so instead of burying their kings and his servers they started cremating their dead with his surviving lovers. The Scythians were warrior tribes and they were given a status of warrior castes in Hindu religious hierarchy. Many of the Rajput clans are believed to originate from the Scythians. Later on other castes who claimed warrior status or higher also adopted this custom.

This custom was more dominant among the warrior communities in north India, especially in Rajasthan and also among the higher castes in Bengal in east India. Among the Rajputs of Rajasthan, who gave lot of importance to valor and self sacrifice, wives and concubines of the nobles even committed suicide, when they came to know that their beloved died in battlefield? In other parts of India it was comparatively low. And among the majority of Indian communities it did not exist at all. A few rulers of India tried to ban this custom. The Mughals tried to ban it. The British, due to the efforts of Hindu reformers like Raja Ram Mohan Roy outlawed this custom in 1829.

There aren't exact figures about the number of *Sati* incidences. In general, before this custom was outlawed in 1829, there were a few hundred officially recorded incidences each year. Even after the custom was outlawed, this custom did not vanish completely. It took few decades before this custom almost vanished. But still there are rare incidences in which the widow demands to voluntary commit *Sati*. In 1987 an eighteen years old widow committed *Sati* in a village of Rajasthan with the blessing of her family members. In this incidence the villagers took part in the ceremony, praising and supporting the widow for her act. In October 1999 a woman hysterically jumped on her husband's pyre surprising everyone. But this incidence was declared suicide and not *Sati*, because this woman was not compelled, forced or praised to commit this act.

In different communities of India, *Sati* was performed for different reasons and different manners. In communities where the man was married to one wife, the wife put an end to her life on the pyre. But even in these communities not all widows committed *Sati*. Those women who committed *Sati* were highly honored and their families were given lot of respect. It was believed that the woman who committed *Sati* blessed her family for seven generations after her. Temples or other religious shrines were built to honor the *Sati*. In communities were the ruler was married to more than one wife; in some cases only one wife was allowed to commit *Sati*. This wife was normally the preferred wife of the husband.

This was some kind of honor for the chosen wife and some kind of disgrace for the other wives. In other communities some or all of the wives and mistresses were immolated with the husband. And in some cases even male servants were immolated with the kings. This kind of *Sati* in which the wives and servants were treated as the ruler's property intensifies the theory that *Sati* was introduced to India by the Scythian invaders of India. In some very rare incidences mothers committed *Sati* on their son's pyre and in even more rare cases husbands committed *Sati* on their wives pyres. Today *Sati* is illegal, it is also generally looked down upon but it continues to exist in the rural corners of our country. One still does hear of stray incidents of woman being forced to or trying to commit *Sati*. The country owes the abolition of this deplorable practice to the crusading efforts of Raja Rammohan Roy the 18th century social reformer.

Hand-prints are available in a temple symbolizing women who have performed *Sati*. There are many monuments erected in the Middle Ages which are dedicated to those women who committed *Sati* (Jauhar) when their honour was in danger of being violated by Saracenic princelings. These temples are called *Sati*-Mata mandirs. The reasons why this practice could have come into being are many. But the principal among them could be identified in the same milieu which gave birth to dowry. Closer examination of this practice of immolation supports this inference. Immolation as a widely prevalent practice can be seen only since the mediaeval period but there are reasons which trace its origins in antiquity.

Even a casual observer will notice that immolation is more prevalent among the higher martial caste. Among the lower castes and aboriginal tribes it is nearly absent. The prevalence of *Sati* among the higher castes is no co-incidence. As mentioned earlier, among the higher castes, a bride was looked upon as a burden as she represented a drain on the family's income while not contributing anything towards it. If this was her status as a bride, it is not surprising that if she had the misfortune to become a widow, her presence in the family was dreaded. And apart from being considered an object of ill omen, her presence after her husband demise was a dead weight to her in-laws family.

A widow's status as an unwanted burden was also a result of the taboos that prevented a widow from participating in the household work as her touch, her voice, her very appearance was considered unholy, impure and something that was to be shunned and abhorred. Thus without her husband a woman's existence was not tolerated and an extreme but logical outcome of this was immolation. Other auxiliary reasons also went into making immolation a prevalent practice. The near impossibility of widow re-marriage arising from the taboos and prejudices that sanctified virginity of a bride was an important reason. Another reason could be the non-recognition of the individuality of a woman who was considered part and parcel of her husband, without whom she was a nullity.

This attitude of looking at women is visible in the legal literature (Dharmashastra) of antiquity. The *Manusmriti* considered to be one of the most important legal texts guiding ancient Indian polity has injunctions which reflect this attitude. It says "a woman is undeserving for independence" (Ne stree svatantyam arahathi). Beliefs that a widow, especially a young one would fall into immoral practices for sensual pleasures were also used to stoke the fires of *Sati*. Strangely enough this logic was never applied to the stronger sex. Widowers were never an under-privileged lot. But the most visible factor that perpetrated *Sati* was the 'halo of honour' given to it.

Especially in the medieavel ages *Sati* was given the status of an act of honour. This was mainly so among the Rajput martial caste of northern India among whom *Sati* took the form of a collective suicide after a battle in which male members had suffered death at the enemy's hands. *Sati* was even committed by women before their husbands were actually death when their city or town was beseiged by the enemy and faced certain defeat. This form of *Sati* was more popularly known as Jouhar. The Jouhar committed by Rant Padmini of Chittor when faced by the prospect of dishonour at the hands of a Sultan from Delhi has been immortalised in Indian history.

In those days North India was under foreign subjugation. The most powerful kingdomset up by the invaders was the Sultanate of Delhi. But in Rajputana, the Rajputs had defiantly preserved their writ by resisting the Delhi Sultans. One such Rajput kingdom was at Chittor. In those days of the aribitrary feudal power structure, any feudal lord who took a fancy for any lady would claim her for himself even at the cost of killing her husband if she happened to be married or even by waging a war if she was queen or princess one such lady of unsurpassable beauty was the Rana of Chittor named Padmini.

Chittor was under the Rule of King Ratnasen, a brave and noble warrior-king. Apart, from being a loving husband and a just ruler, Ratansen was also a patron of the arts. In his court were many talented People one of whom was a musician named Raghav Chetan. But unknown to anybody, Raghav

Chetan was also a sorcerer. He used his evil talents to run down his rivals and unfortunately for him was caught red-handed in his dirty act of arousing evil spirits. On hearing this King Ratansen was furious and he banished Raghav Chetan from his kingdom after blackening his face with face and making him ride a donkey.

This harsh Punishment earned king Ratansen an uncompromising enemy. Sulking after his humiliation, Raghav Chetan made his way towards Delhi with -the aim of trying to incite the Sultan of Delhi Allah-ud-din Khilji to attack Chittor. On approaching Delhi, Raghav Chetan settled down in one of the forests nearby Delhi which the Sultan used to frequent for hunting deer. One day on hearing the Sultan's hunt party entering the forest, Raghav-Chetan started playing a melodious tone on his flute. When the alluring notes of Raghav-Chetan flute reached the Sultan's party they were surprised as to who could be playing a flute in such a masterly way in a forlorn forest.

The Sultan despatched his soldiers to fetch the person and when Raghav-Chetan was brought before him, the Sultan Allah-ud-din Khilji asked him to come to his court at Delhi. The cunning Raghav-Chetan asked the king as to why he wants to have an ordinary musician like himself when there were many other beautiful objects to be had. Wondering what Raghav-Chetan meant, Allah-ud-din asked him to clarify. Upon being told of Rani Padmini's beauty, Allah-ud-din's lust was aroused and immediately on returning to his capital he gave orders to his army to march on Chittor. But to his dismay, on reaching Chittor, Allah-ud-din found the fort to be heavily defended. Desperate to have a look at the legendary beauty of Padmini, he sent word to King Ratansen that he looked upon Padmini as his sister and wanted to meet her.

On hearing this, the unsuspecting Ratansen asked Padmini to see the 'brother'. But Padmini was more wordly-wise and she refused to meet the lustful Sultan personally. But on being persuaded she consented to allow Allah-ud-din to see her only in a mirror. On the word being sent to Allah-ud-din that Padmini would see him he came to the fort with his selected his best warriors who secretly made a careful examination of the fort's defences on their way to the Palace. On seeing Padmini, in the mirror, the lustful 'brother', Allah-ud-din Khilji decided that he should secure Padmini for himself. While returning to his camp, Allah-ud-din was accompanied for some way by King Ratansen.

Taking this opportunity, the wily Sultan treacherously kidnapped Ratansen and took him as a prisoner into his camp and demanded that Padmini come and surrender herself before Allah-ud-din Khilji, if she wanted her husband King Ratansen alive again. Allah-ud-din showed his true colours and demanded that Padmini be given to him and in return Ratnasen was to get his liberty. Word was sent into the palace about the Sultan's demand.

The Rajput generals decided to beast the Sultan at his own game and sent back a word that Padmini would be given to Ala-ud-din the next morning. On the following day at the crack of dawn, one hundred and fifty palaquins (covered cases in which royal ladies were carried in medieveal times) left the fort and made their way towards Ala-ud-din's camps. The palanquins stopped before the tent where king Ratansen was being held prisoner. Seeing that the palanquins had come from Chittor; and thinking that they had brought along with them his queen, king Ratansen was mortified. But to his surprise from the palanquins came out, not his queen and her women servants but fully armed soldiers, who quickly freed; Ratansen and galloped away towards Chittor on horses grabbed from Ala-ud-din's stables.

On hearing that his designs had been frustrated, the lustful Sultan was furious and ordered his army to storm Chittor. But hard as they tried the Sultans army could not break into the fort. Then Ala-ud-din decided to lay seige to the fort. The siege was a long drawn one and gradually supplied within the fort were depleted. Finally King Ratnasen gave orders that the Rajputs would open the gates and fight to finish with the besieging troops. On hearing of this decision, Padmini decided that with their menfolk going into the unequal struggle with the Sultan's army in which they were sure to perish, the women of Chittor had either to commit suicides or face dishonour at the hands of the victorious enemy.

The choice was in favour of suicide through Jauhar. A huge pyre was lit and followed by their queen; all the women of Chittor jumped into the flames and deceived the lustful enemy waiting outside. With their womenfolk dead, the men of Chittor had nothing to live for. Their charged out of the fort and fought on furiously with the vastly powerful array of the Sultan, till all of them perished. After this phyrrhic victory the Sultan's troops entered the fort only to be confronted with ashes and burnt bones of the women whose honour they were going to violate to *sati*sfy their lust. These women who committed Jawhar had to perish but theirmemory has been kept alive till today by bards and songs which glorify their act which was right in those days and circumstances. Thus a halo of honour is given to their supreme sacrifice.

But this halo of honour has to be seen in the light of the above compulsions of alien rule in India during the medieveal ages. From the 13th century onwards up to the coming of the British, the position of women was insecure due to the arbitrary power structure associated with the feudal society and the rule of the Sultans of Delhi. Although during the reign of the later Mughals the situation had improved relatively, women in the medieaval ages were often exposed to the lust of feudal overlords. Their insecurity increased after the demise of their husbands. This compulsion which was resultant of a particular age was by far the most important reason for the prevalence of *Sati* during the middle ages.

Although the Mughal emperor Akbar tried to curb this practice, he could not eradicate it completely. As long as circumstances made necessary the existence of such an anomalous and inhuman practice, all efforts to stamp it out were bound to fail. But with the passing of the feudal power structure and entry of the industrial age under the British, the compulsions of the medieaval age which helped the existence of *Sati* were no longer there. Hence the efforts of Raja

Rammohan Roy succeeded while those of Emperor Akbar could not. One last reason that needs to be mentioned in this context is that of grief and remorse experienced by a widowed lady.

Women as such are more sensitive and emotional than menu this explains in part the readiness of some woman to commit *Sati*. But it should be borne in mind that the proportion of voluntary *Sati* was far less and the reasons behind voluntary *Sati* though facts were blown out of proportion to justify this practice. However, in conclusion it can be observed that a complexity of factors contributed over different periods to make *Sati* a prevalent custom.

THE COMMISSION OF SATI (PREVENTION) ACT, 1987 (NO. 3 OF 1988)

An Act to provide for the more effective prevention of the commission of sati and its glorification and for matters connected therewith or incidental thereto.

Whereas *sati* or the burning or burying alive of widows or women is revolting to the feelings of human nature and nowhere enjoined by any of the religions of India as an imperative duty;

And whereas it is necessary to take more effective measure to prevent the commission of sati and its glorification;

Be it enacted by Parliament in the Thirty-eighth Year of Republic of India as follows:

PART I

Preliminary

1. Short title, extent and commencement. - (1) This Act may be called the Commission of Sati (Prevention) Act, 1987.

(2) It extends to the whole of India except the State of Jammu and Kashmir.

(3) It shall come into force in a State on such date as the Central Government may, by notification in the Official

Gazette, appoint, and different dates may be appointed for different States.

2. Definitions. - (1) In this Act, unless the context otherwise requires.-

(a) "Code" means the Code of Criminal Procedure, 1973 (2 of 1974);

(b) "Glorification" in relation to sati, whether such sati, was committed before or after the commencement of this Act, includes, among other things.-

(i) The observance of any ceremony or the taking out of a procession in connection with the commission of sati; or

(ii) The supporting, justifying or propagating the practice of sati in any manner; or

(iii) The arranging of any function to eulogise the person who has committed sati; or

(iv) The creation of a trust, or the collection of funds, or the construction of temple or other structure or the carrying on of any form of worship or the performance of any ceremony thereat, with a view to perpetuate the honour of, or to preserve the memory of, a person who has committed sati;

(c) "Sati" means the burning or burying alive of -

(i) Any widow along with the body of her deceased husband or any other relative or with any article, object or thing associated with the husband or such relative; or

(ii) any woman along with the body of any of her relatives, irrespective of whether such burning or burying is claimed to be voluntary on the part of the widow or the women or otherwise;

"Special Court" means a Special Court constituted under Sec.9;

(e) "Temple" includes any building or other structure, whether roofed or not, constructed or made to preserve the memory or a person in respect of whom sati has been committed or used or intended to be used for the carrying on of any form of worship or for the observance of any ceremony in connection with such commission.

(2) Words and expressions used but not defined in this Act and defined in the Indian Penal Code (45 of 1860) or in the Code shall have the same meanings as are respectively assigned to them in the Indian Panel Code or the Code.

PART II

Punishment for offences relating to Sati

3. Attempt to commit *sati*.- Notwithstanding anything contained in the Indian Penal Code (45 of 1860), whoever attempts to commit *sati* and does any act towards such commission shall be punishable with imprisonment for a term which may extend to one year or with fine or with both:

Provided that the Special Court trying an offence under this section shall, before convicting any person, take into consideration the circumstances leading to the commission of the offence, the act committed, the state of mind of the person charge of the offence at the time of the commission of the act and all other relevant factors.

4. Abetment of *sati*.- (1) Notwithstanding anything contained in the Indian Penal Code (45 of 1860), if any person commits *sati*, whoever abets the commission of such *sati*, either directly or indirectly, shall be punishable with death or imprisonment for life and shall also be liable to fine.

(2) If any person attempts to commit *sati*, whoever abets such attempt, either directly or indirectly, shall be punishable with imprisonment for life and shall also be liable to fine.

Explanation. - For the purposes of this section, any of the following acts or the like shall also be deemed to be an abetment, namely:

(a) Any inducement to a widow or woman to get her burnt or buried alive along with the body of her deceased husband or with any other relative or with any article, object or thing associated with the husband or such relative, irrespective of whether she is in a fit state of mind or is labouring under a state of intoxication or stupefaction or other cause impeding the exercise of her free will;

(b) Making a widow or woman believe that the commission of *sati* would results in some spiritual benefit to her or her deceased husband or relative or the general well being of the family;

(c) Encouraging a widow or woman to remain fixed in her resolve to commit *sati* and thus instigating her to commit *sati;*

(d) Participating in any procession in connection with the commission of *sati* or aiding the widow or woman in her decision to commit *sati* by taking her along with the body of her deceased husband or relative to the cremation or burial ground;

(e) Being present at the place where *sati* is committed as an active participant to such commission or to any ceremony connected with it;

(f) Preventing or obstructing the widow or woman from saving herself from being burnt or buried alive;

(g) Obstructing, or interfering with, the police in the discharge of its duties of taking any steps to prevent the commission of *sati.*

5. Punishment for glorification of *sati*.- Whoever does any act for the glorification of *sati* shall be punishable with imprisonment for a term which shall not be less than one year but which may extend to seven years and with fine which shall not be less than five thousand rupees but which may extend to thirty thousand rupees.

PART III

Powers of Collector or District Magistrate to prevent offences relating to Sati

6. Power to prohibit certain acts.- (1) where the Collector or the District Magistrate is of the opinion that *sati* or any abetment thereof is being, or is about to be committed, he may,

by order, prohibit the doing of any act towards the commission of *sati* by any person in any area or areas specified in the order.

(2) The Collector or the District Magistrate may also, by order, prohibit the glorification in any manner of *sati* by any person in any area or areas specified in the order.

(3) Whoever contravenes any order made under sub-section (1) or sub-section (2) shall, if such contravention is not punishable under any other provision of this Act, be punishable with imprisonment for a term which shall not be less than one year but which may extend to seven years and with fine which shall not be less than five thousand rupees but which may extend to thirty thousand rupees.

7. Power to remove certain temples or other structures.- (1) The State Government may, if it is satisfied that in that any temple or other structure which has been in existence for not less than twenty years, any form of worship or the performance of any ceremony is carried on with a view to perpetuate the honour of or to preserve the memory of, any person in respect of whom *sati* has been committed, by order, direct the removal of such temple or other structure.

(2) The Collector or the District magistrate may, if he is satisfied in any temple or other structure, other than that referred to in sub-section (1), any form of worship or the performance of any ceremony is carried on with a view to perpetuate the honour of, or to preserve the memory of, any person in respect of whom *sati* has been committed, by order, direct the removal of such temple or other structure.

(3) Where any order under sub-section (1) or sub-section (2) is not complied with, the State Government or the Collector or the District Magistrate, as the case may be, shall cause the temple or other structure to be removed through a police officer not below the rank of a Sub-Inspector at the cost of the defaulter.

8. Power to seize certain properties. - (1) Where the Collector or the District Magistrate has reason to believe that

any funds or property have been collected or acquired for the purpose of glorification of the commission of any *sati* or which may be found under circumstances which create suspicion of the commission of any offence under this Act, he may seize such funds or property.

(2) Every Collector or District Magistrate acting under sub-section (1) shall report the seizure to the Special Court, if any, constituted to try any offence in relation to which such funds or property were collected or acquired and shall await the orders of such Special Court as to the disposal of the same.

PART IV

Special Courts

9. Trial of offences under this Act. - (1) Notwithstanding anything contained in the Code, all offences under this Act shall be triable only by a Special Court constituted under this section.

(2) The State Government shall, by notification in the official Gazette, constitute one or more Special Courts for the trial of offences under this Act and every Special Court shall exercise jurisdiction in respect of the whole or such part of the State as may be specified in the notification.

(3) A Special Court shall be presided over by a judge to be appointed by the State Government with the concurrence of the Chief Justice of the High Court.

(4) A person shall not be qualified for appointment as a judge of a Special Court unless he is, immediately before such appointment, a Sessions Judge or an Additional Sessions Judge in any State.

10. Special Public Prosecutions. - (1) For every Special Court, the State Government shall appoint a person to be a Special Public Prosecutor.

(2) A person shall be eligible to be appointed as a Special Public Prosecutor under this section only if he had been in

practice as an advocate for not less than seven years or has held any post for a period of not less than seven years under the State requiring special knowledge of law.

(3) Every person appointed as a Special Public Prosecutor under this section shall be deemed to be a Public Prosecutor within the meaning of Cl. (u) of Sec. 2 of the Code and the Provisions of the Code shall have effect accordingly.

11. Procedure and powers of Special Courts.-(1) A Special Court may take cognizance of any offence, without the accused being committed to it for trial, upon receiving a complaint of facts which constitute such offence, or upon a police report of such facts.

(2) Subject to the other provisions of this Act, a Special Court shall for the purpose of the trial of any offence, have all the powers of a Court of Session and shall try such offence as if it were a Court of Session, so far as may be, in accordance with the procedure prescribed in the Code for trial before a Court of Session.

12. Power of Special Court with respect to other offences.- (1) When trying any offence under this Act, a Special Court may also try any other offence with which the accused may, under the Code, be charged at the same trial if the offence is connected with such other offence.

(2) If, in the course of any trial of any offence under this Act it is found that the accused person has committed any other offence under this Act or any other law, a Special Court may convict such person also of such other offence and pass any sentence authorised by this Act or such other law for the punishment thereof.

(3) In every inquiry or trial, the proceedings shall be held as expeditiously as possible and, in particular, where the examination of witnesses has begun, the same shall be continued from day to day until all the witnesses in attendance have been examined, and if any Special Court finds the adjournment of the same beyond the following date to be necessary, it shall record its reasons for doing so.

13. Forfeiture of funds or property – Where a person has been convicted of an offence under this Act, the Special Court trying such offence may, if it is considered necessary so to do, declare that any funds or property seized under Sec. 8 shall stand forfeited to the State.

14. Appeal. Notwithstanding anything contained in the Code, an appeal shall lie as a matter of right from any judgement, sentence or order, not being an interlocutory order, of a Special Court to the High Court both of facts and on law.

(2) Every appeal under this section shall be preferred within a period of thirty days from the date of judgment, sentence or order appealed from:

Provided that the High Court may entertain an appeal after the expiry of the said period of thirty days if it is satisfied that the appellant had sufficient cause for not preferring the appeal within the period of thirty days.

PART V

Miscellaneous

15. Protection of action taken under this Act. - No suit, prosecution or other legal proceeding shall lie against the State Government or any officer or authority of the State Government for anything which is in good faith done or intended to be done in pursuance of this Act or any rules or orders made under this Act.

16. Burden of proof. - Where any person is prosecuted of an offence under Sec. 4, the burden of proving that he had not committed the offence under the said section shall be on him.

17. Obligation of certain persons to report about the commission of offence under this Act. - (1) All officers of Government are hereby required and empowered to assist the police in the execution of the provisions of this Act or any rule or order made there under.

(2) All village officers and such other officers as may be specified by the Collector or the District Magistrate in relation

to any area and the inhabitants of such area shall, if they have reason to believe or have the knowledge that *sati* is about to be, or has been, committed in the area shall forthwith report such fact to the nearest police station.

(3) Whoever contravenes the provision of sub-section (1) or sub-section (2) shall be punishable with imprisonment of either description for a term which may extend to two years and shall also be liable to fine.

18. Person convicted of an offence under Sec. 4 to be disqualified form inheriting certain properties. A person convicted of an offence under sub-section (1) of Sec. 4 in relation to the commission of *sati* shall be disqualified from inheriting the property of the person in respect of whom such *sati* has been committed or the property of any other person which he would have been entitled to inherit on the death of person in respect of whom such *sati* has been committed.

Amendment of Act 43 of 1951. In the Representation of the People Act, 1951.-

(a) In Sec. 8, in sub-section (2) after the proviso, the following proviso shall be inserted, namely;

"Provided further that a person convicted by a Special Court for the contravention of any of the provisions of the Commission of Sati (Prevention) Act, 1987 shall be disqualified from the date of such conviction and shall continue to be disqualified for a further period of five years since his release";

(b) In Sec. 123 after Cl. (3-A), the following clause shall be inserted, namely:

"(3-B) The propagation of the practice or the commission of *sati* or its glorification by a candidate or his agent or any other person with the consent of the candidate or his election agent for the furtherance of the prospects of the election of that candidate or for prejudicially affecting the election of any candidate.

Explanation. - For the purpose of this clause, "*sati*" and "glorification" in relation to *sati* shall have the meanings respectively assigned to them in the Commission of *Sati* (Prevention) Act, 1987."

20. Act to have overriding effect.- The provision of this Act or any rule or order made thereunder shall have effect notwithstanding anything inconsistent therewith contained in any enactment other than this Act or in any instrument having effect by virtue of any enactment other than this Act.

21. Power to make rules.-(1) The Central Government may, by notification in the Official Gazette, make rules for carrying out the provisions of this Act.

(2) Every rule made under this section shall be laid, as soon as may be after it is made, before each House of Parliament, while it is in session, for a total period of thirty days which may be comprised in one session or in two or more successive sessions, and if, before the expiry of the session immediately following the session or the successive sessions aforesaid, both Houses agree in making any modification in the rule or both Houses agree that the rule should not be made, the rule shall thereafter have effect only in such modified form or be of no effect, as the case may be; so however, that any such modification or annulment shall be without prejudice to the validity of anything previously done under that rule.

Repeal of existing laws. - (1) All laws in force in any State immediately before the commencement of this Act in that State which provide for the prevention or the glorification of *sati* shall, on such comment, stand repealed.

(2) Notwithstanding, such repeal, anything done or any action taken under any law repealed under sub-section (1) shall be deemed to have been done or taken under the corresponding provisions of this Act, and, in particular, any case taken cognizance of by a Special Court under the provisions of any law so repealed and pending before it immediately before the commencement of this Act in that State shall continue to be dealt with by that Special Court after such commencement as if such Special Court had been constituted under Sec. 9 of this Act.

COMMISSION OF SATI (PREVENTION) RULES, 1988

G.S.R. 360(E), dated 21st March, 1988.- In exercise of the powers conferred by Sec. 21 of the Commission of *Sati* (Prevention) Act, 1987 (3 of 1988), the Central Government hereby makes the following rules, namely:

1. Short title and commencement.

(1) These rules may be called the Commission of *Sati* (Prevention) Rules, 1988.

(2) They shall come into force on the date of their publication in the Official Gazette.

2. Definitions.

(1) In these rules, unless the context otherwise requires,- "Act" means the Commission of *Sati* (Prevention) Act, 1987 (3 of 1988);

"Prohibitory order" means an order issued under Sec. 6;

"Section" means section of the Act.

(2) Words and expressions used but not defined in these rules and defined in the Act shall have the same meanings as are respectively assigned to them in the Act.

3. Delegation of power to prohibit certain acts.- (1) The State Government may, by order and subject to such conditions as it may deem fit to impose, direct that the powers of the Collector or the District Magistrate under Sec. 6 may also be exercised by such other officers not below the rank of the village officers.

4. Prohibitory orders under Sec. 6, how made.- (1) Every prohibitory order under Sec. 6 shall be made by beat of drum or other customary mode, in the concerned village, or in case of town or city, in the locality in which the act prohibited is likely to occur or has taken place.

(2) The prohibitory order shall be displayed at some conspicuous place in the area or areas to which such acts

relates and a copy thereof shall also be displayed in the office of the officer issuing the prohibitory order and such display shall be taken as a sufficient notice to all persons concerned in the area of areas to which such order relates.

5. Manner of making order for removal of temples or structures under sub-section (1) of Sec. 7- (1) Before making any order under sub-section (1) of Sec. 7 for removal of any temple or structure, the State Government or any other officer authorized by the State Government in this behalf, shall give at least ninety days' notice to the person or persons involved in the acts complained of, and also to the owners and occupiers of the temple or structure proposed to be removed.

(2) The notice under sub-rule (1) shall specify:

1. The temple/structure proposed to be removed, its location and other particulars,

2. The owners/occupiers of the temple/structure, and

3. The specific instance or instances or worship or ceremony contravening the provisions of Sec.7.

(3)The Government or the officer authorized by the State Government in this behalf shall, after giving reasonable opportunity of being heard to the persons specified in the notice, order the removal of the temple or structure through a police not below the rank of the Sub-Inspector.

6. Manner of making order for removal of temples or structures under sub-section (2) of Sec. 7.-

(1) After issue of a prohibitory order under Sec. 6, the Collector or the District Magistrate, or such other officer as directed by the State G overnment by order under rule 3 shall, before making any order for removal of any temple or structure under sub-section (2) of Sec. 7 give at least ninety days' notice to the owners and occupiers of the temple or structure proposed to be removed.

(2) The Collector of the District Magistrate, or such other officer as directed by the State Government by order under rule3, shall follow the provisions of sub-rules (2) and (3) of rule 4 in the case of orders made under this rule.

7. Inventory and forfeiture of the property of temple or structure.- As soon as the order of removal of the temple or structure is executed, the State Government or the Collector or the District Magistrate, or as the case may be, the officer as directed by the State Government by order under rule 3, shall prepare an inventory of all the material and other property obtained after removal of such temple or structure specifying in it the place where it is lodged or kept, and shall forward the intimation thereof to the Special court for declaration of forfeiture of the said material or property to the State under Sec. 13, if the Special Court considers it necessary so to do, and shall also give a copy of the inventory to the owners/ occupiers of the temple/structure removed.

6

Hindu Female Mystics

Some scientists see mysticism as a mental illness. Certainly some mystics have been rather strange. Still, enough psychologists have accepted the reality of the mystical experience, and have theorized extensively about it. The accepted definition of mysticism involves (a) experience of unity with all beings; (b) a powerful influence on the mystic's way of thinking; (c) distinct knowledge conferred by the experience; (d) time/space distortion, and (e) a sense of sacredness. Philosopher/psychologist William James wrote that mysticism involved states of consciousness ranging from the non-religious to the religiously profound. James believed that mystical experiences are possible when our "field of consciousness" expands.

His ideas parallel those of Patricia Diane Cota-Robles, director of the New Age Study of Humanity's Purpose and author of several books on consciousness. "Mystic is a word used to describe someone who is reaching a higher level of our natural human potential." Author Carol Huffstickler, a yogini and Kabbalistic scholar, concurs: "I find that visionaries, prophets, and mystics have always been a vital albeit unacknowledged part of the human race. Their business has been to know a 'Truth' ahead of others, and impart it in their own unique fashion to the culture of their time."

Some psychotic episodes bear an uncomfortable resemblance to mystical experience. We hear about psychotics who slay their families because "God [or the Devil] told them to." Schizophrenics sometimes see visions; hear voices, experience time/space displacement. One difference involves the personality of the individual. Is he able to function in everyday life? Does she use common sense? By this standard, the ragged bag lady shuffling along the street talking to unseen companions is probably psychotic, while my own mentor, Marcia Moore, a renowned yogini, undoubtedly was not. She wrote books, gave lectures, organized workshops and other events, while running a busy household. Still, there are psychologists who distrust the mental state even of the Marcia's of the world. To them, anyone who reports experiences that cannot be verified scientifically should be carefully watched- if not institutionalized.

A large percentage of mystics are women. Neurological studies of male and female brains reveal that women have better communication via the corpus callosum between the left and right brain. Dreams and visions are the domain of the right brain, while verbal communication is ruled by the left. This implies that while men may have as many mystical experiences as women, women might have a slight edge when it comes to remembering, making sense of and communicating their mystical experiences. In Biblical times, Moses' sister Miriam, the military leader Deborah, and the tailor's wife Huldah were revered as prophetesses. The mediums who served as mouthpieces for the Oracle of Apollo at Delphi were all women. Recent scholarship suggests that in the early Christian church, St. Mary Magdalene was Christ's most intelligent and well-loved Apostle.

Women mystics of the Middle Ages have in recent years been given the attention they deserve. Perhaps the most famous is Hildegard of Bingen (1098-1179), from Germany. Hildegard, a skilled artist who painted beautiful illuminations of her mystical visions, wrote several treatises on what they revealed. She was also a gifted musician whose songs are popular today among music and meditation enthusiasts. On the other side of the world, in India, in the 1400's, Lalleshwari, or Lall, a devotee of the god Shiva, was pursuing her own spiritual path. Fleeing an unhappy marriage, she searched for a guru, finally finding Shrii Siddhanath. Under his tutelage, she attained God-realization, and became one of the most celebrated of spiritual poets.

A century later another great female mystic was born in India. Mira, called affectionately Mirabai, was a devotee of the god Krishna. Also trapped in a loveless marriage, Mirabai became a student of the female guru Jhala Rani. Later Mira left her home and embraced the life of a wandering ascetic. She eventually settled in Vrindvan, the legendary home of the child Krishna, where she is believed to have attained self-realization. Her poems are the result of this enlightenment:

O Krishna, O All-Pervading One,
My love is for thee alone.
When love has once set in, my dearest,
Do not break it off,
But go on increasing thy affection instead.

GARGI VACHAKNAVI

Gargi Vachaknavi was an ancient Indian female philosopher, daughter of sage Vachaknu, and born in the family of Garga, circa 800 - 500 BCE. Gargi is mentioned in the Sixth and the Eighth Brahmana of Brihadaranyaka Upanishad, where the *brahmayajna*, a philosophic congress organized by King Janaka of Videha is described, she challenged the sage Yajnavalkya with perturbing questions on the *atman* (soul). In Vedic literature, she is honored as one of the great natural philosophers. Gargi composed several hymns that questioned the origin of all existence. Yogayajnavalkya Samhita, a classical text on Yoga is a dialogue between sage Yajnavalkya and Gargi. Gargi was one of the Navaratnas in the court of King Janaka of Mithila.

MAITREYI

Maitreyi was a Vedic philosopher from ancient India. She was the second wife of famous sage and philosopher,

Yajnavalkya, the first being Katyayanee. Maitreyi was well-versed in Vedas and associated scriptures and was called *brahmavadini* or "one who speaks like God" by people of her time. About ten hymns in Rig Veda are accredited to Maitreyi.

According to legend, Maitreyi really did not want to marry Yajnavalkya, but she wanted to live with him as his disciple and a spiritual companion to do *sadhana* or spiritual development. She went to Yajnavalkya's wife, Katyayanee and expressed her desire to live with her husband, and with Katyayanee's consent, she became his companion.

AKKA MAHADEVI

Akka Mahadevi Born in Udatadi (or Udugani) near the ancient city of Banavasi (in Shikaripura taluk Shimoga district) was a prominent figure and Kannada poet of the Veerashaiva Bhakti movement of the 12th century Karnataka. Her Vachanas, a form of didactic poetry are considered her greatest contribution to Kannada Bhakti literature. In all she wrote about 430 Vachanas which is relatively fewer than that compared to other saints of her time. Yet the term 'Akka' (elder Sister) which is an honorific given to her by great Veerashaiva saints like Basavanna, Cenna Basavanna, Kinnari Bommayya, Siddharama, Allamaprabhu and Dasimayya speaks volumes of her contribution to Kannada literature and the history of Karnataka.

She is said to have accepted the god Shiva ('Chenna Mallikarjuna') as her mystical husband (similar to how centuries later Meera, a 16th century saint, considered herself married to Krishna). Much about her early life is not known, nor did she live long. She is a prominent figure in the field of female emancipation and a person of mystical vision. A household name in Karnataka, she had said that she was a woman only in name and that her mind, body and soul belonged to Lord Shiva. During a time of strife and political uncertianity in the 12th century, she launched a movement that made her an inspiration for woman empowerment and enlightenment. It is commonly known that she took part in many gatherings of learned at the *Anubhavamantapa* in Kudala sangama to debate about philosophy and attainment of spiritualism.

In search for her eternal soul mate, she made the animals, flowers and birds her friends and companions, rejecting family life and worldly attachment. The time was marked as height of foolishness of varnashrama dharma which only supported the three upper castes of Hindu society in India and suppressed the shudras and women. Akka was a revelation here in that she not only rose for emancipation but also has sung vachanas which are so simple but of highest order.

It is said that Mahadevi was married by arrangement to Kausika (false, she never got married since her child hood she believed the god channamallikarjuna, the name given by her to her ishtalinga.), a local king. There were immediate tensions, however, as Kausika was a Jain, a group that tended to be wealthy and was, as a result, much resented by the rest of the population. Much of Akka's poetry explores the themes of rejecting mortal love in favor of the everlasting, "illicit" love of God, and this seems to be the path she chose as well.

She ran away from her life of luxury to live as a wandering poet-saint, traveling throughout the region and singing praises to her Lord Shiva. She travelled widely in search of emancipation and finally became a *Sanyasini* (woman saint) before settling down in Basavakalyana, Bidar district. Her non-conformist ways caused a lot of consternation in a conservative society and even her eventual guru Allama Prabhu had to initially face difficulties in enlisting her in the gatherings at Anubhavamantapa. A true ascetic, Mahadevi is said to have refused to wear any clothing-a common practice among male ascetics, but shocking for a woman. Legend has it that due to her true love and devotion with God her whole body was protected by hair. One of her famous vachana has a reason for this also which translates as

People,
male and female,

blush when a cloth covering their shame
comes loose
When the lord of lives
lives drowned without a face
in the world, how can you be modest?
When all the world is the eye of the lord,
onlooking everywhere, what can you
cover and conceal?

Her poetry exhibits her love for Chenna Mallikarjuna and harmony with nature and simple living.

She Sang:

For hunger, there is the village rice in the begging bowl,
For thirst, there are tanks and streams and wells
For sleep temple ruins do well
For the company of the soul I have you, Chenna Mallikarjuna

Some scholars estimate she lived for only twenty five years. She is believed to have disappeared in the banana groves at Shreeshaila, in Andhra Pradesh while in ecstasy entering mahasamadhi (divine union) with a flash of light.

FAMOUS VACHANAS BY AKKA

Thanu karagadavaralli pushpavanolleyayya neenu
Mana karagadavaralli Gandhakshateyanollayya neenu
Arivu kanthereyadavaralli Arathiyanollayya neenu
Parinamigalalladavaralli Naivedyavanollayya neenu
Bhavashuddhavilladavaralli Dhupavanollayya neenu
Hrudaya kamalavilladavaralli iralollayya neenu
Ennalli enuntendu karasthaladali imbugonde,

HeLa Channamallikarjuna............

Mane Mane thappadanthe beduvanthe madayya
Bedidode annavanu ikkadanthe madayya
Ikkidode nelake biluvanthe madayya
Nelake biddode nanettikomba munna shuni ettikombanthe madayya
channamallikarjuna

Thanu karagadavaraqlli pushpavanolleyayya neenu
Mana karagadavaralli Gandhakshateyanollayya neenu
Arivu kanthereyadavaralli Arathiyanollayya neenu
Parinamigalalladavaralli Naivedyavanollayya neenu
Bhavashuddhavilladavaralli Dhupavanollayya neenu
Hrudaya kamalavilladavaralli iralollayya neenu
Ennalli enuntendu karasthaladali imbugonde,
Hela Channamallikarjuna............

Kayakke neLalagi kadithu maye
kalakke manavagi kadithu maye
manake nenahagi kadithu maye
nenahinge arivagi kadithu maye
jagada janguLigaLige bengolanethi kadithu maye
chenna mallikarjuna neenoDDida mayeya aru gelalararu

beTTada mElondu maneya mADi mrugaga Liganjido Dentayya
samudrada taDiyalli maneya mADi nore terega Liganjido Dentayya
santeya naDuve maneya mADi shabdakke nAchdo Dentayya
chenna mallikArjuna dEva kELayya

JANABAI

Janâbâi was a Marâthi religious poetess in the Hindu tradition in India, who was born likely in the seventh or the eighth decade of the 13th century. According to folklore, she died in 1350. Janabai was born in Gangâkhed, Mahârâshtra to a couple with first names *Damâ* and *Karund*. Under the caste system which rigidly existed in India, the couple belonged to the lowest caste. After her mother died, her father took her to Pandharpur. Since her childhood, Janabai worked as a maidservant in the household of *Dâmâsheti*, who lived in Pandharpur and who was the father of the prominent Marathi religious poet Nâmdev. Janabai was likely a little older than Namdev, and attended to him for many years.

Pandharpur has high religious significance especially among Marathi-speaking Hindus. Janabai's employers, Damasheti and his wife, *Gonâi*, were very religious. Through the influence of the religious environment around her and her innate inclination, Janabai was all along an ardent devotee of Lord Vitthal, and she was also gifted with poetic talent. Though she never had any formal schooling, she thus composed many high-quality religious verses of the *abhang* form. Fortuitously, some of her compositions got preserved along with those of Namdev. Authorship of about 300 *abhang* is traditionally attributed to Janabai. However, researchers believe that quite a few of them were in fact compositions of some other writers.

Along with Dnyâneshwar, Nâmdev, Eknâth, and Tukaram, Janabai has a revered place in the minds of Marathi-speaking Hindus who belong especially to the *wârakari* sect in Maharashtra. In accord with a tradition in India of assigning the epithet *sant* to persons regarded as thoroughly saintly, all of the above religious figures including Janabai are commonly attributed that epithet in Maharashtra. Thus, Janabai is routinely referred to as *Sant Janabai*.

LALLESHWARI

Lalleshwari (1320 – 1392) also known as *Lalla* or Lal Ded was a Hindu saint-poetess and a mystic of the Kashmiri Shaivite sect. She is a creator of the mystic poetry called vatsun or *Vakhs*, literally 'speech'. Known as Lal Vakhs, her verses are the earliest compositions in the Kashmiri language and are an important part in history of Kashmiri literature. Lal Ded and her mystic musings continue to have a deep impact on the psyche of Kashmiri common man, and the 2000 National Seminar on her held at New Delhi, led to the release of book *Remembering Lal Ded in Modern Times*. A solo play in English, Hindi and Kashmiri, titled, 'Lal Ded' based on her life, has been performed by actress Mita Vashisht, all over India, since 2004.

Lalleshwari was born in Pandrethan (ancient Puranadhisthana) some four and a half miles to the southeast of Srinagar. She married at age twelve, but her marriage was unhappy and she left home at twenty-four to take sanyas (renunciation) and become a disciple of the Shaivite guru Siddha Srikantha (Sed Bayu). She continued the Mystic tradition of Shaivism in Kashmir. Many legends and stories remain about Lalla. One in particular tells of how Lalla, who ignored the normal convention of dress, choosing to wander around naked, was teased by several children. A nearby cloth merchant scolded the children for their disrespect. Lalla asked the merchant for two lengths of cloth, equal in weight. That day as she walked around naked, she wore a piece of cloth over each shoulder, and as she met with respect or scorn, she tied a knot in one or another. In the evening, she brought the cloth back to the merchant, and asked him to weigh them again. The cloths were equal in weight, no matter how many knots were in each. Respect and scorn have no weight of their own. Her poems (called *vakhs*) have been translated into English by Richard Temple, Jia Lal Kilam, Coleman Barks, and Jaishree Odin.

LAL VAKH

Lal Vakh, literally mean sayings of Lal or Lal Ded:

LAL VAKH IN KASHMIRI

Yi yi karu'm suy artsun

yi rasini vichoarum thi mantar

yihay lagamo dhahas partsun
suy Parasivun tanthar -138
Whatever work I did became worship of the Lord;
Whatever word I uttered became a mantra;
Whatever this body of mine experienced became
the sadhana-s of Saiva Tantra
illumining my path to Parmasiva. -138

MIRABAI

Mirabai (1498-1547CE) (alternate orthographies: Meera; Mira; Meera Bai) was a Hindu mystical poetess, philosopher and sage. Her compositions are popular throughout India. She is held to have been a disciple of Ravidas. She composed between 1200 to 1300 prayerful songs called *bhajans*. These bhajans are in the *bhakti* tradition, and most passionately praised Lord Krishna. The extant version of her poems is in a Rajasthani dialect of Hindi and in Gujarati. Many of the details of her life are pieced together from her poetry and the stories later recounted by members of her community. While her hagiography is held as truth by followers of the bhakti tradition, the historical authenticity of most of her story is the subject of scholarly debate.

Mirabai was born in Kudki, a little village near Merta, Rajasthan, which is presently in Pali district. Her father was Ratan Singh, a descendant of Rao Rathor, the founder of Jodhpur. When Mirabai was only 3 years old, a wandering sadhu came to her family's home and gave a doll of Krishna to her father. Her father took this is as a special blessing, but was initially unwilling to give it to his daughter, because he felt she would not appreciate it. However Mira had, at first sight, become deeply enamoured with this doll. She refused to eat until the doll was given to her. To Mira, this figure of Krishna embodied his living presence. She resolved to make Krishna her lifelong friend, lover, and husband. Throughout her turbulent life she never wavered from her youthful commitment.

On one occasion when Mira was still young she saw a wedding procession going down the street. Turning to her mother she asked in innocence, "Who will be my husband?" Her mother replied, half in jest, half in seriousness. "You already have your husband, Sri Krishna." Mira's mother was supportive of her daughter's blossoming religious tendencies, but she passed away when she was only young. At an early age Mira's father arranged for her to be married to Prince Bhoj Raj, who was the eldest son of Rana Sanga of Chittor. They were an influential Hindu family and the marriage significantly elevated Mira's social position. However Mira was not enamoured of the luxuries of the palace. She served her husband dutifully (Folklore suggest she didn't do so and even refused to accept Prince as her husband), but in the evening she would spend her time in devotion and singing to her beloved Sri Krishna. While singing devotional *bhajans*, she would frequently lose awareness of the world, entering into states of ecstasy and trance.

However her new family did not approve of her piety and devotion to Krishna. To make things worse Mira refused to worship their family deity, Goddess Durga. She said she had already committed herself to Krishna. Her family became increasingly disapproving of her actions, but the fame and saintly reputation of Mirabai spread throughout the region. Often she would spend time discussing spiritual issues with sadhus and people would join in the singing of her bhajans. However this just made her family even more jealous. Mira's sister-in-law Udabai started to spread false gossip and defamatory remarks about Mirabai. She said Mira was entertaining men in her room. Her husband, believing these stories to be true, tore into her room with sword in hand. However he saw Mira only playing with a doll. No man was there at all. Yet throughout these hysterical slanders Mirabai remained unmoved by both the criticism and praise of the world.

Mira's fame spread far and wide her devotional bhajans were sung across northern India. It is said that the fame and spirituality of Mirabai reached the ears of the Moghul Emperor

Akbar. Akbar was tremendously powerful, but he was also very interested in different religious paths. However, he and Mirabai's family were the worst enemies. Visiting Mirabai would cause problems for both Akbar and Mirabai, but Akbar was determined to see Mirabai, the Princess Saint. Disguised as a beggar, he travelled with Tansen to visit Mirabai. Akbar was so enamoured of her soulful music and devotional singing that before leaving, he placed a priceless necklace at her feet; unfortunately, the necklace revealed about the visit to Mirabai's husband Bhoj Raj, who was furious that a Muslim and his own arch-enemy had seen his wife.

Bhoj Raj ordered Mirabai to commit suicide by drowning herself in a river. Mirabai intended to honour her husband's command, but as she was entering the river, Sri Krishna appeared to her and commanded her to leave for Vrindavan where she could worship him in peace. So with a few followers, Mirabai left for Vrindavan, where she spent her time in devotion to Sri Krishna. After a while her husband repented, feeling that his wife was actually a real saint. Thus he travelled to Vrindavan and asked her to return to him. Mirabai agreed, much to the displeasure of the rest of her family. However, Mira's husband died soon after, fighting in battles with the Moghul emperors. This made the situation even worse for Mirabai. Her father in law, Rana Sanga, saw her husband's death as a way to be rid of Mirabai. He commanded her to commit *sati*. However Mirabai, with the inner direct assurance of her beloved Sri Krishna, said that she would not do this. Her real husband, Sri Krishna had not died.

After this experience, her family continued to torture her. They restricted her movements and sought to make her life as uncomfortable as possible. Yet in the face of all these trials and tribulations, she remained detached from her physical suffering. Nothing disturbed her inner connection to Govinda (Krishna as young cowherd boy). Legend says that twice her family tried to kill her: once with a venomous snake and once with a poisonous drink. On both occasions, Mirabai, protected by the Grace of Sri Krishna, came to no harm.

However the relentless torments and hostility interfered with her life of devotion and contemplation on Krishna. She sought the advice of learned men and saints. They advised her to leave the palace and return to Vrindavan. Secretly with some followers she slipped out of the palace and escaped to the holy city of Vrindavan. In Vrindavan Mirabai was free to worship Giridhara (Govinda) to her heart's content. She would spend her time singing bhajans and in ecstatic communion with Krishna. Like a true bhakti she worshipped God wholeheartedly. The riches of the world offered no attraction to Mirabai; her only *satis*faction came from her single minded devotion to Sri Krishna. Her soul was ever yearning for Krishna. She considered herself to be a gopi of Vrindavan, mad only with pure love for Krishna.

Even learned sadhus would come to her for inspiration. There is a story of one respected spiritual master who refused to speak to Mirabai because she was a woman. Mirabai replied there was only one real man in Vrindavan, Krishna; everyone else was a gopi of Krishna. On hearing this spiritual teacher accepted the wisdom of Mirabai and agreed to talk to her. Later Mirabai would become his student. Vaishnava records indicate that the name of that Spiritual Master is Rupa Goswami, a disciple of Sri Krishna Caitanya.

Mirabai belongs to the Saguna class of worshippers of Brahman. Theologically, they believed that between *atman* and *paramatma* (here the Sanskrit *Parama-* carries approximately the same meaning as Latin *Trans-*), this physical body is the only wall, and upon death the atman and paramatman will combine, just as a pot filled with water is placed in pond and if the pot breaks the water inside (atman) will combine with the water outside (Parama Atman). Mirabai's poetry holds love for Krishna closer to her heart than the love for friends and family. She perceived Krishna to be her husband, lover, lord and master. The unique characteristic of Mirabai's poetry is the use of complete surrender to her love for Krishna.

Her longing for union with Krishna is predominant in Mira's poetry who says she wants to be "coloured with the colour of dusk" (dusk being the symbolic colour of Krishna). She believed that in her previous life she was one of the several gopis in Vrindavan, in love with Krishna. Much like the gopis, as mentioned in the life of Krishna, Mirabai looked upon Krishna as her lover, seeking spiritual and physical union with him. Her writings were at the same time, spiritual and highly devotional. Mirabai's songs portray a personal universe where the only existence was that of Krishna - her sole object of desire.

A Mirabai poem is traditionally called a *pada*, a term used by the 14th century preachers for a small spiritual song. This is usually composed in simple rhythms and carries a refrain within itself. Her collection of songs is called the *Padavali*. The typicality of Indian love poetry of those days was used by Mirabai but as an instrument to express her deepest emotions felt for her ishta-devata. Her typical medium of singing was *Vraja-bhasha*, a dialect of Hindi spoken in and around Vrindavan (the childhood home of Krishna), sometimes mixed with Rajasthani.

An example poem:

That dark dweller in Brajj

Is my only refuge.

O my companion,

Worldly comfort is an illusion,

As soon you get it, it goes.

I have chosen the indestructible for my refuge,

Him whom the snake of death

Will not devour.

My beloved dwells in my heart all day,

I have actually seen that abode of joy.

Mira's lord is Hari, the indestructible.

My lord, I have taken refuge with Thee,

Your dasi.

The poetry of Mirabai has been translated by Robert Bly in his *Mirabai Versions* (New York; Red Ozier Press, 1984). Composer John Harbison adapted Bly's translations for his *Mirabai Songs.*

There is a documentary film *A Few Things I Know About Her* by Anjali Panjabi. Some say: "In love, her form of devotion and its essence, Mira sought release from the cycle of birth and death : 'Jana Mira Kun Girdhara milaya, dukha metan sukha bheri, Ruma ruma sata bhayi ura mein, miti gayi phera pheri' – the moment Mira met Girdhara, sorrows vanished and happiness emerged, all agitations of mind and body extinguished, and the cycle of birth and death is destroyed."

MOTHER MEERA

Mother Meera, born Kamala Reddy (b. 26 December, 1960) is believed by her devotees to be an embodiment (avatar) of the Divine Mother (Shakti). Born in Chandepalle a small village in Nalgonda district of Andhra Pradesh, India, she had her first samâdhi, a state of complete spiritual absorption, at the age of six, which lasted for a whole day. When she was 12 her uncle Bulgur Venkat Reddy met her for the first time, and immediately recognized in her the girl of his visions. He became convinced that she is the Divine Mother and started to take care of her, allowing her to unfold her inner experiences. Her parents Antamma and Veera Reddy live in Madanapalle, Chittoor district of Andhra Pradesh.

In 1974, Mr. Reddy brought Mother Meera to the Sri Aurobindo Ashram in Pondicherry, India, of which he was a member. There she first met Westerners and started to give Darshan. She is however not associated with the Sri Aurobindo Ashram today. In 1979 she was invited by her first devotees to Canada, where she went several times. Meanwhile Reddy's health started to deteriorate. In 1981 she made her first trip to West Germany, where she together with Mr. Reddy and her close companion Adilakshmi settled down a year later. She married a German in 1982. Mr. Reddy died in 1985 and was buried in the local cemetery in Dornburg-Thalheim, Hesse.

Currently she gives Darshan (literally seeing, primarily in a spiritual context) at Schloss Schaumburg in Balduinstein, a small town in Germany. She also visits the United States on a regular basis.

Mother Meera receives thousands of visitors of all religions for darshan which she conducts in total silence. Her darshan consists of a ritual, where she will touch a person's head, and then look into their eyes. During this process, she reportedly 'unties knots' in the person's subtle system and permeates them with light. She doesn't charge any money for doing so and she will not give lectures. Mother Meera's reported task on Earth was in calling down a dynamic light-force from the Supreme (Paramatman - the supreme Self) in collaboration with other saints and divine beings, as she says, making spiritual progress on earth easier. About this light she says:

"Like electricity, the Light is everywhere, but one must know how to activate it. I have come for that." (Answers, Part I.)

Through Japa, the mental remembrance of *any* Divine Name or Mantra, which may be done informally, and whenever convenient, people could open themselves up to this Light. She does not claim to be a guru or have followers. To be connected to her work, people do not have to recognize her. Her teaching is mainly related to Bhakti, that is devotion to God, and in that she accepts all denominations. Mother Meera does not belong to any particular tradition, except for certain closeness to the work of Sri Aurobindo and the Mother, whom she had allegedly met in their subtle bodies, when she was a child, visiting their Samadhi (grave).

After splitting from Mother Meera, the writer and former follower Andrew Harvey wrote *The Sun at Midnight*. In it, Harvey accused Meera of homophobia, saying that Mother Meera disapproved of Harvey's marriage to another man. In his first book about her, *Hidden Journey*, Harvey had originally praised her as an avatar, attributing his own claimed enlightenment to her. Harvey's accusation of homophobia is disputed. One of Harvey's former lovers, the writer Mark

Matousek (1997), said that: "I do know that the idea that she's homophobic is completely ridiculous. For God's sake, we were served breakfast in bed together in her house."

MATA AMRITANANDAMAYI

Mâtâ Amritanandamayî Devi is an Indian spiritual leader revered as a saint by her followers, who also know her as "Amma", "Ammachi" or "Mother". She is widely respected for her humanitarian activities and is known as "the hugging saint". Mata Amritanandamayi was born *Sudhamani* in the small village of Parayakadavu (now partially known as Amritapuri), near Kollam, Kerala in 1953. Sudhamani was born to a fishing family of the Arayan caste. Her schooling ended when she was nine, and she began to take care of her younger siblings and the family domestic work full-time.

She is said to have had many mystical experiences as a child. Since 1981, she has been teaching spiritual aspirants all over the world. She founded a worldwide organization, the Mata Amritanandamayi Mission Trust, which is engaged in many spiritual and charitable activities. She addressed the United Nations General Assembly and was recognised as a universal mother figure.

International events:

- 1993, Chicago: speech at the "Parliament of the World's Religions" 100th Anniversary.
- 1995, New York: address at the Interfaith Celebrations at the 50th Anniversary of the UN.
- 2000, New York: keynote address at the Millennium Peace Summit, UN General Assembly.
- 2002, Geneva: keynote address at the Global Peace Initiative of Women innaugural meeting at the UN in Geneva.
- 2002, Geneva: "Gandhi-King Award for Non-Violence" from The World Movement for Non-Violence at UN headquarters.

- 2004, Barcelona, Parliament of World Religions.
- 2006, New York, James Parks Morton Interfaith award.

Recognition:

In 1993, she was one of the representatives of Hinduism at the Parliament of the World's Religions in Chicago. Mata Amritanandamayi was the keynote speaker at the Global Peace Initiative of Women, at the UN in Geneva, Switzerland held in October 2002. This was an initiative of the UN' Millennium World Peace Summit, in which Mata Amritanandamayi spoke in August 2000. In 2002 Mata Amritanandamayi was presented with the Gandhi-King Award for Non-Violence by The World Movement for Nonviolence at the UN General Assembly Hall (Palais Des Nations) in Geneva in recognition of her lifelong work in furthering the principles of non-violence. The three previous recipients of the award were Kofi Annan, Nelson Mandela, and primatologist Dr. Jane Goodall.

In 2006, Amma was honoured with the 4th Annual James Parks Morton Interfaith Award at the Interfaith Centre, New York. The Interfaith Award annually honors global leaders who forward the ICNY-mission of promoting peace, interfaith understanding and action through social and cultural programs. Some others who had previously accepted the awards are former US President Bill Clinton, Dalai Lama, Dr. Mohamed ElBaradei, Shirin Ebadi, Archbishop Desmond Tutu and famous Indian musician Pandit Ravi Shankar. In Oct 2007, Amma was awarded for her humanitarian activities at human rights film festival, Cinema Verite, in Paris. Actress Sharon Stone presented the award.

In March, 2008, in Jaipur, Rajasthan, India, Amma gave the keynote address for the Global Peace Initiative of Women's international conference entitled "Making Way for the Feminine for the Benefit of the World Community". She is also considered by some to be an avatar of the Great Mother.

The first set of monastic disciples of Mata Amritanandamayi came to her in the late 1970s. Today, they as well as other disciples and devotees look after the ashram's multifaceted activities. The first disciple to be initiated as a sanyasi was Swami Amritaswarupananda. Other senior disciples are Swami Paramatmananda, Swami Ramakrishnananda, Swami Purnamritananda, Swami Turiyamritananda, Swami Amritatmananda, Swami Pranavamritananda, Swamini Atmaprana and Swamini Krishnamritaprana. The ashram, known as the Mata Amritanandamyi Math (or Ashram), is located in Amritapuri. Bramachari Dayamrita Chaitanya is one of Amma's senior disciples stationed at the MA Center located in San Ramon, CA. He is in charge of all activities performed by the MA center in the US and all branch groups. Brahmacharini Dipamrita Chaitanya is in charge of the French ashram in Pontguin, France.

Mata Amritanandamayi is known to the world media as 'the hugging saint'. She offers a hug to everyone who approaches her and in India she has been known to individually hug over 50,000 people in a day, sitting sometimes for over 20 hours. Worldwide, Mata Amritanandamayi is said to have hugged at least 30 million people in the past 30 years. "Darshan – The Embrace," a film on the life of Mata Amritanandamayi, was officially selected for showcasing at the 2005 Cannes Film Festival. Jan Kounen, an award winning filmmaker who was born in Netherlands and is based in France, directed the film. Manuel De La Roche of France is the producer.

Jan Kounen and his crew began shooting the footage for the film in 2003 during Amritavarsham50, Mata Amritanandamayi's 50th birthday celebrations in Kochi. The team also traveled with her on her Indian and International tours in order to complete the movie. About the film, Kounen says, "When I first took up the project and started filming, I thought, 'Amma is a good person, doing good things, in turn I can do something good for her'. But as it went on, I realized, no, I am the one who is receiving the gift".

Mata Amritanandamayi Math's website describes various charitable and humanitarian projects undertaken by the organization. Examples include a program to build 100,000 homes for the poor; hospitals; orphanages; hospices; women's shelters; pension disbursements for widows; community aid centers; homes for the aged; eye clinics; and speech therapy centers. Many of Amma's centers in the US run 'Mother's Kitchen', or 'vegetarian soup-kitchens', where volunteers prepare and serve meals to the poor and needy. The M.A. Math runs around 100 schools, 20 temples, a super-speciality hospital in Kochi, feeds thousands from its kitchen, provides pensions every year to over 15,000 widows, builds 25,000 houses annually for the homeless and has 35 Amma welfare centres worldwide to spread her spiritual message.

M.A. Math announced a billion rupees (23 million dollars) in aid to the victims of the 2004 tsunami. The Math's relief work is happening in Kerala, Tamil Nadu, Pondicherry, and Andaman & Nicobar Islands and in Sri Lanka. In September 2005, Mata Amritanandamayi donated $1,000,000 to the Bush-Clinton Hurricane Katrina fund. She also sent a top aide to the devastated areas soon after the storm struck in the United States to assess the kind of help needed by victims. In October 2005, thousands of blankets were sent and distributed to the survivors of the Kashmir and Pakistan earthquake.

Matruvani is a monthly magazine featuring accounts of Ammachi's religious and humanitarian activities and stories by devotees. It is published by the Amritapuri Ashram in both Indian and European languages. *Matruvani* was first published in 1984. The magazine has been translated into English, Malayalam, Tamil, Kannada, Telugu, Marathi, Gujarati, Bengali and Hindi. *European Matruvani* is also published in French, German, Italian, Finnish and Spanish. Also published is a quarterly international magazine is known as "Immortal Bliss".

A book critical of the Mata Amritanandamayi ashram written by the Kerala-based head of the Indian Rationalist Association Sreeni Pattathanam led a political furor when the State government sanctioned prosecution of Pattathanam, the owner of the publishing company and the printer of the book. The order followed directions from the Kerala High Court to the State's Home Department for considering an application by a high ranking devotee and inmate of the Mata Amritanandamayi Ashramam, T.K. Ajan, to criminally prosecute the three, based on criticisms found in the book. The order ultimately received international attention, and was rescinded after criticism by Humanists, Rationalists, writers, and the Communist Party.

SHREE MA

Shree Ma is a Hindu Mystic who was born near Kamakhya, Assam, India. She was descended from the family of the famous Bengali mystic, Ramprasad Sen. Shree Ma's great uncle was Atulananda Saraswati, a Sannyasi or renunciate who never married, but spent his entire life wandering from place to place. One of her aunts was Renuka Sen, a famous poet and friend and inspiration in the life of Rabindranath Tagore. The author of her biography, Swami Satyananda Saraswati, writes that she was born in the year when there was a great earthquake in Assam. Many records were destroyed in the earthquake and so there is no factual evidence to verify her date of birth. He adds that her birth could be somewhere between 1938 and 1948, although it could easily be earlier or later.

From her earliest years her only desire was to meditate, merging her own being in the universal being the Hindus call Brahman [i.e. God]. Inspired by the 19th century Bengali mystic, Sri Ramakrishna Paramahamsa , she left her family's home. She lived in the forests and foothills of Kamakhya and Himalayas where she performed intense sadhana. She meditated for long periods without moving and became absorbed in the silence of deep meditation. In this period, she ate practically nothing except sandal paste mixed with water, tulsi [basil] leaves and occasional juice fed to her by disciples and devotees. Because of her intense tapasya [austerity], her body weight reduced to little more than 60 pounds.

People, who saw her in samadhi [deep communion with God] for hours and days at a time, called her the Goddess of the Mountain, The Goddess of the River, or simply Shree Ma, the Respected Holy Mother. After several years, she began to roam throughout India in temples, forests, fields and homes, conducting pujas and archana to the Divine Mother, reading from the Chandi Path, a famous Hindu scripture that describes the Divine Mother Durga's manifestations on Earth. Sometimes she would also sing bhajans [divine hymns] all night, and devotees, filled with bhakti [devotion], would gather to be in her presence.

In 1980, in a small temple in Bakreswar, West Bengal, Shree Ma met Swami Satyananda Saraswati. Born and educated in America, the latter had worked for several major corporations in managerial positions before traveling to India in the mid 1960s. At a time when journeying throughout Middle Asia was arduous at best, he had traveled an unbeaten path to India's interior where he studied with a number of gurus, coming to embrace the worship of Chandi and the sacred fire ceremony, the yagya, as his primary system of worship and meditation, while undertaking great austerities in the process. On his journey he became proficient in numerous languages including Bengali, Hindi, Latin, Hebrew, Pahari, Urdu and several dialects of Indian languages among others, and developed a deep passion for Sanskrit.

After this meeting, the two traveled together throughout India, sharing dharma even when, due to cultural clashes and unrest, their own lives were at risk. It was in the early eighties that Shree Ma, in communion with her guru Ramakrishna Paramahamsa, was instructed to move to America to share divine love and to teach the meaning of dharma. In 1984, with no capital and few possessions they left the shores of India for the West Coast of the United States. Shunning self promotion and publicity, they lived a very simple life dedicated to daily worship, preferring to own little, and to offer all to God. They undertook the Sahasra Chandi Yagya, a three year fire ceremony and worship of the Goddess, without setting foot outside from the humble temple grounds they established in Martinez, California.

The temple itself contained numerous beautiful murtis, statues fashioned from clay by Ma and Swami's own hands.

As the word of Shree Ma's presence in the Bay area spread, thousands of seekers found their way to the humble grounds of the Devi Mandir. Shree Ma teaches that every home is an ashram, a place of worship, every resident is a priest or priestess, and that all acts of life can be service to God and expressions of devotion. Life itself is worship. Shree Ma has recorded CDs of her own compositions, songs of Ramprasad Sen, and traditional Hindu Mantras such as Om, Gayatri, and Navarna.

Her Biography, entitled, *Shree Ma: The Life of a Saint*, by Swami Satyananda Saraswati was published in 1997. Shree Ma has been featured in a book by Linda Johnsen entitled "Daughters of the Goddess: Women Saints of India" published by Yes International Publications in 1994. She has also been featured in numerous articles in magazines such as Yoga Journal, Hinduism Today, Yoga International, East West Journal, New Realities, Challenge, and in newspapers such as the *Times of India, Contra Costa Times, India West* and the *Ananda Bazar Patrika.*

SARADA DEVI

Sarada Devi, born Saradamani Mukhopadhyaya, was the wife and spiritual counterpart of Ramakrishna Paramahamsa, a nineteenth century mystic of Bengal. Sarada Devi is also reverentially addressed as the Holy Mother (*Sri Ma*) by the followers of the Ramakrishna monastic order. Sarada Devi played an important role in the growth of the Ramakrishna Movement. Sarada Devi was born in Jayrambati.

At the age of five she was betrothed to Ramakrishna, whom she joined at Dakshineswar when she was in her late teens. According to her traditional biographers, both lived lives of unbroken continence, showing the ideals of a householder and of the monastic ways of life. After Ramakrishna's death, Sarada Devi stayed most of the time either at Jayrambati or at the Udbodhan office, Calcutta. The disciples of Ramakrishna regarded her as their own mother, and after their guru's passing looked to her for advice and encouragement. The followers of the Ramakrishna movement regard Sarada Devi as an incarnation of the Divine Mother.

Saradamani Devi was born of Brahmin parents as the eldest daughter on December 22, 1853, in the quiet village of Jayrambati in present day West Bengal, India. Her parents, Ramchandra Mukhopadhyaya and Syamasundari Devi, were poor but pious. Her father Ramchandra earned his living as a farmer and through the performance of priestly duties. According to traditional accounts, Ramachandra and Syamasundari had visions and supernatural events foretelling the birth of a divine being as their daughter.

Sarada lived the simple life of an Indian village girl. As a child Sarada- then known as Saradamani- was fascinated by traditional Hindu folklore and narratives. As in the case of most girls of rural upbringing, she did not receive any formal education but learned to serve others as she helped her mother run a large household and looked after her younger brothers. During the terrible famine of 1864, Sarada worked ceaselessly as her family served food to hungry people. She was interested in the clay models of goddesses Kali and Lakshmi, which she worshiped regularly. She is said to have started meditating from her childhood and traditional accounts recount her mystic visions and experiences. According to Sarada Devi, she used to see a bevy of eight girls of her age coming from an unknown place, and escorted her in the chores during her childhood.

Ramakrishna- then known as Gadadhar Chattopadhaya and a priest of the Dakshineswar Kali Temple since 1855- was practicing spiritual austerities. His mother and brother thought that a marriage would be a good steadying effect on him, by diverting his attention away from spiritual austerities and visions. It is reported that Ramakrishna himself indicated Saradamani as the bride. In May 1859, Sarada was betrothed to Ramakrishna. Sarada was 5 years old and Ramakrishna was 23 then, but the age difference was typical for 19th century rural Bengal.

After the betrothal, Sarada was left to the care of her parents and Ramakrishna returned to Dakshineswar. Sarada next met Ramakrishna when she was fourteen years old, and she spent three months with him at Kamarpukur. There, Ramakrishna imparted Sarada instructions on meditation, spiritual life. Ramakrishna's frequent *samadhi* (ecstasy) and unorthodox ways of worship led some onlookers to doubt his mental stability, while others regarded him as a great saint. Sarada joined Ramakrishna at Dakshineswar in 1872 on her own accord when she was eighteen, after hearing these rumors about his mental health. She found Ramakrishna to be a kind and caring person.

At Dakshineswar, Sarada Devi stayed in a tiny room in the *nahabat* (musical tower). Sarada Devi stayed at Dakshineswar until 1885, except for short periods when she visited her village Jayrambati. By this time Ramakrishna had already embraced the monastic life of a sannyasin; as a result, the marriage was never consummated. As a priest, Ramakrishna performed the ritual ceremony- the *Shodashi Puja* where Sarada Devi was made to sit in the seat of goddess Kali, and worshiped as the Divine mother. According to Saradananda a direct disciple of Ramakrishna, Ramakrishna married in order to show the world an ideal of a sexless marriage. Ramakrishna regarded Sarada as the incarnation of Divine Mother, addressing her as *Sree Ma* (Holy Mother) and it was by this name that she was known to Ramakrishna's disciples.

Sarada Devi's day began at 3 am. After finishing her ablutions in the Ganges, she would practice *japa* and meditation until daybreak. Ramakrishna taught her the sacred *mantras*, and instructed her how to initiate people and guide them in spiritual life. Sarada Devi is regarded as Ramakrishna's first disciple. Except for her hours of meditation, most of her time was spent in cooking for Ramakrishna and the growing number of his devotees. While Sarada Devi remained completely in the background, her unassuming but warm personality attracted some female devotees to become her lifelong companions.

During Ramakrishna's last days, during which he suffered from throat cancer, Sarada Devi played a important role in nursing him and preparing suitable food for him and his disciples. It is reported that after Ramakrishna's passing away in August 1886, when Sarada Devi tried to remove her bracelets as the customs dictated for a widow, she had a vision of Ramakrishna in which he said, "I have not passed away, I have gone from one room to another." According to her, whenever she thought of dressing like a widow, she had a vision of Ramakrishna asking her not to do so. After Ramakrishna's death, Sarada Devi continued to play an important role in the nascent religious movement. She remained the spiritual guide of the movement for the next thirty four years.

After Ramakrishna's death, Sarada Devi began her pilgrimage through North India, accompanied by a party of women disciples including Lakshmi Didi, Gopal Ma, and Ramakrishna's householder and monastic disciples. The party visited the Vishwanath Temple of god Shiva at Banaras and the city of Ayodhya, which is associated with life of god Rama. Later, she visited Vrindavan which is associated with god Krishna. According to traditional accounts, at Vrindavan, she experienced *nirvikalpa samadhi* and began her role as *guru*. She initiated several of the Ramakrishna's disciples including Mahendranath Gupta, Yogen with a *mantra*. According to her traditional biographers and disciples, to call her "Mother" was no mere expression of respect and all those who met her became aware of a maternal quality in her.

After the pilgrimage, Sarada Devi stayed alone in Kamarpukur, Ramakrishna's native village. There, she endured poverty, verging on starvation for a year. In 1888, when the news reached the lay and monastic disciples of Ramakrishna that she needed their care and attention, they invited her to Calcutta and arranged for her stay. Swami Saradananda built a permanent house for Sarada Devi in Calcutta. The house was named the Udbodhan House, after the Bengali monthly magazine conducted by the Ramakrishna Math. It is also called *Mayerbati* ("Holy Mother's House"), where she spent the longest period of her life outside Jayrambati.

At Udbodhan House, Sarada Devi was accompanied by other women disciples of Ramakrishna, Gopal Ma, Yogin Ma,

Lakshmi Didi and Gauri Ma being the best known. An increasing number of people began to flock for guidance, instructions and spiritual initiation. Other Western women followers of Ramakrishna Order including Sister Nivedita and Sister Devamata formed close relationship with her. According to her biographers, her innate motherliness put visitors at ease. Swami Nikhilananda, her direct disciple writes, "Though she had no children of the flesh, she had many of the spirit." She regarded all her disciples as her own children.

Sarada Devi received the highest reverence from the Ramakrishna Order and its devotees. Ramakrishna had bade her continue his mission after his passing away and wanted his disciples not to make any distinction between himself and her. According to her devotees and traditional biographers, the hospitality of Sarada Devi was unique and was characterized by motherly care and solicitude. Traditional accounts recount the mystical experiences of her devotees. Some dreamt of her as a goddess in human form though they had never seen her picture before. Others reportedly received their initiation from her in their dream. One such example is of Girish Chandra Ghosh, the father of Bengali drama, who reportedly saw Sarada Devi in a dream when he was nineteen years old and received a *mantra,* and when he met her many years later, to his astonishment it was the same person in the dream.

Sarada Devi spent her final years moving back and forth between Jayrambati and Calcutta. In January 1919, Sarada Devi went to Jayrambati and stayed there for over a year. During the last three months of her stay, her health seriously declined. Her strength was greatly impaired and she was brought back to Calcutta on February 27, 1920. For the next five months she continued to suffer. Before her death, she gave the last advice to the grief stricken devotees, "But I tell you one thing- if you want peace of mind, do not find fault with others. Rather see your own faults. Learn to make the whole world your own. No one is a stranger my child: this whole world is your own!" This is considered as her last message to the world. She died at 1.30 am on July 20, 1920. Her body was cremated at the Belur Math.

Sarada Devi did not write any books and her utterances and reminiscences have been recorded by her disciples including Swami Nikhilananda, Swami Tapasyananda. Though uneducated Sarada Devi's spiritual insight and utterances are highly regarded by scholars like Gayatri Chakravorty Spivak, who writes, "We have bits and peices of her exquisite remarks as testimony."

- Practise meditation, and by and by your mind will be so calm and fixed that you will find it hard to keep away from meditation.
- The mind is everything. It is in the mind alone that one feels pure and impure. A man, first of all, must make his own mind guilty and then alone can he see another man's guilt.
- "I tell you one thing. If you want peace of mind, do not find fault with others. Rather see your own faults. Learn to make the whole world your own. No one is a stranger, my child; the whole world is your own."
- One must have devotion towards one's own *guru*. Whatever may be the nature of the *guru*, the disciple gets salvation by dint of his unflinching devotion towards his *guru*.

Sarada Devi played an important role as the advisory head of an nascent organization that became a monastic order devoted to social work- the Ramakrishna Mission. Gayatri Spivak writes that Sarada Devi "performed her role with tact and wisdom, always remaining in the background." She also initiated several prominent monks into the Ramakrishna Order. Swami Nikhilananda, who was a freedom fighter and a follower of Mahatma Gandhi, accepted Sarada Devi as his *guru* and joined the Ramakrishna Order. He eventually founded the Ramakrishna-Vivekananda Center in New York.

Though uneducated herself, Sarada Devi advocated education for women. She entrusted Devamata with the implementation of her dream- a girl's school on the Ganges, where Eastern and Western pupils could study together. In 1954, Sri Sarada Math and Ramakrishna Sarada Mission, a monastic order for women was founded in the honor of Sarada Devi.

CHIDVILASANANDA

Swami Chidvilasananda is the monastic name of Malti Shetty (Mumbai, India, June 24, 1955), who is the current guru of the Siddha Yoga lineage (*parampara*) established, by Swami Muktananda. Malti Shetty was the oldest child of a Mumbai restaurateur, who with his wife was devotees of Swami Muktananda in the 1950s. Malti was brought the first time to the Gurudev Siddha Peeth *ashram* at Ganeshpuri when she was five years old. During her childhood, her parents brought her, her sister and two brothers to the ashram on weekends.

After she had been initiated by Muktananda through *shaktipat* at age fourteen, Malti would move to the ashram as a formal disciple and yoga student. Muktananda soon made her his official English language translator and she accompanied him on his three world tours. In May 3, 1982, Malti Shetty was initiated as a sannyasin into the Saraswati order, taking vows of poverty, celibacy and obedience, and acquiring the title and monastic name of Swami Chidvilasananda, (literally, "bliss of the play of consciousness").

She was later to be also called Gurumayi by her devotees. At this time Muktananda formally designated her as one of his successors, along with her brother Subhash Shetty, by this time known as Swami Nityanand.

Swami Chidvilasananda provided a unique description of the spiritual initiation she received from Swami Muktananda in 1982:

> All of a sudden, my Guru, my Baba,
>
> Placed his hand on my head.
>
> Streaks of fire exploded from his palm.
>
> The house of my individuality was set ablaze.
>
> Everything I had was burned away.

Muktananda died a few months later. In 1985, there was a split between the two co-gurus and Swami Chidvilasananda became the sole head of Siddha Yoga. Swami Chidvilasananda renamed the South Fallsburg, New York ashram Shree Muktananda Ashram, in honor of her guru, Swami Muktananda. In 1992 she incorporated the PRASAD Project in the United States. The PRASAD project is an NGO in Special Consultative Status with the Economic and Social Council of the United Nation. In 1997 she founded the *Muktabodha Indological Research Institute* with its own publishing imprint, Agama Press.

7

Women in the Saiva/ Sakta Ethos

We have so far discussed the Hindu view of art mainly from the internal evidence of the art itself. There remains, what is more exactly pertinent to the title of these chapters, to discuss the Hindu Esthetic as it is expressly formulated and elaborated in the abundant Sanskrit and Hindi literature on Poetics and the Drama. We shall find that general conclusions are reached which are applicable, not only to literature, but to all arts alike. The discussion begins with the Defence of Poesy. This is summed up in the statement that it may contribute to the achievement of all or any of the Four Ends of Life.

A single word rightly employed and understood is compared to the 'cow of plenty,' yielding every treasure; and the same poem that is of material advantage to one, may be of spiritual advantage to another or upon another occasion. The question follows: What is the essential element in poetry? According to some authors this consists in style or figures, or in suggestion (vyanjana, to which we shall recur in discussing the varieties of poetry). But the greater writers refute these views and are agreed that the one essential element in poetry 2 is what they term Rasa, or Flavour.

With this term, which is the equivalent of Beauty or Esthetic Emotion in the strict sense of the philosopher, must be considered the derivative adjective rasavant Especially Visvanatha in the Sahitya Darpana, ca. 1450 A. D. (trans. Bibliotheca Indica, Ballantyne) and also in the Agni Purana, and the Vyakti Viveka. As remarked by W. Rothenstein, "What is written upon a single work should enable people to apply clear principles to all works they may meet with" (Two Drawings by Hok'sai, 1910). Also Benedetto Croce, "laws relating to special branches are not conceivable".

Such words as saundarya and rupa should be translated as loveliness or charm. No one suggests that metre makes poetry. This error was hardly to be expected in a country where even the dryest treatises on law and logic are composed in metre. Metrical poetry is padya kavya, prose poetry is gadya kavya, but it is rasa that makes them poetry. 'having rasa/ applied to a work of art, and the derivative substantive rasika, one who enjoys rasa, a connoisseur or lover, and finally rasasvadana, the tasting of rasa, i.e., aesthetic contemplation.

A whole literature is devoted to the discussion of rasa and the conditions of its experience. The theory, as we have remarked, is worked out in relation to poetry and drama, especially the classic drama of Kalidasa and others. When we consider that these plays are essentially secular in subject and sensuous in expression, the position arrived at regarding its significance will seem all the more remarkable.

Aesthetic emotion rasa is said to result in the spectator rasika though it is not effectively caused, through the operation of determinants (vibhava}, consequents {anubhava}, moods (bhava} and involuntary emotions (sattvabhava} Thus:

Determinants: the aesthetic problem, plot, theme, etc., viz: the hero and other characters and the circumstances of time and place. In the terminology of Croce these are the "physical stimulants to aesthetic reproduction."

Consequents: deliberate manifestations of feeling, as gestures, etc.

Moods: transient moods (thirty-three in number) induced in the characters by pleasure and pain, e. g., joy, agitation, impatience, etc. Also the permanent (nine), viz: the Erotic, Heroic, Odious, Furious, Terrible, Pathetic, Wondrous and Peaceful.

Involuntary Emotions: emotional states originating in the inner nature; involuntary expressions of emotion such as horripilation, trembling, etc. (eight in all). In order that a work may be able to evoke rasa one of the permanent moods must form a master-motif to which all other expressions of emotion are subordinate. That is to say, the first essential of a rasavant work is unity.

As a king to his subjects, as a guru to his disciples, Even so the master-motif is lord of all other motifs. If, on the contrary, a transient emotion is made the motif of the whole work, this "extended development of a transient emotion tends to the absence of rasa," or as we should now say, the work becomes sentimental. Pretty art which emphasizes passing feelings and personal emotion is neither beautiful nor true: it tells us of meeting again in heaven; it confuses time and eternity, loveliness and beauty, partiality and love.

Let us remark in passing that while the nine permanent moods correspond to an identical classification of rasas or flavours as nine in number, the rasa of which we speak here is an absolute, and distinct from any one of these. The 'nine rasas 'are no more than the various colourings of one experience, and are arbitrary terms of rhetoric used only for convenience in classification : just as we speak of poetry categorically as lyric, epic, dramatic, etc., without implying that poetry is anything but poetry. Rasa is tasted beauty is felt only by empathy, 'einfiihlung' (*sadharana*); that is to say by entering into, feeling, the permanent motif ; but it is not the same as the permanent motif itself, for, from this point of view, it matters not with which of the permanent motifs we have to do.

It is just here that we see how far Hindu Aesthetic had now departed from its once practical and hedonistic character: the Dasarupa declares plainly that Beauty is absolutely independent of the sympathetic "Delightful or disgusting, exalted or lowly, cruel or kindly, obscure or refined, (actual) or imaginary, there is no subject that cannot evoke rasa in man." Of course, a work of art may and often does afford us at the same time pleasure in a sensuous or moral way, but this sort of pleasure is derived directly from its material qualities, such as tone or texture, assonance, etc., or the ethical peculiarity of its theme, and not from its aesthetic qualities: the aesthetic experience is independent of this, and may even, as Dhanamjaya says, be derived in spite of sensuous or moral displeasure.

Incidentally we may observe that the fear of art which prevails amongst Puritans arises partly from the failure to recognize that aesthetic experience does not depend on pleasure or pain at all: and when this is not the immediate difficulty, then from the distrust of any experience which is "beyond good and evil" and so devoid of a definitely moral purpose. The tasting of rasa the vision of beauty is enjoyed, says Visvanatha, "only by those who are competent thereto": and he quotes Dharmadatta to the effect that "those devoid of imagination, in the theatre, are but as the wood-work, the walls, and the stones."

It is a matter of common experience that it is possible for a man to devote a whole life time to the study of art, without having once experienced aesthetic emotion: "historical research" as Croce expresses it, "directed to illumine a work of art by placing us in a position to judge it, does not alone suffice to bring it to birth in our spirit," for "pictures, poetry, and every work of art produce no effect save on souls prepared to receive them."

Visvanatha comments very pertinently on this fact when he says that "even some of the most eager students of poetry are seen not to have a right perception of rasa." The capacity and genius necessary for appreciation are partly native ('ancient') and partly cultivated ('contemporary'): but cultivation alone is useless, and if the poet is born, so too is the rasika, and criticism is akin to genius. Indian theory is very clear that instruction is not the purpose of art. On this point Dhanamjaya is sufficiently sarcastic: "As for any simple man of little intelligence," he writes, "who says that from dramas, which distil joy, the gain is knowledge only, as in the case of history and the like (mere statement, narrative, or illustration) homage to him, for he has averted his face from what is delightful."

The spectator's appreciation of beauty depends on the effort of his own imagination, "just as in the case of children playing with clay elephants." Thus, technical elaboration (realism) in art is not by itself the cause of rasa: as remarked by Rabindranath Tagore "in our country, those of the audience who are appreciative, are content to perfect the song in their own mind by the force of their own feeling."

This is not very different from what is said by Sukracharya with reference to images: "the defects of images are constantly destroyed by the power of the virtue of the worshipper who has his heart always set on God." If this attitude seems to us dangerously uncritical, that is to say dangerous to art, or rather to accomplishment, let us remember that it prevailed everywhere in all periods of great creative activity: and that the decline of art has always followed the decline of love and faith.

Tolerance of an imperfect work of art may arise in two ways: the one uncritical, powerfully swayed by the sympathetic, and too easily *sati*sfied with a very inadequate correspondence between content and form, the other creative, very little swayed by considerations of charm, and able by force of true imagination to complete the correspondence of content and form which is not achieved or not preserved in the original.

Uncritical tolerance is content with prettiness or edification, and recoils from beauty that is 'difficult': creative tolerance is indifferent to prettiness or edification, and is able from a mere suggestion, such as an awkward 'primitive' or a broken fragment, to create or recreate a perfect experience. "Also, "the permanent motif becomes rasa through the rasika's own capacity for being delighted not from the character of the hero to be imitated, nor because the work aims at the production of aesthetic emotion." How many works which have "aimed at the production of aesthetic emotion," that is to say, which were intended to be beautiful, have failed of their purpose!

The degrees of excellence in poetry are discussed in the Kavya Prakasa and the Sahitya Darpana. The best is where there is a deeper significance than that of the literal sense. In minor poetry the sense overpowers the suggestion. In inferior poetry, significantly described as 'variegated' or 'romantic' (chitra}, the only artistic quality consists in the ornamentation of the literal sense, which conveys no suggestion beyond its face meaning. Thus narrative and descriptive verse take a low place, just as portraiture does in plastic art: and, indeed, the Sahitya Darpana excludes the last kind of poetry altogether.

It is to be observed that the kind of suggestion meant is something more than implication or double entendre: in the first case we have to do with mere abbreviation, comparable with the use of the words et cetera, in the second we have a mere play on words. What is understood to be suggested is one of the nine rasas.

It is worth noting that we have here a departure from, and I think, an improvement on Croce's definition 'expression is art.' A mere statement, however, completely expressive, such as: "The man walks/' or (a+b) 2 = a 2 +2ab+b 2, is not art. Poetry is indeed a kind of sentence 1: but what kind of sentence?" A sentence ensouled by rasa, 2 i.e., in which one of the nine rasas is implied or suggested: and the savouring of this flavour, rasasvadana, through empathy, by those possessing the necessary sensibility is the condition of beauty.

What then are rasa and rasasvddana, beauty and aesthetic emotion? The nature of this experience is discussed by Visvanatha in the Sahitya Darpana: "It is pure, indivisible, self-manifested, and compounded equally of joy and consciousness, free of admixture with any other perception, the very twin brother of mystic experience (Brahmasvadana sahodarah), and the very life of it is supersensuous (lokottara) wonder."

Further, "It is enjoyed by those who are competent thereto, in identity, just as the form of God is itself the joy with which it is recognized." For that very reason it cannot be an object of knowledge, its perception being indivisible from its very existence. Apart from perception it does not exist. It is not on that account to be regarded as eternal in time or as interrupted: it is timeless. It is again, supersensuous, hyperphysical (alaukika), and the only proof of its reality is to be found in experience. Religion and art are thus names for one and the same experience an intuition of reality and of identity.

This is not, of course, exclusively a Hindu view: it has been expounded by many others, such as the Neo-platonists, Hsieh Ho, Goethe, Blake, Schopenhauer and Schiller. Nor is it refuted by Croce. It has been recently restated as follows: "In those moments of exaltation that art can give, it is easy to believe that we have been possessed by an emotion that comes from the world of reality. Those who take this view will have to say that there is in all things the stuff out of which art is made reality. The peculiarity of the artist would seem to be that he possesses the power of surely and frequently seizing reality (generally behind pure form), and the power of expressing his sense of it, in pure form always I".

Here pure form means form not clogged with unsesthetic matter such as associations. It will be seen that this view is monistic: the doctrine of the universal presence of reality is that of the immanence of the Absolute. It is inconsistent with a view of the world as absolute maya, or utterly unreal, but it implies that through the false world of everyday experience may be seen by those of penetrating vision (artists, lovers and philosophers) glimpses of the real substrate. This world is the formless as we perceive it, the unknowable as we know it.

Precisely as love is reality experienced by the lover, and truth is reality as experienced by the philosopher, so beauty is reality as experienced by the artist: and these are three phases of the Absolute. But it is only through the objective work of art that the artist is able to communicate his experience, and for this purpose any theme proper to himself will serve, since the Absolute is manifested equally in the little and the great, animate and inanimate, good and evil.

We have seen that the world of Beauty, like the Absolute, cannot be known objectively. Can we then reach this world by rejecting objects, by a deliberate purification of art from all associations? We have already seen, however, that the mere intention to create beauty is not sufficient but there must be an object of devotion. Without a point of departure there can be no flight and no attainment: here also "one does not attain to perfection by mere renunciation."

We can no more achieve Beauty than we can find Release by turning our backs on the world: we cannot find our way by a mere denial of things, but only in learning to see those things as they really are, infinite or beautiful. The artist reveals this beauty wherever the mind attaches itself: and the mind attaches itself, not directly to the Absolute, but to objects of choice. Thus we return to the earth. If we supposed we should find the object of search elsewhere, we were mistaken.

The two worlds, of spirit and matter, Purusha and Prakriti, are one: and this is as clear to the artist as it is to the lover or the philosopher. Those Philistines to whom it is not so apparent, we should speak of as materialists or as nihilist's exclusive monists, to whom the report of the senses is either all in all or nothing at all. The theory of rasa set forth according to Visvanatha and other sestheticians, belongs to totalistic monism; it marches with the Vedanta.

In a country like India, where thought is typically consistent with itself, this is no more than we had a right to expect. It is very generally held that natural objects such as human beings, animals or landscapes, and artificial objects such as factories, textiles or works of intentional art, can be classified as beautiful or ugly. And yet no general principle of classification has ever been found: and that which seems to be beautiful to one is described as ugly by another. In the words of Plato "Everyone chooses his love out of the objects of beauty according to his own taste."

To take, for example, the human type: every race, and to some extent every individual, has a unique ideal. Nor can we hope for a final agreement: we cannot expect the European to prefer the Mongolian features, or the Mongolian the European. Of course, it is very easy for each to maintain the absolute value of his own taste and to speak of other types as ugly; just as the hero of chivalry maintains by force of arms that his own beloved is far more beautiful than any other. In like manner the various sects maintain the absolute value of their own ethics. But it is clear that such claims are nothing more than statements of prejudice, for who is to decide which racial ideal or which morality is "best"?

It is a little too easy to decide that our own is best; we are at the most entitled to believe it the best for us. This relativity is nowhere better suggested than in the classic saying attributed to Majnun, when it was pointed out to him that the world at large regarded his Laila as far from beautiful. "To see the beauty of Laila/' he said, "requires the eyes of Majnun."

It is the same with works of art. Different artists are inspired by different objects; what is attractive and stimulating to one is depressing and unattractive to another and the choice also varies from race to race and epoch to epoch. As to the appreciation of such works, it is the same; for men in general admire only such works as by education or temperament they are predisposed to admire. To enter into the spirit of an unfamiliar art demands a greater effort than most are willing to make.

The classic scholar starts convinced that the art of Greece has never been equalled or surpassed, and never will be; there are many who think, like Michelangelo, that because Italian painting is good, therefore good painting is Italian. There are many who never yet felt the beauty of Egyptian sculpture or Chinese or Indian painting or music: that they have also the hardihood to deny their beauty, however, proves nothing. It is also possible to forget that certain works are beautiful: the eighteenth century had thus forgotten the beauty of Gothic sculpture and primitive Italian painting, and the memory of their beauty was only restored by a great effort in the course of the nineteenth.

There may also be natural objects or works of art which humanity only very slowly learns to regard as in any way beautiful; the western aesthetic appreciation of desert and mountain scenery, for example, is no older than the nineteenth century; and it is notorious that artists of the highest rank are often not understood till long after their death. So that the more we consider the variety of human election, the more we must admit the relativity of taste.

And yet there remain philosophers firmly convinced that an absolute Beauty (rasa} exists, just as others maintain the conceptions of absolute Goodness and absolute Truth. The lovers of God identify these absolutes with Him (or it) and maintain that He can only be known as perfect Beauty, Love and Truth. It is also widely held that the true critic (rasika) is able to decide which works of art are beautiful (rasavant) and which are not; or in simpler words, to distinguish works of genuine art from those that have no claim to be so described.

At the same time we must admit the relativity of taste, and the fact that all gods (devas and Isvaras) are modelled after the likeness of men. It remains, then, to resolve the seeming contradictions. This is only to be accomplished by the use of more exact terminology. So far have I spoken of 'beauty' without defining my meaning, and have used one word to express a multiplicity of ideas. But we do not mean the same thing when we speak of a beautiful girl and a beautiful poem; it will be still more obvious that we mean two different things, if we speak of beautiful weather and a beautiful picture.

In point of fact, the conception of beauty and the adjective "beautiful" belong exclusively to aesthetic and should only be used in aesthetic judgment. We seldom make any such judgments when we speak of natural objects as beautiful; we generally mean that such objects as we call beautiful are congenial to us, practically or ethically. Too often we pretend to judge a work of art in the same way, calling it beautiful if it represents some form or activity of which we heartily approve, or if it attracts us by the tenderness or gaiety of its colour, the sweetness of its sounds or the charm of its movement.

But when we thus pass judgment on the dance in accordance with our sympathetic attitude towards the dancer's charm or skill, or the meaning of the dance, we ought not to use the language of pure aesthetic. Only when we judge a work of art aesthetically may we speak of the presence or absence of beauty, we may call the work rasavant or otherwise; but when we judge it from the standpoint of activity, practical or ethical, we ought to use a corresponding terminology, calling the picture, song or actor "lovely," that is to say lovable, or otherwise, the action "noble," the colour "brilliant," the gesture "graceful," or otherwise, and so forth.

And it will be seen that in doing this we are not really judging the work of art as such, but only the material and the separate parts of which it is made, the activities they represent, or the feelings they express. Of course, when we come to choose such works of art to live with, there is no reason why we should not allow the sympathetic and ethical considerations to influence our judgment. Why should the ascetic invite annoyance by hanging in his cell some representation of the nude or the general select a lullaby to be performed upon the eve of battle?

When every ascetic and every soldier has become an artist there will be no more need for works of art: in the meanwhile ethical selection of some kind is allowable and necessary. But in this selection we must clearly understand what we are doing, if we would avoid infinity of error, culminating in that type of sentimentality which regards the useful, the stimulating and the moral elements in works of art as the essential. We ought not to forget that he who plays the villain of the piece may be a greater artist than he who plays the hero. For beauty in the profound words of Millet, does not arise from the subject of a work of art but from the necessity that has been felt of representing that subject.

We should only speak of a work of art as good or bad with reference to its aesthetic quality; only the subject and the material of the work are entangled in relativity. In other words, to say that a work of art is more or less beautiful, or rasavant, is to define the extent to which it is a work of art, rather than a mere illustration. However important the element of sympathetic magic in such a work may be, however important its practical applications, it is not in these that its beauty consists. What, then, is Beauty, what is rasa, what is it that entitles us to speak of diverse works as beautiful or rasavant? What is this sole quality which the most dissimilar works of art possess in common?

Let us recall the history of a work of art. There is (1) an aesthetic intuition on the part of the original artist, the poet or creator; then (2) the internal expression of this intuition, the true creation or vision of beauty, (3) the indication of this by external signs (language) for the purpose of communication, the technical activity; and finally, (4) the resulting stimulation of the critic or rasika to reproduction of the original intuition, or of some approximation to it.

The source of the original intuition may, as we have seen, be any aspect of life whatsoever. To one creator the scales of a fish suggest a rhythmical design, another is moved by certain landscapes, a third elects to speak of hovels, a fourth to sing of palaces, a fifth may express the idea that all things are enlinked, enlaced and enamoured in terms of the General Dance, or he may express the same idea equally vividly by saying that "not a spar- row falls to the ground without our Father's knowledge."

Every artist discovers beauty, and every critic finds it again when he tastes of the same experience through the medium of the external signs. But where is this beauty? We have seen that it cannot be said to exist in certain things and not in others. It may then be claimed that beauty exists everywhere; and this I do not deny, though I prefer the clearer statement that it may be discovered anywhere. If it could be said to exist everywhere in a material and intrinsic sense, we could pursue it with our cameras and scales, after the fashion of the experimental psychologists: but if we did so, we should only achieve a certain acquaintance with average taste we should not discover a means of distinguishing forms that are beautiful from forms that are ugly.

Beauty can never thus be measured, for it does not exist apart from the artist himself, and the rasika who enters into his experience. All architecture is what you do to it when you look upon it. Did you think it was in the white or grey stone or the lines of the arches and cornices? All music is what awakes in you when you are reminded of it by the instruments, it is not the violins and the cornets... nor the score of the baritone singer and it is nearer and further than they matter.

When every sympathetic consideration has been excluded, how- ever, there still remains a pragmatic value in the classification of works of art as beautiful or ugly? But what precisely do we mean by these designations as applied to objects? In the works called beautiful we recognize a correspondence of theme and expression, content and form: while in those called ugly we find the content and form at variance. In time and space, however, the correspondence never amounts to an identity: it is our own activity, in the presence of the work of art, which completes the ideal relation, and it is in this sense that beauty is what we "do to" a work of art rather than a quality present in the object.

With reference to the object, then "more" or "less" beautiful will imply a greater or less correspondence between content and form, and this is all that we can say of the object as such: or in other words, art is good that is good of its kind. In the stricter sense of completed internal aesthetic activity, however, beauty is absolute and cannot have degrees. The vision of beauty is spontaneous, in just the same sense as the inward light of the lover (bhakta). It is a state of grace that cannot be achieved by deliberate effort; though perhaps we can remove hindrances to its manifestation, for there are many witnesses that the secret of all art is to be found in self-forgetfulness.

And we know that this state of grace is not achieved in the pursuit of pleasure; the hedonists have their reward, but they are in bondage to loveliness, while the artist is free in beauty. It is further to be observed that when we speak seriously of works of art as beautiful, meaning that they are truly works of art, valued as such apart from subject, association, or technical charm, we still speak elliptically. We mean that the external signs poems, pictures, dances, and so forth are effective reminders. We may say that they possess significant form. But this can only mean that they possess that kind of form which reminds us of beauty, and awakens in us aesthetic emotion.

The nearest explanation of significant form should be such form as exhibits the inner relations of things; or, after Hsieh Ho, "which reveals the rhythm of the spirit in the gestures of living things." All such works as possess significant form of linguistic; and, if we remember this, we shall not fall into the error of those who advocate the use of language for language's sake, nor shall we confuse the significant forms, or their logical meaning or moral value, with the beauty of which they remind us.

Let us insist, however, that the concept of beauty has originated with the philosopher, not with the artist: he has been ever concerned with saying clearly what had to be said. In all ages of creation the artist has been in love with his particular subject when it is not so, we see that his work is not 'felt' he has never set out to achieve the Beautiful, in the strict aesthetic sense, and to have this aim is to invite disaster, as one who should seek to fly without wings. It is not to the artist that one should say the subject is immaterial: that is for the philosopher to say to the philistine who dislikes a work of art for no other reason than that he dislikes it.

The true critic (rasika) perceives the beauty of which the artist has exhibited the signs. It is not necessary that the critic should appreciate the artist's meaning every work of art is a kamadhenu, yielding many meanings for he knows without reasoning whether or not the work is beautiful, before the mind begins to question what it is "about." Hindu writers say that the capacity to feel beauty (to taste rasa) cannot be acquired by study, but is the reward of merit gained in a past life; for many good men and would-be historians of art have never perceived it.

The poet is born, not made; but so also is the rasika, whose genius differs in degree, not in kind, from that of the original artist. In western phraseology we should express this by saying that experience can only be bought by experience; opinions must be earned. We gain and feel nothing merely when we take it on authority that any particular works are beautiful. It is far better to be honest, and to admit that perhaps we cannot see their beauty.

A day may come when we shall be better prepared. The critic, as soon as he becomes an exponent, has to prove his case; and he cannot do this by any process of argument, but only by creating a new work of art, the criticism. His audience, catching the gleam at second-hand but still the same gleam, for there is only one has then the opportunity to approach the original work a second time, more reverently. When I say that works of art are reminders, and the activity of the critic is one of reproduction, I suggest that the vision of even the original artist may be rather a discovery than a creation.

If beauty awaits discovery everywhere, that is to say that it waits upon our recollection: in aesthetic contemplation as in love and knowledge, we momentarily recover the unity of our being released from individuality. There are no degrees of beauty; the most complex and the simplest expression remind us of one and the same state. The sonata cannot be more beautiful than the simplest lyric, nor the painting than the drawing, merely because of their greater elaboration.

Civilized art is not more beautiful than savage art, merely because of its possibly more attractive ethos. A mathematical analogy is found if we consider large and small circles; these differ only in their content, not in their circularity. In the same way, there cannot be any continuous progress in art. Immediately a given intuition has attained to perfectly clear expression, it remains only to multiply and repeat this expression. This repetition may be desirable for many reasons, but it almost invariably involves a gradual decadence, because we soon begin to take the experience for granted.

The vitality of a tradition persists only so long as it is fed by intensity of imagination. What we mean by creative art, however, has no necessary connection with novelty of subject, though that is not excluded. Creative art is art that reveals beauty where we should have otherwise overlooked it, or more clearly than we have yet received. Beauty is sometimes overlooked just because certain expressions have become what we call "hackneyed"; then the creative artist dealing with the same subject restores our memory.

The artist is challenged to reveal the beauty of all experiences, new and old. Many have rightly insisted that the beauty of a work of art is independent of its subject, and truly, the humility of art, which finds its inspiration everywhere, is identical with the humility of Love, which regards alike a dog and a Brahman and of Science, to which the lowest form is as significant as the highest. And this is possible, because it is one and the same undivided all. "If a beauteous form we view, 'Tis His reflection shining through."

It will now be seen in what sense we are justified in speaking of Absolute Beauty, and in identifying this beauty with God. We do not imply by this that God (who is without parts) has a lovely form which can be the object of knowledge; but that in so far as we see and feel beauty, we see and are one with Him. That God is the first artist does not mean that He created forms, which might not have been lovely had the hand of the potter slipped: but that every natural object is an immediate realization of His being.

This creative activity is comparable with aesthetic expression in its non-volitional character; no element of choice enters into that world of imagination and eternity, but there is always perfect identity of intuition-expression, soul and body. The human artist who discovers beauty here or there is the ideal guru of Kabir, who "reveals the Supreme Spirit wherever the mind attaches itself." The Early Buddhist view of art is strictly hedonistic. Just as little as Early Buddhism, dreamed of an expression of its characteristic ideas through poetry, drama, or music, so little was it imagined that the arts of sculpture and painting could be anything but worldly in their purpose and effect.

The arts were looked upon as physical luxuries, and loveliness as a snare. 'Beauty is nothing to me says, the Dasa

Dhamma Sutta, "neither the beauty of the body nor that that comes of dress." The Brethren were forbidden to allow the figures of men and women to be painted on monastery walls, and were permitted only representations of wreaths and creepers.

The psychological foundation of this attitude is nowhere more clearly revealed than in a passage of the *Visuddhi Magga*, where we find that painters, musicians, perfumers, cooks, and elixir-prescribing physicians are all classed together as purveyors of sensuous luxuries, whom others honour "on account of love and devotion to the sensations excited by forms and other objects of sense."

This is the characteristic Hinayana position throughout, and it is, of course, conspicuous also in the Jaina system, and in certain phases of Brahmanical thought, particularly in the period contemporary with early Buddhism. It is only in the third and second centuries BC. that we find the Buddhists patronizing craftsmen and employing art for edifying ends.

From what has just been said, however, it will be well understood that there had not at this time come into being any truly Buddhist or Brahmanical idealistic art; and thus "Early Buddist" art was necessarily the popular Brahmanical art and animistic art of the day, adapted to Buddhist requirements. The only exception to this rule is that special phase of Early Buddhist art which is represented by the capital of the Asoka columns, of which the forms are not merely non-Buddhist, but of extra-Indian origin.

8

Varieties of Hindu Female Asceticism

Throughout the history of Hinduism ascetic ideals have maintained so strong a hold on the minds of the cultured and uncultured classes alike that it may be well to devote some attention to the subject of asceticism itself. There is no land in the world in which ascetic practices have been so widely followed. To the mind of the Hindu, the life of the sannyasi who has freed himself from all human ties, and stripped himself of all -that ministers to physical comfort and well-being, has almost always seemed to be the highest. There are many who in the full vigour of their life have not been able to bring themselves to the point of breaking family and social ties, who, when death is near, take refuge in the estate of the sannyasi after the manner of those souls described by Milton, who dying put on the weeds of Dominic or Francis.

And there are multitudes that pass through life, engaging in all its social activities, who hope for another life in which they shall be more favourably situated for the casting off of worldly goods and worldly ties. Even in their case the ascetic element is not wholly lacking, as is evidenced by the fasts and penances to which so many of them submit themselves. We have further to remember the widespread practice of Yogic exercises, inspired by a purpose not essentially different. All this is an expression of a deeply rooted belief in the efficacy of discipline or negation of the flesh as an aid to the attainment of the highest.

The rationale of Hindu asceticism has already been made sufficiently clear. It has its justification in a widely accepted philosophical theory of the nature of reality. It was certainly no philosophical theory that originally gave rise to it. It was rather the practice that suggested the theory: or, if this statement seems too strong, it may at least be said that the practice gave a great impetus to the development of the theory. But the theory has in turn reinforced the practice, in a measure refined it, and provided for it a justification in reason which is lacking to ascetic practices followed to this day by more primitive peoples. Hindu asceticism in its distinctive form can therefore be justly criticized only if it is considered in relation to the intellectual basis on which it rests.

It is well, however, to bear in mind the fact that ascetic elements have found a place in the ideals of men apart from considerations so fundamental. Almost universal among primitive peoples are certain forms of ascetic practice, inspired by motives magical or sacrificial. Such practices were followed in India in ancient times; and they have persisted to the present day. So far as such motives have been operative, we have in Hindu asceticism the same spirit as that manifested in the ascetic practices followed in connexion with ancient Greek, Phrygian, and Egyptian cults. Further, asceticism has found a place in some form or other within most, if not all, of the higher religions of the world. Mahommedanism has its feast of Ramazan, observed so religiously by all believers; and it has its faqirs. Christendom has had its great company of anchorites and monks, and its hair shirts and whips and other instruments for the subduing of the flesh. And it has numbered within it men like St. Simeon Stylites, who in their efforts to free themselves from the dominion of the body, have gone to the wildest extremes of self-denial and self-torture.

There are, of course, distinctions which must be recognized between the ascetic practices which have been followed in connexion with different religions; and even in connexion with the same religion. There has been considerable confusion as to what is to be included under the head of ascetic practices. Some would include acts of self-restraint which amount to nothing more than the curbing of wanton desires or the girding of the mind and body to distasteful tasks. Certain Indian writers of modern times would go so far as to include work for the development of the material resources of their country. This is obviously far too wide a denotation to give to the term asceticism, for it would be thus made to cover all effort that is inspired by any purpose. Yet it is not easy to draw a clear line of division.

There may seem to be a world of difference between the man who sacrifices a meal that a hungry neighbour may be fed and him who betakes himself to monastic life, between the man who abstains from alcoholic liquors and him who abstains from all but the barest necessaries of existence. Yet, after all, it depends chiefly on the motive whether there is or is not. It is curious to find that so many people have failed to grasp this elementary distinction, and to observe the impression made on a certain type of mind by certain forms of self-sacrifice apart from any consideration of the motives inspiring it. This, it may be remarked in passing, is an interesting evidence of the strength of the ascetic 'instinct in human nature. We shall not here attempt any-thing as precarious as a definition of asceticism, but shall content ourselves with drawing certain distinctions between motives to self-denial and austerity, which must be held clearly in view if we are to arrive at any satisfactory estimate of the moral value of the practices in question.

In the first place, a broad general division may be made among motives to asceticism according as the good aimed at is that of the individual or of society. The history of Christian asceticism furnishes us with examples of both classes of motives. When St. Francis of Assisi subjected himself to privations and hardships, he did so in the service of Christ among men. This motive led to acts of remarkable self-sacrifice- the sharing of his single garment with another, the continual submission of himself to all kinds of indignities and privations. He found satisfaction in this life, and he even maintained that in these things is perfect joy. Yet suffering was not endured for its own sake but for the sake of others. Jesus illustrates the other askesis when He says: If thy right hand causeth thee to stumble, cut it off, and cast it from thee: for it is profitable for thee that one of thy members should perish, and not thy whole body goes into hell (Matt. v. 30).

It will be seen that in both of these cases the motive is an ethical one. In the one case it is the good of others that is directly sought, one enduring suffering or want that others may suffer less. In the other case it is self-discipline, undertaken not for the mere sake of casting off, but for the better government and direction of the individual's activities as a whole. It will be observed that in Christian morality these motives are not in antagonism to each other, and it could be shown that a self-discipline which has no social reference, however widely it may be practised, is not in accordance with the fundamental principles of the Christian religion. Yet the two motives can be distinguished.

In Hindu asceticism the social motive has been but little apparent. It is only in quite recent times that the idea of suffering and sacrifice for the sake of others has laid powerful hold on the mind of any large section of the Hindu people. The other motive, however, of the discipline of the individual soul, has operated powerfully. The aim has been to break down all that has been understood to interfere with the freedom of the soul, and as an aid to the attainment of this end there have been practised in India forms of self-mortification and penance which have few parallels in the whole history of human conduct.

It is unnecessary to recapitulate here what has been said in earlier chapters regarding the various ramifications of the ascetic idea, or of the various ends which it has been believed possible for the individual to attain through various practices—the power to coerce the gods and the power to bend nature to ones will, to which they have been supposed to give access. In so far as these have been the ends sought, we must look on these practices as not in themselves strictly moral, and what ethical value they may have come to have must be regarded as in a way accidental. Yet it may be claimed that just as the alchemy which was practised with a view to the discovery of the philosophers stone led to the discovery of other things of more solid and lasting value, so these crude ascetic practices contributed to the realization of ends attainable through the curbing of the desires and the mortification of the flesh, higher than the mere subjugation to ones arbitrary capricious will of the powers that govern the universe.

It is to the highest ideals sought through asceticism within Hinduism to which in a critical study our attention should be chiefly directed. The Christian would demand that the Christian mind should be judged not by reference to such vagaries as those presented by the lives of men like St. Simeon Stylites, but ultimately by reference to the teaching and practice of Christ, and the Hindu may similary claim that there is an essential and an accidental in Hindu practice, through whatever process the essential may have come to be discovered, and however much the accidental may have at times obscured the essential. So we may leave aside the primitive expressions of Hindu asceticism, whether appearing early in time or persisting to the present day.

Asceticism, so defended, has been believed to have value in the way of discipline for the soul in two ways. On the one hand, Yogic practices and less extravagant forms of self-restraint have the effect, if not of leading to freedom, of raising the soul to a higher position in future births. On the other hand, the breaking of all worldly ties is a condition of the attainment of final deliverance. These two ideas are not contradictory to each other, but are in their main principle in harmony, for the ultimate goal is in both cases the same. This is well brought out regarding the Yoga philosophy with its ascetic exercises by Max Muller, when he says:

It is to serve as a Taraka, as a ferry, across the ocean of the world, as a light by which to recognize the true independence of the subject from any object ; and as a preparation for this, it is to serve as a discipline for subduing all the passions arising from worldly surroundings.

The reference here is to the Yoga philosophy and to its peculiar metaphysical position, but there are similar ideas of the value of physical discipline in connexion with the other systems. It is true that the method by which this discipline works is connected with the doctrine of karma, the merit of particular acts becoming the property of the agent, and this explanation of the relation of act to agent we have already seen reason to reject. But the principle might be maintained apart from this, and it might be held that ascetic practices have a kathartic value, which is conserved through succeeding births, on grounds which would be free from the difficulties which beset the doctrine of karma in its familiar form. Indeed, there seems to be ground for believing that in certain places there is an implied distinction between the effect of certain kinds of austerities and penances, which are the fruit of desire as are other acts, and which accordingly have their appropriate fruits in future births, and that of actions which are the expression of the mortification of desire, though the process may not have reached completion.

Whether this be so or not, we can see how it is possible for some to regard Hindu asceticism in its higher forms as moral discipline, aiding the soul to that more and more complete severance from the world which will issue finally in that act of insight in which worldly ties shall be completely broken, the illusion of individuality dispelled, and freedom attained. On such grounds the claim may be made that Hindu asceticism has high ethical value. Whether we can admit this or not will depend on the view we take of certain considerations to which attention must now be directed. We have already considered the general bearings of Hindu philosophical thought on ethics, and we have come to the conclusion that it provides no satisfactory basis for a theory of morals. But it may be replied that we have taken too narrow a view of morality, and that the recognition of an end to the attainment of which ascetic discipline is so valuable a means, implies that a place has been given to moral effort which has been far too little regarded.

The Christian admits that if the right hand proves an occasion of stumbling it should be cut off, and so does the Hindu. Where is the difference? It would not be quite true to reply that the Christian believes in sacrifice with a view to the attainment of a greater good, for the Hindu would answer that he believes in greater sacrifice with a view to the attainment of a still greater good. So the question would resolve itself again into that of the specific nature of the good to be attained. Dr. Rabindranath Tagore has well described the Hindu position when he says:

In the typical thought of India it is held that the true deliverance of man is the deliverance from avidya, from ignorance.

It is not in destroying anything that is positive and real, for that cannot be possible, but that which is negative, which obstructs our vision of truth. When this obstruction, which is ignorance, is removed, then only is the eyelid drawn up which is no loss to the eye. With part of this we should probably all agree. The moral life is carried on through the negating of the lower that the higher may find its true expression. But what is not made clear by typical Indian thought, in spite of all that Dr. Rabindranath has said, is that there are lower and higher forms of activity. Indian asceticism has most normally found its justification in the idea that it is an aid to the cutting of the roots of desire, to the negation of all activity. The right hand is cut off not that the individual may be helped in the task of directing better the activities of the body, but because its activities from their very nature lead the soul astray. Looked at from this point of view, Hindu asceticism is no longer a moral discipline. It is in its essential nature non-moral.

The case may be stated in a slightly different way. Can we have a true morality that is not social, that is not based on an assumption of the permanent worth of individuality and of society? Can we have a true good that is not a social good?

In our Western thought self-sacrifice has seldom been regarded as an end in itself. It has been practised with a view to a fuller realization of the self. It is the lower and more capricious selves that men have sought to slay, making of them stepping-stones to higher things. The true self has been conceived as social. It finds its true expression in activities which bring it into various relationships with other selves. This thought again is connected with the conception of reality as a unity in diversity, To Hindu thought; on the other hand, reality has commonly appeared to be a unity without diversity, or a plurality of existences ultimately without diversity.

So asceticism has served as a means not to the stripping of the individual life of hindrances to its true expression of itself within a society of selves, but to the destruction of selfhood itself so far as it is individual. In the light of this the moral life may be held to find its highest expression in asceticism, but we would reply that this is not morality in the sense in which the term has been used traditionally, or in any sense which the etymology of the term justifies. A true morality involves recognition of the worth of individuality, and of the value of society as the sphere in which it finds its true expression. Hindu thought provides us with no philosophy of society, for its system of dharma is not a philosophy. So we are led to the conclusion that Hindu asceticism as defended by philosophic thought does not partake of the nature of ethical activity.

Asceticism in the form of yoga and meditation possibly goes back to the earliest period of Indian history. Seals depicting a figure sitting in what looks like a yogic pose have been found at sites of the Indus Valley Civilization dating to the second millennium B.C.E. In the texts of the early Vedas (c. 1500–c. 1000 B.C.E.), ascetic practices appear in a variety of contexts. References are made to long-haired silent sages (*munis*), clad in soiled yellow garments or naked, who are depicted as having supernatural powers, acquired perhaps as a result of their ascetic practices. The early texts also tell of the shadowy wandering ascetics (*vratyas*), who seem to have also practiced physical austerities.

The Vedas in some places say that the deities gained their status, or even created the entire universe, through the power of their inner, ascetic heat (*tapas*), acquired through the rigorous practice of physical and spiritual self-discipline and mortification of the body. The term *tapas* derives from a Sanskrit root meaning to heat up or burn, and refers to any one of a variety of ascetic methods for achieving religious power. In the Rig Veda, Indra is said to have achieved his divine place through the practice of asceticism and the generation of this powerful "heat," while elsewhere in that ancient work are encountered cosmogonic hymns that attribute the origins of the universe to the Primal One who creates by "heating up ascetic heat."

The metaphysical qualities of both truth and order are said to have derived from ascetic heat, and the ancient Indian seers (*rishis*) also were supposed to have achieved their powers through ascetic heat. This notion of ascetic heat as a creative, or even coercive, religious force was to persist in Indian religious thinking through subsequent centuries to the present. One may gain ascetic heat through a variety of ascetic techniques, including fasting, chastity, and various yogic techniques such as breath control (*pranayama*), and through it the adept can procure tremendous supernatural powers and even the status of a god.

In the Upanishads, epics, and other Sanskrit texts one often learns of various ascetics who force their way into heaven and become gods through the power of their ascetic heat. Deities such as Shiva were especially associated with this power of ascetic heat, derived from proficiency in yoga, meditation, and extreme austerities. Various classes of ascetics (*tapasvins*, "specialists in the practice of *tapas* ") eventually arose in Hindu India and are sometimes enumerated. They are mainly differentiated by the form of austerities they engage in. Some ascetics, for example, stay totally stationary for years at a time or remain standing or in water for weeks on end. Some ascetics subsist solely on fruits, wild plants, and roots or they live only on grain left in the fields.

Among the most famous are ascetics who practice the "five fires" ritual (building four fires around themselves, with the sun as the fifth) and "spike-lying" ascetics who sleep on beds of nails. A second strand of asceticism within the Hindu tradition might better be termed "renunciation." Such renunciation can be either *tyaga* (relinquishing a desire for actions to produce effects) or *samnyasa* (abandoning family, social, economic life, and the ritual activity associated with the householder's way of life), in order to pursue single-mindedly the ultimate goals of religion. World renouncers seem to have been a feature of Indian religious life since very early times. Already mentioned above are the silent sages and wandering ascetics discussed in the Vedas. Later texts depict a wide variety of renouncers, hermits, and ascetic "orders" living in the jungles and forests.

Among such ascetics were those who, with or without their wives, live on wild fruits and plants and maintain a ritual sacrificial fire; those who are "god-possessed" but perform the Vedic rituals; those with matted hair who wear bark clothing; those who sleep on the ground, eat only what drops from trees and plants, and regulate their meals according to the waxing and waning of the moon; those who wander from one monastery to another, eating only eight mouthfuls of food per day; those who remain naked, live under trees or in graveyards, and remain indifferent to what they eat or receive from others; renouncers who wear red and beg only at the homes of high-caste Brahmins; and radical ascetics who do not remain more than a day in any one place and live on cow urine and feces.

Renunciation (and the values and practices associated with it, especially nonviolence [*ahimsa*], vegetarianism, lack of possessions, and begging for a living) came to play an enormously influential role in Hinduism from the time of the Upanishads onwards. Not only were there dedicated ascetics and renunciates who committed their lives to this kind of religious practice; even those who chose to remain householders were influenced by renunciatory values. From a very early date, then, Hinduism was shaped by asceticism and renunciation. Yet the Hindu tradition also had dissenting voices. The religion was somewhat divided about the value and necessity of asceticism and the renunciatory lifestyle. Some ancient texts condemn renunciation in general. (In the Hindu epic *Mahabharata,* one of the heroes of the epic goes so far as to say that renunciation is only for those who have failed in worldly affairs.)

More often, texts condemn renunciation by householders those with families to support and occupations to fulfill. Indeed, Hindu texts written in the wake of the wanderer movement often extolled the householder's life of marriage, reproducing, and raising children. In the *Dharma Sutras* the householder stage is sometimes said to be the only legitimate or best stage of lifebetter even than the stage of pursuing the ultimate religious goal of final liberation from rebirth. Those in all other stages of life (the student, forest dweller, and world renouncer) depend on the householder, in part because it is the householder who feeds or donates to them when they beg from him:

> A householder alone offers sacrifices. A householder afflicts himself with austerities. Of the four stages of life, therefore, the householder is the best. As all rivers and rivulets ultimately end up in the ocean, so people of all stages of life ultimately end up with the householder. As all creatures depend on their mothers for their survival so all mendicants depend on householders for their survival.

As another text puts it, when "carried out with zeal," the householder stage of life procures both happiness in this life and heaven in the next:

> Just as all living creatures depend on air in order to live, so do members of the other stages of life subsist by depending on householders. Since people in the other three stages of life are supported every day by the knowledge and food of the householder, therefore the householder stage of life is the best. It must be carried out with zeal by the man who wants to win an incorruptible heaven [after death] and endless happiness here on earth.

Nevertheless, one also finds ascetic and renunciatory values- especially nonviolence (*ahimsa*), but also nonpossession and ascetic heat- included in ethical lists that seem generally applicable to all, no matter what stage of life they are in. Indeed, even the householder's life came to include certain kinds of austerities, especially as a way of penance and cleansing one's conscience: "If his mind-and-heart is heavy because of some act that he has committed, he should generate the inner heat [*tapas*] [prescribed] for it until he is *sat*isfied.... Those who have committed major crimes and all the rest who have done what should not be done are freed from that guilt by well-generated inner heat".

From an early age in the history of Hinduism there was also recognition that one could live two basic kinds of religious lives within the boundaries of the religion: a life of engagement and a life of disengagement. Both were usually regarded as legitimate (although some texts do weight one or the other more heavily), and both were accorded Vedic authority and pedigree. Both were also generally regarded as efficacious- according to the following text, engagement leading to a state of equality with the gods, and disengagement to a transcendent condition beyond the world of *samsara*:

There are two kinds of Vedic activity: the one that brings about engagement [in worldly action] and the rise of happiness, and the one that brings about disengagement [from worldly action] and the supreme good. The activity of engagement is said to be driven by desire in this world and the world beyond; but the activity of disengagement is said to be free of desire and motivated by knowledge. The man who is thoroughly dedicated to the activity of engagement becomes equal to the gods; but the man who is dedicated to disengagement passes beyond the five elements.

Reconciling these two apparently different modes of religious life was not always easy, however. On the face of it, the life of engagement and the life of disengagement appear to be incompatible- the one involved in the world of activity and *karma*, and the other attempting to renounce such activity and free oneself of *karma*. One of the principal methods for synthesizing the two was the system of the four stages of life (*ashramas*) - perpetual student, householder, forest dweller, and world renouncer- developed especially in the *Dharma Sutras*. In some texts the four states of life seem to have been regarded as four different types of life that a student could pursue after study with a teacher. In other cases, however, the early authorities insisted that there is only one legitimate stage of life, that of the householder.

Finally, however, the tradition settled into conceptualizing the system of stages of life as progressive and more or less incumbent upon all upper-caste Hindus. This framework of stages of life could then be used to affirm life in the world (by emphasizing that all must pass through the householder stage of life before renunciation) while still incorporating the values and practices of asceticism into the ideal life of the Hindu practitioner. Three of the four classical stages of life emphasized ascetic practices, as will be seen, while the system also validated, and indeed insisted upon, the legitimacy of and need for the nonrenunciatory householder stage.

In the ideal structure laid out in Hindu texts, the first stage of life is that of a student. A young boy is given over to a teacher (*guru*), whom he lives with and serves for many years while studying the sacred Vedas under the teacher's guidance. The lifestyle assigned to this stage of life is one of austerity, asceticism, and discipline. Not only should the student remain chaste for the duration of this period; he should also observe a variety of other restraints and avoidances:

The chaste student of the Veda who lives with his guru should obey these restraints, completely restraining the cluster of his sensory powers to increase his own inner heat.... He should avoid honey, meat perfume, garlands, spices, women, anything that has gone sour, and violence to creatures that have the breath of life; anointing [his body with oil], putting make-up on his eyes, wearing shoes, and carrying an umbrella; desire, anger, and greed; dancing, singing, and playing musical instruments; gambling, group arguments, gossip, telling lies, looking at women or touching them, and striking another person. He should always sleep alone and never shed his semen, for by shedding his semen out of lust he breaks his vow.

Another text gives a slightly different list of observances, vows, and practices, but similarly emphasizes the importance of an austere life dedicated to self-restraint, the cultivation of virtue, and obedience to the teacher:

> Now the rules for the studentship are discussed. He shall obey his teacher, except when ordered to commit crimes which cause loss of caste. He shall do what is serviceable to his teacher, he shall not contradict him. He shall always occupy a couch or seat lower than that of his teacher. He shall not eat food offered at a sacrifice to the gods or the ancestors, nor pungent condiments, salt, honey, or meat. He shall not sleep in the daytime. He shall not use perfumes. He shall preserve chastity. He shall not embellish himself by using ointments and the like. He shall not wash his body with hot water for pleasure. But, if it is soiled by unclean things, he shall clean it with earth or water, in a place where he is not seen by a guru.
>
> Let him not sport in the water whilst bathing; let him swim motionless like a stick.... Let him not look at dancing. Let him not go to assemblies for gambling, etc., or to crowds assembled at festivals. Let him not be addicted to gossiping. Let him be discreet. Let him not do anything for his own pleasure in places which his teacher frequents. Let him talk with women so much only as his purpose requires. Let him be forgiving. Let him restrain his organs from seeking illicit objects. Let him be untired in fulfilling his duties; modest; possessed of self-command; energetic; free from anger; and free from envy.

Also among the duties laid out for those in the student stage of life is begging for a living- more precisely, begging and then turning over the proceeds to the teacher. Begging, for the religious student and other renunciates who legitimately live by such means, was said to be like fasting:

> He should fetch a pot of water, flowers, cow dung, clay, and sacrificial grass, as much as are needed, and go begging

every day. A chaste student of the Veda, purified, should beg every day from the houses of people who do not fail to perform Vedic sacrifices and who are approved of for carrying out their own innate activities. He should not beg from his guru's family or from the relatives of his mother or father, but if he cannot get to the houses of others he should avoid each of these more than the one that precedes it. And if there are none of the people mentioned above, he should beg from the whole village, purified and restrained in his speech, but he should avoid those who have been indicted.... When he is under the vow [of a chaste student] he should make his living by begging, nor should he eat the food of just one person; when begging is the livelihood of a person under a vow it is traditionally regarded as equal to fasting.

When the student reaches marriageable age, he should take a wife and start a family, eschewing, by and large, renunciatory and ascetic practices in favor of the pursuit of private gain (*artha*) - understood as material prosperity, self-interest, political advantage, and in general getting ahead in the world. Hinduism thus recognizes making a good living (in an acceptable occupation) and taking care of one's family as important and indeed religiously enjoined goals of life. Private gain is listed as one of the three "ends of life" in Hindu texts, the other two being the pursuit of religious duty (*dharma*) and the pursuit of pleasure (*kama*). And while following the dictates of religious duty is obviously of great importance for one's spiritual well-being and can involve certain ascetic practices, especially for purification and penance, the pursuit of pleasure and creature comforts is to be fully embraced in the householder stage of life. In some texts, private gain is in fact the most important of these ends of life: "Of the three ends of human life, material gain is truly the most important.... For the realization of religious duty and pleasure depend on material gain".

But, according to the scheme of the ideal stages of life, when the householder has completed this stage of life (upon the birth of grandchildren), he should begin to withdraw from the world and once more cultivate a more ascetic lifestyle.

After finishing the life of a student and after marrying and raising a family as a householder, a man may enter the third stage of life, that of the forest dweller. This stage of life, like that of the student, is characterized by ascetic practices and detachment from the world, including the renunciation of cultivated food (in favour of wild food that grows in the jungle) and of all possessions:

> After he has lived in the householder's stage of life in accordance with the rules in this way, a twice-born Vedic graduate should live in the forest, properly restrained and with his sensory powers conquered. But when a householder sees that he is wrinkled and gray, and [when he sees] the children of his children, then he should take himself to the wilderness. Renouncing all food cultivated in the village and all possessions, he should hand his wife over to his sons and go to the forest- or take her along.... He should eat vegetables that grow on land or in water, flowers, roots, and fruits, the products of pure trees, and the oils from fruits.... He should not eat anything grown from land tilled with a plough, even if someone has thrown it out, nor roots and fruits grown in a village, even if he is in distress [from hunger].

Subsistence on gathered food that grows naturally and spontaneously in the wild can be supplemented with food obtained by begging. The begged food, however, should be only enough for "bare subsistence" and should be obtained from the right donors:

> He should get food for bare subsistence by begging from priests who are ascetics themselves, from householders, and from other twice-born forest-dwellers. Or a man who lives in the forest may get [food] from a village, receiving it in the hollow of a leaf or in his hand or in a broken clay dish, and eat [only] eight mouthfuls of it. To perfect himself, a priest who lives in the forest must follow these and other preparations for consecration, as well as the various revealed canonical texts of the Upanishads, and those that sages and priestly householders have followed, to increase learning and inner heat and to clean the body.

The final stage of life is that of the world renouncer, who continues and furthers the ascetic practices of the forest dweller: "And when he has spent the third part of his lifespan in the forests in this way, he may abandon all attachments and wander as an ascetic for the fourth part of his lifespan" (*Manu,* 6.33). In this stage, the renouncer sends his wife away to live with his sons and performs a ceremony equivalent to his own funeral, stating that from this time on "no one belongs to me, and I belong to no one." Dying to his social persona, the wandering hermit from this time forth may no longer return to his previous home and should live entirely detached from the things of this world, owning nothing, alone and without companions, perfectly content and indifferent. He should beg but once a day, and he should not be "addicted to food" or hope for lots of alms or be disappointed should he receive nothing.

He should always go all alone, with no companion, to achieve success; realizing that success is for the man who is alone, he neither deserts nor is deserted. The hermit should have no fire and no home, but should go to a village to get food, silent, indifferent, unwavering and deep in concentration. A skull-bowl, the roots of trees, poor clothing, no companionship, and equanimity to everything- this is the distinguishing mark of one who is freed.

He should not welcome dying, nor should he welcome living, but wait for the right time as a servant waits for orders.... He should live here on earth seated in ecstatic contemplation of the soul, indifferent, without any carnal desires, with the soul as his only companion and happiness as his goal.... He should go begging once a day and not be eager to get a great quantity, for an ascetic who is addicted to food becomes attached to sensory objects, too.... He should not be sad when he does not get anything nor delighted when he gets something, but take only what will daily sustain his vital breath, transcending any attachment to material things.

The system of stages of life was the principal way in which Hinduism reconciled the apparently contradictory pulls of its life-affirming and world-renouncing strains. But there was also another way of reconciling the householder and renunciatory ways of life in the classical texts of Hinduism. This is the yoga of action (*karma yoga*) in the *Bhagavad Gita*. As opposed to the renunciation *of* action characteristic of ascetics and world renouncers, the *Bhagavad Gita* advocates a renunciation *in* action: one performs one's duties in society but dedicates the fruits of all action to God.

THE ROLE ASCETICISM IN HINDUISM

Religious life in early Vedic period was characterized by rituals. Vedic people performed rituals to deal with the uncertainties of life. Those who possessed the knowledge of rituals enjoyed special privileges. Kings and nobility vied with one another, seeking their help and intervention in invoking gods for peace and prosperity, victory against enemies and insurance against natural calamities, disease and danger. During this period Vedic religion suffered from a preponderance of the procedural and material aspects of rituals and ritual purity rather than the spiritual and metaphysical aspects of transcendental experience and self realization.

PHILOSOPHICAL NOTIONS ABOUT RITUALS

In the later Vedic period philosophical speculation about rituals gained ground. We see a symbolic correlation emerging between the mechanical aspects of rituals and the deeper issues of human existence. In the Aranyakas and the Upanishads we find a reevaluation of the knowledge of rituals and its subordination to the spiritual knowledge of the self or the knowledge of atman and Brahman. The knowledge of ritual still mattered in society. But in the minds of the seers, who lived in the forests, it was lower knowledge compared to the higher knowledge of self. Emphasis was now more on the internalization of rituals and control of mind and body by withdrawing the senses, practicing yoga of self control, inner purity, proper conduct and renunciation.

There was speculation about the role of karma, bondage to the cycle of births and deaths and a permanent solution to the problem of human suffering. In the ritual of life, the outer was meant to be sacrificed for the inner and the lower for the higher. In the microcosm of the individual, the seers found a new universe, inhabited by divinities and energies corresponding with those of the cosmos, giving them enough justification for the internalization of ritual as an act of personal sacrifice and inner purification to achieve self-realization. We are not sure how this reorientation in purpose and perception took place. Probably it was a reaction against the growing popularity of some ascetic traditions in the subcontinent which called for a change in their approach from the outer aspects of life to the inner.

THE RISE OF ASCETICISM AND RENOUNCER TRADITIONS

In the Upanishads and the Aranyakas we find echoes of the growing importance of asceticism against the backdrop of a society that was preoccupied with the performance of rituals and the wealth that accrued out of them. Urban settlements, expansion of empires, frequent wars and trade with foreign countries added to the complexity of life and necessitated a change in outlook and the need for a religious tradition that would act like a balm soothing the agitated nerves and helping people cope with the problems of death and disease.

Asceticism was thus a natural outcome of a tradition that was steeped in empty ritualism and failed to satisfy the spiritual needs of life. It emerged as a reactionary and evolutionary process against the simplistic and outdated solutions offered by Vedic religion.

It attempted to resolve the problems of human suffering, catastrophes, death and disease from a wider perspective, which the Vedic mantras could not resolve despite the blessings of the priests and the money paid to them. By 6th century BC dissolution with the Vedic tradition reached its culmination. Hundreds of ascetic sects and new religious traditions sprouted all over the subcontinent and challenged its authority. Buddhism and Jainism posed a much greater threat to Vedic ritualism, offering at the same time more appealing and intellectually satisfying alternative solutions to the problems of human misery and suffering.

These sects appealed to all sections of society ignoring the caste distinctions. They viewed the problem of human suffering as a product of ignorance and tried to interpret the relationship between the individual and the rest of the world in terms of illusion and duality.

They speculated upon the permanence or impermanence of individual self, the universal self and the relationship between the two. They attempted to analyze the nature of human personality and its constituent parts and principles. They pondered upon the role of nature in the creation of life and whether there was something beyond and above nature that regulated the process of creation. Out of this churning of the human thought, which was perhaps unprecedented in the religious history of mankind, starting roughly from about 1000 BC to 600 BC, emerged many powerful and brilliant concepts like yoga, karma, maya, prakriti and bondage, which constituted the core of Hinduism in subsequent times.

The rise of ascetic sects coincided with growing skepticism about Vedic traditions. The idea that individuals were born repeatedly through the mechanism of karma in order to fulfill the purpose of their creation gained ground give rise to many schools of philosophy. They offered a plethora or metaphysical explanations to explain the origin of life and the evolutionary process in which individual souls advance from one level to another through a laborious process of pain and suffering. Makkhali Gosala (560-484 B.C.) of the Ajivika sect, Vardhamana Mahavira (547-467 B.C.), the 24th Thirthankara of Jainism, and the Buddha (550-483 B.C.) the founder of Buddhism were some of the great personalities who belonged to this period of great introspection and spiritual enquiry preceding the Mauryan empire.

These spiritual leaders set a personal example by renouncing the comforts of worldly life which the Vedic priests hankered after. They showed least consideration for caste distinctions and the social order upheld religiously by the Vedic society.

They renounced the world, practiced detachment and indulged in various kinds of austerities ranging from the extreme measures of self-torture and self-immolation to the more moderate measures of fasting and restraint. They practiced yoga, meditation concentration as means of self-control. They debated among themselves trying to disapprove their opponents. Some of them even plotted against their opponents with diabolical schemes to discredit them in the eyes of the public. Their philosophy was borne out of their personal experience. It touched the hearts of many because of its direct appeal and emphasis on the problem of human suffering.

SIMILARITIES AMONG THE ASCETIC SECTS

The Vedic tradition collectively referred the wandering ascetics as Sramanas or those who labored (srama) for their liberation. The sramanas dotted the length and breadth of the subcontinent, propagating a diverse range of beliefs. Some of them like the Ajivakas, the Kapalikas and the Kalamukhas belonged to theistic sects. They believed in god and soul and worshipped the universal self as a personal god. Some like the Lokayatas, Charvakas and the Jainas belonged to atheistic sects. They did not believe in an absolute God as the cause of all causes. Some of them believed in the existence of soul and afterlife, but others like the lokayatas believed in neither souls nor life after death.

Some like the Buddhists had an ambivalent approach towards an absolute self and maintained silence, considering it to be an irrelevant subject in the matter of liberation. The vedic people treated the sramanas conditionally without wasting an opportunity to scorn those whom they detested or feared, using derogatory epithets such as yatis (wanderers), vratyas (untouchables) and ajivikas (beings lacking in vitality). Greater the alienation of the ascetics from the Vedas, the stronger was their reaction and criticism. Some sects focused on the urban communities, while some preferred to stay in seclusion maintaining secrecy.

The Buddha and Mahavira focused mainly on the urban communities, while Gosala preferred to stay away from them. He even questioned the intentions of Mahavira in spreading his beliefs. Despite these differences, the ascetic sects agreed on some fundamental ideas and concepts, which are mentioned below. Interestingly, they also constitute the core beliefs of modern day Hinduism

1. Suffering (dukha) is an integral part of human life and it is aggravated by the action of the senses and desires. Man should not aim for acquisition of wealth and empires but complete liberation from the very need to strive and achieve.
2. Individual actions (karma) would result in bondage. Practice of virtue through restraining of the senses and detachment from the sense objects would lead to emancipation from suffering
3. The body, the mind and the senses are impediments in cultivating higher awareness. They need to be restrained through various means such as austerities or practice of yoga or meditation to achieve the transcendental state of liberation.
4. Identification of oneself with the false self will result in bondage. When this identity is removed liberation is achieved.

ASCETICISM VS BRAHMANISM

The rise of asceticism posed many challenges to the established traditions of Brahmanism. By the time Alexander came to India with his army, the popularity of asceticism was so evident that it was the individual ascetics, probably the Jain ascetics, living in isolation in deep forests, who attracted his attention rather than the rituals of the traditional Vedic society. With its emphasis on rites and rituals, the inviolable supremacy of the Vedas, varnas (castes), purusharthas (the four aims of life), varnasharama dharma (the four stages of human life) and the rites of passage, Brahmanism found itself isolated and challenged by the new traditions that were slowly finding acceptance in both rural and urban areas.

Brahmanism met the challenge posed by the ascetic sects by drawing strength from the Vedas and finding answers in the Upanishads which had the depth and the vision to match their arguments and speculation. The idea of asceticism and renunciation that seemed so opposed to Brahmanism on the surface was actually the same ideals propounded in the Upanishads and practiced by Vedic seers for centuries. For the puritanical followers of Vedism, harassed by the notions of empty ritualism and self-interest, the Upanishads provided justification to strike a conciliatory approach towards some of the ascetic movements and acknowledge them as movements with in its own tradition. Those that did not fit into the philosophical notions and the world view of the Vedas were either ignored or condemned.

This strategy brought new vigor into Brahmanism, increased the breadth and scope of its vision and resulted in the assimilation of many new traditions such as Vaishnavism, the Puranic (adi) Saivism, and many concepts of Jainism, some practices of the Ajivilkas and the six schools of philosophy including the Yoga of Patanjali as inseparable trends with in its own tradition. The Bhagavadgita is a fine example of how these different traditions were assimilated into one acceptable and integrated philosophy without compromising the authority of the Vedas.

If Buddhism and Jainism escaped the same fate and maintained their distinction as separate religious traditions, it was mainly because of the charismatic appeal of the Buddha and Mahavira and the missionary zeal with which they and their followers propagated their beliefs and maintained their identities giving little scope for the possibility of any reconciliation. In Yoga and Samkhya, Vedism found a simple but effective reconciliation between the mind and the body and the tenets of the Samhitas and the deeper philosophy of the Upanishads. Integration of these two into Vedic religion ensured the continuity of an age old tradition that was obsessed with rituals and its progression, with few adjustments, into a more viable and intellectually satisfying alternative, without undermining the authority of the Vedas and the body of rituals it upheld.

THE KESHINS OF THE RIGVEDA

In the Tenth Mandala of the Rigveda there is a hymn addressed to a special class of ascetics (munis) known as keshins, who wore long locks of hair, practiced breath control and possessed supernatural abilities to transcend time and space. The keshins or munis are extolled in the following manner:

1. He with the long loose locks supports Agni, and moisture, heaven, and earth:
   He is all sky to look upon: he with long hair is called this light.
2. The Munis, girdled with the wind, wear garments soiled of yellow hue.
   They, following the wind's swift course go where the Gods have gone before.
3. Transported with our Munihood we have pressed on into the winds:
   You therefore, mortal men. Behold our natural bodies and no more.
4. The Muni, made associate in the holy work of every God,
   Looking upon all varied forms flies through the region of the air.
5. The Steed of Vata, Vayu's friend, the Muni, by the Gods impelled,
   In both the oceans hath his home, in eastern and in western sea.
6. Treading the path of sylvan beasts, Gandharvas, and Apsarases,
   He with long locks, who knows the wish, is a sweet most delightful friend
7. Vayu hath churned for him: for him he poundeth things most hard to bend,

When he with long loose locks hath drunk, with Rudra, water from the cup.

There is no doubt from the hymn that the munis were an important class of ascetics revered by the Vedic people for their association with the rituals and the holy work of every god. The munis had supernatural powers, with which they could travel in the air and fly like the Gandharvas and the Apsaras, looking at the forms upon the earth. When they, with (their minds focused on) Rudra, drank waters (breathed in pranic energy or life energy) from the cup (of life), that is when they practiced some form of kundalini or breath control, vayu (air) did wonders for them accomplishing the most difficult things.

KESHINS WERE WORSHIPPERS OF LORD SIVA

The kesins were not mentioned by the Rigvedic seers with disdain but with reverence. There is also a word of caution for the mortal men who cannot see them (or their hidden powers) beyond their natural bodies for who they truly are. Their supernatural ability is mentioned in association with Vayu or wind god alluding to some ancient form of breathing practices that gave them the special ability to transcend their minds and bodies. They probably worshipped Rudra or Siva who himself possessed long locks and was a real keshin.

As they drew in their breath and held it for long at will, Vayu obliged them and did wonders for them. The Keshins were mysterious beings and the fact that they were mentioned in the Rigveda in association with Rudra compounds the mystery. The hymn probably alludes to the increasing influence of Saiva sects upon Vedic tradition which is also confirmed by the descriptions of Siva in the Svetavatara Upanishad as Brahman himself.

VRATYAS

The Atharvaveda mentions vratyas as a band of ascetic warriors who practiced a tradition of their own which was probably a mixture of early forms of tantricism and ceremonial worship of ancient deities through magical rituals. According to some historians the Vratyas were probably an early band of Vedic Aryans who were excommunicated by their successors for some religious reasons. One of the arch enemies of Indra was Vratasura whom Indra slew in order to release waters from the clouds. Symbolically Vratasura was considered to be a dark cloud and Indra as the ruler of heavens slew him to release the waters and make the earth fertile.

We are not sure whether the Vratyas were connected to Vratasura in any way. The Vedic scriptures made a provision to readmit vratyas into Vedic society through purification rituals. Some historians believe that vratyas started the tradition of warrior ascetics and that the present vedic practice of doing vrata (a sacrificial ceremony of longer duration) seeking favors from a personal deity is probably an ancient tradition practiced by the Vratyas and adopted by Vedic tradition subsequently. It is also possible that the Vratyas were probably early worshippers of Siva and mother goddess and had some close affinity with early Dravidian tribes who inhabited parts of northern and eastern India.

THE LEGACY OF ASCETICISM

Modern Hinduism owes a great deal to the ancient ascetic sects. Perhaps without contribution from these sects, Hinduism would have been a mere ritualistic tradition. If Vedic rituals provided the body to Hinduism, the ascetic traditions provided the mind and the Vedas the soul to make it a religion of many dimensions and deeper spiritual values.

The *Bhagavadgita* is a summary of the diverse traditions that prevailed in ancient India and their reinterpretation in the light of the Vedas and Vedic beliefs. The six schools of Hindu philosophy, the theories of monism, dualism and qualified monism, owe a great deal to the ancient ascetic traditions which pondered upon the subject of human consciousness and its connection with the universal consciousness.

The Buddha and Mahavira were products of these sects. Before they received enlightenment, they spent considerable time in the company of wandering ascetics, absorbing their knowledge and ideas. The rise of Saivism and Vaishanavism and their assimilation into Vedic religion and the elevation of Vishnu and Siva into Hindu trinity were hastened by the growing popularity of Jainism and Buddhism in the urban areas. With its puritanical features and emphasis on karma and devotion, Vaishnavism matched Jainism emphasizing bhakti as the means of liberation, while with its spiritual depth and meditative approach Saivism matched Buddhism emphasizing jnana or knowledge as the means of liberation. Lord Vishnu and Lord Siva provided the much needed buffer for the Vedic religion against the charismatic appeal of Mahavira and the Buddha in containing the spread of the two religions in the subcontinent.

If Hinduism survived centuries of oppression in the hands of foreign powers that practiced different religions and emerged as a religion of great spiritual depth and vitality, it is because of the contribution made by thousands of ascetics, gurus, babas, yogis, munis and sanyasis in their individual capacities. Through their knowledge and selfless service they kept the tradition alive, invigorating it from time to time by reviving old and forgotten traditions and with new knowledge. They compensated for the lack of central leadership and missionary activity. The ascetics continue to dominate Hinduism even today and have been playing vital role in keeping its traditions and practices alive. Every Hindu ought to salute them for their valuable contribution in keeping Hinduism alive and vibrant.

9

Evolution of Women in Hinduism

FEMALE INFANTICIDE

Female infanticide arose from the general Vedic attitude towards women. The large dowries prescribed by the Vedas meant that a girl was seen as a burden. The woman who gave birth to a daughter was ashamed, and much stigma attached to a lady who only gave birth to daughters. Hence infanticide arose as a convenient way of getting rid of the "burden."Aryan texts sanction this custom:

"Tasmat striyam jatam parasyanti ut pumamsam haranti"(Hence they reject a female child when born, and take up a male.) [Taitt. Samh. VI.5.10.3] [Muir I 26]

A recent U.N. report said that up to 50 million girls and women were missing from India's population, the result of systematic discrimination extending to the abortion of female fetuses. In 1921 there were more than 97 women for every 100 men in India. Seventy years later, the number dropped to 92.7.

CHILD-MARRIAGE

Child marriage of daughters 5-6 years old was common due to the custom of dowry and to avoid scandals. Hindu Law books prescribe that the best partner for a man in one-third his age. Thus a man 18 year old should marry a girl 6 years old! –

"A man, aged thirty years, shall marry a maiden of twelve who pleases him, or a man of twenty-four a girl of eight years of age; if (the performance of) his duties would otherwise be impeded, he must marry sooner."[Manu IX.94]

This was meant to prevent any scandals. Narada states that some of the defects to be avoided in brides are if they already had a relationship with another man or have their minds set on another, they should not be selected [Sheth 67].

WIVES

This is often related to dowry, when the bride's family cannot pay up to the amount demanded by the in-laws. Often the in-laws make demands in excess of those made at the time of marriage. When the deadline specified runs out, the bride is burned in often gruesome fashions. At least 5000 women die each year for not bringing in enough dowries. At least a dozen women die each day in 'kitchen fires,' which are often passed off as accidents, because their in-laws are not satisfied with their dowries. Only a few of the murderers are brought to justice.

WIFE-BURNING

A Hindu-Aryan husband could at any time accuse his wife of infidelity. In case the wife protests her innocence, the council of village elders would then order an ordeal by fire. The accused wife would be required to pass through a blazing flame. Not just death, but any signs of burns would be taken as a sign of guilt and the wife would then have to undergo the penalty for infidelity [EB 8:986 'ordeal']. Adultery carries the death sentence in Aryan law, so either way she would have to pay with her life for her husband's or elders' mere suspicions. The ideal role model for this custom was Sita, Ram's wife. She was required by her spouse, the "ideal husband"of the Hindus, to pass through the fire ordeal after her return from Sri Lanka.

JAUHAR - VARIANT OF SATI

Jauhar refers to the practice of the mass burning of all the wives and daughters in an entire town/district to prevent them from falling into the hands of the enemies. Often the husbands forced their unwilling spouses, sometimes the women practiced it themselves, encouraged by the elders. It is merely a variant of *Sati,* since it occurred in anticipation of the women's widowhood.

WITCH-BURNING

The burning of witches during the Vedic Dark Ages of Indian History (1500 BC - 500 BC) and the later Puranic Dark Ages (100 AD-1000 AD) makes the European Medieval ecclesiastical witch-hunts pale in comparison.

PUNISHMENT OF WOMEN

The wife could suffer seriously cruel punishment for very minor offences.

AMPUTATION OF EARS AND NOSES

Aryan husbands cut off the ears and nose of their wives if they left the house without their prior permission. The *Pancatantra* mentions one such story [Pancatantra p.54, I.7th story "The Weaver's Wife"]. The weaver cut off his wife's nose because she did not respond and he considered her unfaithful. (Actually he cut off the barber's wife's nose that was there instead.) The Ramayana and Lord Rama practiced the cutting off of womens' noses for minor offences, thereby providing divine sanction for the custom. Shurpanakha was a Dravidian lady (referred to as *Rakshis* or female demons by the Aryans) who fell in love with Rama. She proposed to him, but he directed her to his brother Laxman. He cut off her ears and nose for this crime, and Ram condoned this act. [Alld Chmbrs 1036]

DEATH PENALTY

The death penalty was prescribed for Aryan women guilty of infidelity. The *Manu Smrti,* the most authoritative Indo-Aryan law-book, states

"When a woman, proud of her relations [or abilities] deceives her husband (with another man), then the king should [ensure that] she be torn apart by dogs in place much frequented by people"[Manu Smrti 8:371] "And the evil man should be burnt in a bed of red-hot iron"[Manu Smrti 8:371-2]

VIII.371. "If a wife, proud of the greatness of her relatives or (her own) excellence, violates the duty which she owes to her lord, the king shall cause her to be devoured by dogs in a place frequented by many. VIII.372. Let him cause the male offender to be burnt on a red-hot iron bed; they shall put logs under it, (until) the sinner is burned (to death)."[*Manu Smrti* Buhler VIII 371-372]

That this custom was prevalent in the 9the century is confirmed by Arab reports. Merchant Sulaiman, an Arab traveller of the 9th century states that "If any man in the Indies runs away with a wife and abuses her body they kill both him and the woman, unless it be proved that she was forced, then the man only is punished with death; but if the woman consented to the evil deed, they are punished with death, both one and the other."

Ram, the ideal husband, showed little regard to female life. Ram killed Tataka, a "Rakshi." Infidelity to husband was considered a grave sin and it was believed that such women went to Aksaya hell. The husband had the power to curse the wife who was disloyal to him. Thus the sage Gautama cursed his wife Ahalya for sleeping with Indra though through no fault of her own (In the Kautilyan period) if a woman was found guilty of a carnal crime her generative organs were cut off and she was ultimately sentenced to death [Arth.IV.13 in Jain p.164], although it is not clear whether this was only for intercourse with slaves. Not only that, but adultery is defined as the simple touching of clothes and even conversing with men:

- VIII. 356. He who addresses the wife of another man at a Tirtha, outside the village, in a forest, or at the confluence of rivers, suffer (the punishment for) adulterous acts (samgrahana).
- VIII. 357. Offering presents (to a woman), romping (with her), touching her ornaments and dress, sitting with her

on a bed, all (these acts) are considered adulterous acts (samgrahana).

- VIII. 358. If one touches a woman in a place (which ought) not (to be touched) or allows (oneself to be touched in such a spot), all (such acts done) with mutual consent are declared (to be) adulterous (samgrahana). [*Manu* VIII.356-358]

RESTRICTIONS ON WOMEN

NO PROPERTY

Women and Sudras can, in the Aryan-Vaishnava system, have no property: A wife, a son, and a slave, these three are declared to have no property; the wealth which they earn is (acquired) for him to whom they belong. A Brahmana may confidently seize the goods of (his) Sudra (slave); for, as that (slave) can have no property, his master may take his possessions. [*Manu* VIII.416-417]

DRESS AND VEILING

Aryan women had to wear a face-veil when going out. As usual, several observers, seeing Arab women veiled, assumed it must be due to Muslim "contamination."They are not aware that Muslim ladies who do this do it as an act of modesty, and are ignorant of Indian scriptures. Sanskrit literature mentions the:

The practice of using veils by women, particularly in well-to-do families, was in vogue. Prabhakaravardhana's daughter Rajyasri put on a veil when she met her husband, the Maukhari Grahavarman of Kanauj, for the first time. It is known from Vacaspati Misra (9C AD) that women in good families observed the purdah system and did not appear in public without veils... However, Dhoyi, the author of the 12 C poetical work the Pavanaduta, relates that the women of Vijayapura (in Bengal) did not observe the purdah system':

- "Harsha's [1099-1101] [Lohara dynasty] coins [depict] a half cross-legged goddess [and] a veil appears on the head"
- "Gangayadeva's [one of the Kalachuri rulers of Dahala,

the country around Jabalpur in MP] (1019-1042AD) coins... the female is shown as having a veil on her head which hangs down to the shoulders and upper arms"

- "Many of the female figures on the gold coins, like the sculpture and literature of the [Gupta] age, do reflect a somewhat new idea of feminine beauty which we now call classical [thinner and more slender]"

It is now generally accepted that the *purdah* (seclusion and veiling) was existent in India since ancient Aryan times. In fact, certain high-class women refused to entertain strangers. It seems that the bodice was imported by Muslims:

"In several parts of India... bodices [are worn by ladies under the cloth]... this, i am told, is a modern innovation, and borrowed from the Mohamedans."

The Vedas prescribe that a dowry be given by the bride's family to the groom. The Rig Veda states that cows and gifts given by the father of the bride to the daughter accompanied the bride's procession [Rg Ved X.85]. Kakshivat says he became rich by the father-in-law giving him 10 chariots and maids and 1060 cows during the marriage ceremony [Rg Ved I.126] [Apte 13]. The ancient custom is the *kanyadan,* where the father presented his daughter with jewelry and clothes at the time of her marriage and vardakshina, where the father presented the groom with kith and kind are in essence the dowry system.

It may be thought that only the absence of the husband could temporarily alleviate the condition of Aryan women. Alas, even then she was under constant suspicion. To prevent nightly intrigues, she cannot even sleep alone:

"Whilst her husband is absent, she shall sleep with one of her female relatives and not alone"[Vasishta's Padma Purana]

"Husbands are not supposed to have intercourse with a wife who bore only daughters."[*Hindu Law and Custom,* p.145]

GOING OUT AND EDUCATION

Women and Sudras were declared to be unfit for study of their own sacred texts:

"And as women, Sudras and the inferior members of the twice-borne classes were unfitted for hearing the Veda, and were infatuated in desiring the blessings, arising from the ceremonies, the muni, with a vision to their felicity, in his kindness composed the narrative called the Mahabharata."[*Bhag.Pur*. I.4.25]

Also Madhava Acharya stated:

"They [women and Sudras] are debarred... from being competent students of the Veda"[Vedarthaprakasha of Madhava Acharyya on the Taittriya Yajur Veda, quoted in Muir III, p.66]

NO DIVORCE

- Divorce was not permitted.
- No Remarriage

Even if the wife ran away from the harsh husband, she could never get remarried as long as she is in the confines of Hindu tradition.

WIDOWS AND ELDERLY WOMEN

The Aryans, upon their invasion of India 1500 B.C. introduced the horrific custom of *Sati,* i.e. the burning of a woman after the death of her husband. When performed singly it is referred to as *Sati,* when performed en masse by all the women and daughters of a town in anticipation of their widowhood (eg. when the men were to fight a battle against all odds), it is known as Jauhar. It is sanctioned by their most sacred texts, and was practiced from the fall of the Semito-Dravidian Indus Valley civilization to the modern age.

SCRIPTURAL SANCTION

The most sacred of Aryan scriptures are the *Vedas,* and the *Rig Veda,* the oldest Veda, first mentions the custom of *Sati.* The following famous "*Sati* Hymn"of the Rig Veda was (and still is) recited during the actual immolation of the widow [Kane 199-200]:

"Let these women, whose husbands are worthy and are living, enter the house with ghee (applied) as corrylium (to their eyes). Let these wives first step into the pyre, tearless without any affliction and well adorned."[Rig Veda X.18.7]

In recent times some Aryan apologists have arisen who try to prove that this verse does not sanction *sati*. This concept arises from a mistaken reading of the word *agne* or *agneh*, which they believe is *agre*.

This is a wrong interpretation, and other evidence exists that the Aryans definitely practiced *Sati* from the earliest times. They distorted this verse which directs the widow to enter the pyre (*agneh*) so as to mean that the wife was to rise from her pyre and go to the front (*agre*). In addition to these examples, ancient Aryan scripture encourages *Sati*. The Garudapurana favorably mentions the immolation of a widow on the funeral pyre, and states that women of all castes, even the Candalla woman, must perform *Sati*.

The only exceptions allowed by this benevolent author are for pregnant women or those who have young children. If women do not perform *Sati*, then they will be reborn into the lowly body of a woman again and again till they perform *Sati*. [Garudapurana II.4.91-100] [Kane 237] According to Vasishta's Padma-Purana, a woman must, on the death of her husband, allow herself to be burnt alive on the same funeral pyre. The *Vishnusmirti* gives two choices for the widow:

"If a woman's husband dies, let her lead a life of chastity, or else mount his pyre"[*Vishnusmrti* xxv.14] [Clayton 13]

Brahma is one of the main Aryan gods, being the creator of the world (later he was identified as an incarnation of Vishnu). One of the Puranas is named after him, the Brahma Purana. Like other Puranas, it was composed after the Vedas (Pandits hold 4000 B.C., Indologists 700 B.C.) This scripture also sanctions *sati*:

"It is the highest duty of the woman to immolate herself after her husband,"[Br.P. 80.75]

Once again we hear that *Sati* is sanctioned by the Vedas:

"..is enjoined by the Vedas,"[Br.P. 80.75]

And is "greatly reputed in all the worlds"[Br.P. 80.75]

Long life is promised to the *sati*:

"She [the sati] lives with her husband in heaven for as many years as there are pores in the human body, i.e. for 35 million years."[Br.P. 80.76, 80.77]

Vishnu Dharmasutra XXV.14 contains the statement:

On her husband's death, the widow should observe celibacy or should ascend the funeral pyre after him.

Several other scriptures sanction widow-burning. Some of these are as given below [Wilkins]:

- "It is proper for a woman, after her husband's death to burn her in the fire with his copse; every woman who thus burns herself shall remain in paradise with her husband 35,000,000 years by destiny."
- "The wife who commits herself to flames with her husband's copse shall equal Arundathi and reside in Swarga (heaven)."
- "Accompanying her husband, she shall reside so long in Swarga as the 35,000,000 of hairs on the human body.
- "As the snake-catcher forcibly drags the serpent from his earth, so bearing her husband [from hell] with him she enjoys heavenly bliss."
- "Dying with her husband, she sanctifies her maternal and paternal ancestors and the ancestors of him to whom she gave her virginity."
- "Such a wife adorning her husband, in celestial felicity with him, greatest and most admired, shall enjoy the delights of heaven while fourteen Indras reign."
- "Though a husband had killed a Brahman, broken the ties of gratitude, or murdered a friend she expiates the crime."

Thus, it is evident that the custom of *Sati* was introduced by the Aryans since it is encouraged in their scriptures and many goddesses performed the act.

ARYAN SATI GODDESSES

The Aryan origin of *Sati* is evident from the fact that several Aryan ladies and 'goddesses' performed *Sati*:

- Several of Krishna's wives performed *Sati* upon his death, including Rukmini, Rohini, Devaki, Bhadra and Madura [M.Bh. Mausalaparvan 7.18]
- Madri, second wife of Pandu, considered an incarnation of the goddess Dhriti, performed *Sati* [M.Bh. Adiparvan 95.65]
- Rohini, a wife of Vasudev, Krishna's father, who gave birth to Balram (Devki's child) and later became a *Sati*.

"The 8 queens of Krishna, who have been named, with Rukmini at their head, embraced the body of Hari, and entered the funeral fire. Revati also embracing the corpse of Rama entered the blazing pile, which was cool to her, happy in contact with her lord. Hearing these events, Ugrasena and Anakadundubhi, with Devaki and Rohini, committed themselves to the flames."[Vishnu Pur. 5.38] [*Vishnu Pur.* {Wilson} p.481]

ANCIENT TRAVALLERS' ACCOUNTS

Even ancient observers mentioned the barbaric practice of *Sati*. Alexander the Great and the Greeks observed *Sati* in Punjab. The Greek Diodorus Siculus, who lived in the 1st century BC, mentioned the practice of *Sati* in his account of the Punjab in the 4th century BC. Indigenous historical evidence substantiates this, for

"The earliest recorded historical instance of Sati is that of the wife of the Hindu general Keteus, who died in 316 B.C. while fighting against Antigonos. Both his wives were eager to perform *sati*, but as the elder one was with child, only the younger one alone was allowed to carry out her wish."

The *Sati* was customary for the widows of Kshatriyas in the end of the first century BC. *Sati* was performed by all the Aryan races, for it is recorded that the Germanic tribes used to immolate the widows of chieftain to accompany the husband to Valhalla. The Arab writer Al-Beruni mentioned the practice of *Sati* among the Hindus. [AlBer. U II.LXIX; II.LXXIII]

"She [the widow] has only to choose between two things - either to remain a widow as long as ashe lives, or to burn herself, and the latter eventuality is considered preferable... As regards the wives of kings, they are in the habit of burning them whether they wish it or not."[Al-Beruni. II.LXIX]

"Nicolo deo Contei states that as many as 3000 of the wives and concubines of the kings of Vijayanagar were pledged to be burnt with their lord on his death [and often ministers and palace servants accompanied the king in death]."[Basham 188] Strangely the practice increased in popularity in Bengal during the British expansion, despite the best efforts of Ram Mohan Roy to stop it. This is also confirmed by the Abbe DuBois:

"[Sati] is more in vogue on the banks of the Ganges; [while] in Bengal Presidency [only] 706 suttees occurred in 1817 [and in] the Madras Presidency [out of] 30 million inhabitants not 30 allow themselves to be burnt each year."[DuBois 357] "[The wife] must, on the death of her husband, allow herself to be burnt alive on the same funeral pyre [of her husband]."

Sati still continues to this day. In 1990, more than 50 widows were burnt alive in *sati*. [Sonali Verma, Reuter, 12 August 1997, New Delhi] Note: The data gathered for the report of 50 widows burned to death was not gathered on a collective basis, but as data for micro-sections of India.

BIZARRE HYPOTHESES

Several bizarre hypotheses have been set forth to explain the occurrence of *Sati*, often with less than honest intentions. Another silly notion is that the custom of *Sati* started when Hindu society started to "degenerate."[Now, THAT was an oxymoron!] If so, then why do the Vedas take this custom for granted? Why did Krishna's wives perform *sati*? Are we to then conclude that Krishna, an incarnation of Vishnu himself, was a corrupt Hindu? Again, where did this corruption come from? When did it start? If some outsiders, then it must be one of the Greeks, Bactrians, etc. But they came 1000 years after

Krishna! Krishna was one of the earliest Aryan figures, and this story could hence have not been an invention, since the Aryans were very scared of altering anything in their tradition. Hence the Aryans stand condemned for introducing *sati*.

Islamic Khalifat and *Sati*: One far-fetched idea ascribes the origin of *Sati* as being due to the molestation of Hindu women by Muslim men. Needless to say, this would imply the existence of Muslims to molest Krishna's wives, Madri and the galaxy of Vedic Aryan women who performed self-immolation. It also overlooks the accounts by ancient Greeks and Arabs on the prevalence of *Sati*. In fact, the Muslim emperors took active steps to abolish *Sati*. (E.g. Ghiyasudin, Akbar, Muhammad Tughlaq) and the Sufi saints condemned it.

RELIGION

The ascetic emphasis in Aryan Indian religious life led to an extremely negative attitude towards women.

ARYAN VAISHNAVIASM

Vedic Vaishanvism

Women in the Vedic period were harshly treated, as depicted above. The presence of *Sati* was common.

BUDDHISM AND JAINISM

Buddhism and Jainism were both protest movements against the Vedic Vaishnava system. However, they did not lead to any major changes in the status of women. This was due to the emphasis placed by these religions on asceticism. Thus, although *Sati* was opposed by these reformers, yet women were considered as hurdles on the path to liberation. The Buddha was very strict in his insistence on asceticism. He left his home and wife to become attain *nirvana* and considered women a hindrance to that goal:

"Buddha is said to have induced his disciples not to look at a woman or even talk to her"[*Sacred Books of the East*, XI p.91 cited in N.N.Bhatt p.44]

VAISHNAVISM

Women are generally termed as thieves, dacoits, pirates, thirsty tigresses and hypocrite cats in the medieval Nath literature. [Obsc 245] Chaitanya was one of the major saints during the medieval period. He spread Vaishnavism in Eastern India, but aroused the approbation of the Orthodox Aryan-Vaishnavas because he allowed "conversion"from lower castes. Even this "liberal"man had highly negative opinions of women:

"Chaitanya thought it to be a sin to talk, think or even dream of women and that even the sight of a wooden statue of a woman can distract the mind and be responsible for immorality. He advised people to avoid being alone even with their own mother, sister or daughter."[Nand 124-127]

After all, Chaitanya was a Vaihnavite. Gandhi's insistence on strict vegetarianism and celibacy among his disciples was in keeping with the traditions of Vaishnava ascetic ethics [EB 20:528:2a] Gandhi ordered many of the erotic temple sculptures of India to be destroyed. "[A Vedic Graduate] should not look at a naked woman."[Manu 8:453] "Let a decent man ever avoid by night... a loose woman"[V.P. Book III Ch. XII p. 250] "In the Buddhist Age, a slave-girl who was obliged to sleep with her master, was often deprived of her nose and ears by her mistress and there was no law to protect her."[Jain 162]

DRAVIDIAN SHAIVISM

Dravidian women enjoyed much greater freedom than their Aryan counterparts.

REPRESSION AND PERVERSIONS: INCEST

Due to the strict restrictions and regulations one feature arose that is apparently more common in Aryan society than in any other part of the world: incest. References to this practice abound. Often the girls were unwilling, but were then forceed by their brothers/fathers. References abound even in the *Rig Veda*, showing that the perversion of brother-sister incest was introduced by the Aryans (Astaghfirullah al-Azeem):

- Pushan is the lover of his sister [Rg Ved VI.55.4]
- Agni is the lover of his own sister [Rg Ved X.3.3]
- Ashvins are referred to as the sons of Savitar and Ushas who are brother and sister.
- The Ashvisns married Surya and Savitri who is their sister [RV I.116.19].
- Agni is the son of his father and his sister [Rg Ved.I.91.7]
- Yama wards off his sister Yami, saying marriage between brother and sister is forbidden [R.V.X.10]

Father-daughter incest occurs in the famous story of Prajapati (later identified with Brahma, in turn incorporated as an incarnation of Vishnu) and his daughter [RV III.31.1-2]. Moreover, this was punished. Prajapati is thought to have done something wrong, and Prajapati was pierced by Agni as a punishment [Sat.Br. XIII.9] [Apte 63]. It is evident that the strict laws on male-female relations led to the repression of normal practices and the rise of various perversions like brother-sister incest, father-daughter incest etc. Even to this day incest of varying degrees (father-daughter, mother-son, brother-sister, etc.) is extremely common amongst the Indo-Aryans. No other race on earth has ever recorded such a prevalence of this practice. Just as sodomy had its home in Persia, Lesbianism in ancient Lesbos, so incest has its home amongst the Indo-Aryans.

There were exceptions to the rule, even during the Vedic Dark Ages following the collapse of the Indus civilization. Eastern India (Purvadesha), including Bengal, with its majority Mon-Khmer population, was only slightly Aryanized. The Shakti cult (mother-goddess) predominated (75 % of all the idolatrous population is stil Shaktis), and women here had a much higher degree of freedom. Thus for instance they were not required to wear the veil. Shakti (or Tantric) cults involved the worship of women, and the acceptance of their supremacy. Needless to say, the Shakti cult was only limited to Bengal and Assam. The Dravidian women were also freeer. Malabar was a center of the Tantric form of the Shiva-Shakti cult, and matriarchal customs still prevail. Till recently, polyandry existed.

Besides these two islands, the rest of India confirmed to the picture given above. This lasted until the establishment of the Islamic Khalifat of Hindustan in the 12th century A.D. Muslims came to form more than 50 % of the population of Hindustan proper (India north of the Narmada), and under Islam, the status of women improved considerably. In modern times the degradation of women's status is related to the rise in Hindu Fundamentalism (in actual fact, a thinly disguised form of Aryan Fanaticism). The extremist organizations that comprise the Sangh Parivar (BJP, RSS, Bajrang Dal, Ranvir Sena, VHP etc.) are reviving the practice of *Sati*, dowry, female infanticide etc. in various parts of India. Thus, in modern times the status of women has declined sharply due to the activities of Hindu (i.e., Aryan) Fundamentalist organizations.

A wife, a son, a slave, these are declared to have no property; the wealth which they earn is (acquired) for him to whom they belong. Manu 8.416 Manu 8.299 [A wife, a son, a slave, a pupil and a (younger) brother of the full blood, who have committed faults, may be beaten with a rope or a split bambboo. 9.77? When he created them) Manu allotted to women (a love of their) bed, (of their (seat and (of) ornament, impure desires, wrath, dishonesty, malice and bad conduct.

According to Hinduism "a woman is a form of energy (shaktiswarupini) or an aspect of Shakti. She is mata, the Mother Goddess, or Devi the auspicious one. As a young child she is kanya, the goddess Durga. As a wife she is patni and saha dharma charini, a partner in her husband's religious duties. As a mother she is worthy of worship (matrudevobhava). As a child she is supposed to remain in the custody and care of her parents. Once married, she becomes a property and responsibility of her husband, who is supposed to take care of her needs and expectations and keep her in his custody. As his wife, she performs four roles:

- as his servant (dasi) in duty,
- as his minister (mantri) in decision making,
- as a mother (mata) to his children and
- as a lover (rambha) in his bed.

And when she becomes old, she lives in the house of her son or sons and has to lead a very solitary and forlorn life. In ancient times, when a Hindu died, his wife either committed *sati* on his funeral pyre or retired into a life of social damnation, religious contemplation and perennial solitude. Now the situation has changed. *Sati* is illegal and an anathema. A widow can now keep herself busy in many ways, and if she gets an opportunity, like Mrs. Gandhi, she can join politics and dream of becoming the Prime Minister of India!

Historically speaking, whether it was in ancient India or medieval India, the status of women in the subcontinent was never good. A present day woman would feel outraged, and rightly so, if she goes through the contents of the Manusmriti, which is particularly harsh against women and treats them with disdain and suspicion. But we have no evidence to believe that the contents of the book were followed by all sections of the society. Probably the Brahmin women were its worst victims and suffered more compared to women of other castes.

The situation is gradually changing. In a changing world, Hindu society is trying to redefine the role of women in the institution of family and society. Politically Hindu women today enjoy an equal status with men and wider opportunities then their counterparts in many western countries. There is a talk to provide them with new privileges and rights including inheritance rights. But a lot still needs to be done on the social and economic front, because women in Hindu society still suffer from gender bias and a number of other problems such as dowry, inheritance, domestic abuse, sexual exploitation, rape and harassment.

In Hinduism, women are considered a form of energy and are given due importance at every stage of life - as a daughter, as a daughter-in-law and as a mother. Out of these roles some come out as women gurus. During the Vedic times we had seers and philosophers like Ghosha, Apala, Lopamudra, Vishwvara, Surya, Indrani, Yami and Romasha (all women). In a theosophical debate between Shankaracharya and Mandana Mishra (Sanskrit scholars of ancient times), the latter's wife was appointed to be the judge – obviously because of her superior knowledge and spiritual attainments.

In modern times we also have a number of female gurus with large followings. Some of the TV channels like 'Astha and Samskara' in India continue showing the gatherings and preaching of women gurus. Ma Anandmayee, Amma, and Mata Nirmala Devi are famous female gurus. I have attended one of Mata Nirmala Devi's big congregations in New Delhi. Let me tell you about her and her work and how she is helping to change the face of women in the spiritual evolution. Shri Mataji Nirmala Devi was born on March 21, 1923 in Chindawara, India. Her parents called her Nirmala, which means 'Immaculate'. She is married with children and is currently living in Italy. She travels extensively in India and abroad.

Shri Mataji began experimenting with awakening the spiritual power of every human being (which the Hindus call the Kundalini) and was surprised at the results. She experimented first on people near her and noticed they were transformed physically, mentally and spiritually. Slowly she found out that this process had the potential solution for all human problems and decided to make her work more widespread. Since 1970, Shri Mataji Nirmala Devi has been traveling around the world teaching the techniques she developed of Sahaja Yoga meditation (Sahaja is Spontaneous and Yoga is Union with the Self). Large numbers of people acknowledge the value of her teachings and Sahaja Yoga centers are now in more than 75 nations. The yoga and meditation allows people to tap into their inner spiritual power and achieve balance in their physical, emotional, mental and spiritual lives.

Some members of the Hindu faith have accepted Shri Mataji Nirmala Devi's guru status today. Nirmala Devi has dedicated her life to helping with the spiritual ascent of mankind and in doing so has "reclaimed the role of women in the spiritual evolution." Over the past few decades' feminist ideas have to a great extent succeeded in bringing to the fore women's issues in the Western world. It is now proposed that these ideas are to be extended to other areas of the world. Western feminism now seeks to speak for the women who hail from the non-western cultural and religious world as well. What western feminism fails to identify is of course that the status and role of women in Hindu religious culture and civilization has been very different from that of the Western world -where Semitic ideas have played a great role.

Western Feminism also claims that it is relevant to the needs and issues that are important to Hindu women in general. This claim to universality will have to be considered very carefully, so as to ascertain whether the claim is reasonable or merely culturally chauvinistic. The academic fields of Religious Studies, Asian Studies, and Social Studies have a large number of women when it comes to specializing in Hinduism studies, many of them often tend to be devout Christians, strong ideological feminists and occasionally women of Indian origin who tend to hold strident anti-Hindu views. This pronounced asymmetry in numerical strength between those who speak for western religions/ideologies and those who hold Hindu values and culture shows up in the form of Hindu-bashing at human rights seminars, feminist events, religious and social studies conferences.

In American academia, Hinduism has been projected as being responsible for abuse of women. Social ills attributed to Hinduism include *sati,* female infanticide, dowry deaths, and supposed inferiority of Hindu women, caste, and so forth. While these are valid research topics, they do not present the whole picture. Hindu women's issues are stereotyped and politicized. They are often taken out of context and are rarely compared to women's conditions in poor Christian countries or Western nations. Environmental problems in contemporary India are seen as rooted in India's traditions, rather than as an acute phenomenon that has particularly come into prominence over the past 150 years only.

The focus is on caste, cows and curry. Indian philosophical and religious traditions, political institutions, vast cultural influence, maritime reach, civil engineering, scientific and rational thinking is ignored. The motive is to justify the case that globalization equals Westernization - the indigenous cultures are positioned as chronically and systemically flawed. What is rarely presented is that most social ills are either caused by or at least exacerbated by poverty. No historical background of invasions and colonization is presented. While serious scholars act responsibly, in many instances Hinduism is depicted as merely meaningless superstitious rituals. Kali is used to depict scary images and deployed to indicate a negative and violent religion. Simplistic logic is used - Shiva is evil because he is the destroyer and because destruction is evil. Animal symbolism is interpreted to indicate animal worship, or animism.

In contrast to the serious scholars are others who subvert Hinduism by depicting it as an unscientific tradition lacking rational tendencies, compared to superior western intellectual traditions and ideologies. To dismiss Hinduism, it is sometimes portrayed as 'world negating' and socially backward, compared to the 'rational' West. It is said to exploit the underclass. Karma theory is interpreted as fatalism and as accepting one's plight rather than taking responsibility. Hindu society is depicted as having been intrinsically poor throughout its history, without factoring in the massive destruction its academic institutions, multiple invasions and the decimation of its infrastructure by colonialists. All of India's ills are too often placed on Hinduism. By using such one sided and prejudiced views, Hindu tradition and culture is seen in a distorted manner by young students.

This distorted projection of Hinduism has far reaching consequences. Hindu women scholars are under subtle pressure to distance themselves from their own culture and values. The U.S. State Department during the Cold War created and funded many 'Area Studies' to contain the Soviet threat. One of these areas has been the `South Asian' area. This 'South Asian' terminology is now used as a pretext to submerge and drown the concerns and issues that face Hindu women. Hindu women have their own issues and priorities that are different from those of other women in South Asia who belong to non Indic religions.

However, since being 'Hindu' is projected as being backward and retrograde, many women are forced into the rubric of a 'South Asian' identity and have to give up their Hindu values and culture to be accepted. Raised Hindu and Indian at home, many Hindu women have become 'South Asians' on entering college - an identity concocted in the past 25 years! Also, the recent politics in India has served as a welcome pretext for academicians to bash Hindus. Any person who calls herself or himself a Hindu and who questions any theory or misrepresentation of India or Hinduism by Western scholars is to be labeled as a fanatic and dismissed. The result has been that there is no dialogue or interaction. Hindu women in particular have to hide their Hindu identity and accept western ideologies in order to be accepted.

Hindu women have traditionally been the parent who passes down traditions, values, culture, and spirituality to children. Unlike many other religions, Hinduism has had a large number of women who have been major religious leaders, and many Hindu women have risen to prominence in all walks of life - facts conveniently skipped by many modern textbooks. With this neglect from its own scholars, Western Academics have found it very convenient to project their own view of Hinduism and Hindu women. Because of all the reasons cited above, there is a need to establish a forum where Hindu women can find a voice of their own - a forum where Hindu women can interact, discuss issues important to them and project their own unique perspectives, rather than accept ideologies that have been forced upon them.

Many Latin and African women have already launched their own women's movements that challenge this Western feminist hegemonic campaign to mold all women of the world as per some set Western ideology. Some Hindu intellectuals' voices have also emerged individually in recent times. Professor Usha Menon of Drexel University, in the Fall 2000 issue of Daedalus magazine, has an excellent paper on how Western feminism's attempt to portray Hindu women does not speak for most Hindu women - an article that has caused flack from Western feminists. It explains the history of how the colonialists manipulated the Manusmriti text into a tool for governance, including the downgrading of Hindu women. Many other Hindu women have broken away from this power structure and are also demanding self-representation.

The Infinity Foundation proposes a Hindu Women's Think-Tank. This would be non-political, free to borrow ideas from the left and the right, and also free to criticize both. While politicians will come and go, Hinduism is too vast to be contained inside any political ideology. Many well-intended thinkers in the past have hoped to use politics as a distribution channel to spread their ideas, but in the long run this approach is a sellout to the politicians instead. (As an example from another religion, many historians of Christianity feel that while Christians felt glad that they had converted the Roman Emperor Constantine in the 4th century, in fact, it was Rome in the long run that ended up appropriating Christianity and remolding it into a tool for control.) Furthermore, why should free thinking women be held responsible to explain every (mis)deed of one or another political group, and why should irrelevant issues to be used by their opponents as distractions from the main items they wish to focus on in a given situation? In other words, why carry someone else's baggage around?

By no means would this proposed think-tank fight or oppose any political side. It would be an independent voice - in the same manner as Ralph Nader was before he unfortunately entered politics.

Among its activities would be the following:

- It would participate in at least 5 academic panels each year. These would include conferences ranging from religious studies, women's issues, human rights, South Asian studies, anthropology and other relevant fields. The objective would be to provide a Hindu voice as opposed to letting the portrayal be defined and dominated by others, many with their own ideological agendas.
- It would provide mentoring to young women scholars so that they can maintain their self-esteem and do not have to give up their values while seeking legitimacy,

emotional/intellectual support, or advancement in their careers.

- It would encourage high quality research and publish the results. This would include awards and grants to promote authentic portrayals from within the traditions.
- It would also challenge stereotypes and review writings and books.

The Infinity Foundation would evaluate proposals to provide the initial funding and guidance for this. Basing it in India with affiliates elsewhere would make it cost effective, would allow harnessing the huge talent there, would bring greater authenticity as compared to Western-based scholarship, and most of all it would strengthen the Hindu culture at its own roots. It is hoped that such a project would become a worldwide one with centers everywhere.

The intricate dynamics of power and gender has grown to become an increasingly important topic within the realm of present day academia - and justifiably so. Though representing half of the human race, women's voices, needs and inner psyches have, traditionally, been relegated to a place of unimportance in the history of the Western world. Throughout the history of European civilization, the nature of the feminine was misunderstood, neglected and, in some cases, practically demonized. Consequently, for millennia women have been deprived of the power - political, economic, spiritual, and even sexual - which men so take for granted.

Recognizing the imperative need to correct this historic imbalance, many modern Feminist leaders attempted to devise an ideological framework through which they felt that the roots of this imbalance could be properly understood. Additionally, there have been many attempts to wrest control over the primary mechanisms of power, specifically in the political and economic sectors. As a result, what were at one time conceived as the exclusive domains of the male gender has now begun to open up to women. In the modern West, power is no longer equated with the testosterone laden half of the human race. The question, however, is should this have ever been the view of Western civilization?

For while it may have been the tradition in the West to naturally equate power with the masculine, this is not at all a universally held outlook. One world-view which offers us a fresh and radically different approach to the issue of power and the feminine is found in the philosophy and culture of Hinduism - and specifically in the concept of Shakti. Within the metaphysical framework of Shakti, we discover the concept of the feminine as being the very manifestation of power itself.

In this chapter one can accomplish three tasks:

- An examination of the concept of Shakti as found throughout the history and various schools of thought of Hinduism;
- I will explore the historical implications that this concept has contributed in forming the traditional Hindu view of the nature of the feminine and the subsequent role of women; and finally
- I will share some thoughts on the role that the concept of Shakti can potentially play in helping to bring about a reemergence of the much neglected and crucially needed feminine in our own Western culture.

The Sanskrit word Shakti can be translated as meaning "power" or "energy." It is derived from the parasmaipada verb root "shak," which means "to be able," "to do," "to act." This power is witnessed in all the various phenomena of life. It is the force responsible for the growth of vegetation, animals and human beings. It is what is responsible for the movement of all things. The planets revolve around the sun as a result of Shakti. It is Shakti that makes the winds blow and the oceans churn. Shakti is manifest as the very affective ability of all the forces of nature. She is the heat of fire, the brilliance of the sun, the very life force of all living beings. In human beings, she is seen as the power of intelligence (*buddhi*), compassion (*daya*) and divine love (*bhakti*), among her many other functions.

It is the power of Shakti that "...keeps the gods in their position, makes a man virile or makes a sage of a man".

Without the presence of Shakti, all creation would be rendered impotent. Most significantly, Shakti is an exclusively feminine principle. Shakti is synonymous with the great Devi, or the Great Goddess of Hinduism. As such, she is omnipresent in Hindu society via her many forms. She is propitiated by all segments of Hindu society, especially by women. According to Klaus Klostermaier, "...childless women implore her to conceive. In times of epidemics, it is the goddess who is implored to grant health and relief". Shakti has always been a living force throughout the long history of Hinduism.

The importance of goddesses is evident throughout the various sects and schools of thought of Hinduism. Additionally, the presence of goddesses is seen throughout the long literary tradition of India. In the Rig Veda, for example, at least 40 goddesses are mentioned. These include: Sarasvati, goddess of wisdom; Ushas, the dawn; and Aditi, who is depicted as "birthless". The very word "Shakti" itself appears in the Rig Veda some 12 times. Two of the word's derivatives, "shaktivat" and "shakman," respectively appear twice and five times. Part of the Rig Veda is known as the "Devi Sukta" and is certainly recognition of Shakti as a cosmic principle. Shakti is also seen in the later Itihasas, or Epics of India. She is found in the Ramayana, where "...she is called Devi, and is respected by all".

In the *Mahabharata* there are two hymns dedicated to her. The various manifestations of the goddess are ubiquitous throughout the Puranas. Indeed, the Devi Bhagavata Purana is entirely dedicated to her. One would be hard pressed to find a work anywhere in the entirety of Hindu literature in which there is not at least some mention of a feminine power. Hinduism's respect for Shakti is not limited to the religion's literary heritage. The various schools of Indian philosophy (shad-darshanas) also took this principle quite seriously. The Mimamsakas, for example, held that Shakti was no less than the inherent power of all things. The Naiyayika logicians attempted to explain Shakti in terms of being the function or property of any cause. For the Vedanta school, Shakti was

"...conceived as the activity of a cause revealing itself in the shape of an effect". Of all the various schools of Indian philosophy, however, the school most influential in helping to formulate a theory of Shakti was the Samkhya School.

Samkhya teaches the dualistic doctrine of *Prakriti / Purusha.* According to this theory there are two radically distinct principles at play during the creation of the cosmos: matter (*Prakriti*) and spirit (*Purusha*). Prakriti is the primordial matter which is present before the cosmos becomes manifest. It is as a direct result of the devolution of this original material substance that the universe, with all its diversity of names and forms comes into being. Prakriti is seen as being "...the power of nature, both animate and inanimate. As such, nature is seen as dynamic energy". Prakriti is originally passive, immobile and pure potentiality by nature. It is only as a direct result of her contact with the kinetic Purusha that she unfolds into the variagatedness we see before us. Sudhir Gupta explains this process of devolution from the perspective of a Shakta, or a worshiper of Devi, the Great Goddess:

> The universe with all its diversity and multiplicity remains equated in the divine volition as conception before manifestation. It is manifested in the course of basic evolution, started under the influence of the creative volition of the Divine Mother. The Universal Mother in Her Absolute Self admits of no mutability, change or division.

Thus, Shakti is seen as being antecedent to Prakriti, with Shakti being the instrumental cause, in the form of the Devi, or the Great Goddess, and Prakriti serving as the material cause. The idea of Prakriti / Purusha is seen mirrored in another closely allied concept: that of the Divine Consort. According to Hindu teachings, Shakti, energy, cannot exist in a vacuum. If there is energy, it must be someone's energy. Almost every god (deva) of the Hindu pantheon has a feminine companion, a consort, a goddess. This is an idea which is an indispensable element of every major sect of Hinduism. Vishnu, for example, has the goddess Shri (Lakshmi) as his eternal companion. Shiva is accompanied by Parvati, Brahma by Sarasvati, and Krishna by Radha. These goddess-consorts are said to personify nothing less than the essential energy of the god. In the words of Ernest Payne:

> The energy of Vishnu and Shiva was personified as a goddess and identified with Prakriti, the primary source of the universe. The connubial relations between Devi and her husband were held to typify the mystical union of the eternal principles, matter and spirit, which produces the world.

So integral is the relationship between a particular god and his Shakti that one is thought incapable of existing without the other. It is said that in her manifestation as Shiva's consort and source of energy, Shakti is embodied in the "i" of his name. According to the grammatical rules of classical Sanskrit, if a consonant is not followed by a vowel, it is automatically assumed that this consonant is followed by the vowel "a." Consequently, without this "i" in his name, Shiva becomes shava, or a lifeless corpse. Thus it is the feminine principle which is the animating force of life itself. Both the feminine and the masculine are necessarily present in the Divine. This is dramatically illustrated in South Asia in the image of Ardhanarishvara, the representation of God as being half man and half woman. Veneration of God necessarily entails veneration of the Goddess. They are two aspects of the same being and are, as such, mutually dependent upon one another.

The intimacy of god and goddess can be more clearly illustrated by examining one of the stories involving the creation of Devi which is found Devi Bhagavata Purana. Interestingly, although clearly a Shakta Purana, the Devi Bhagavata Purana describes Vishnu / Krishna as being the supreme God who "...is said to be the root and creator of all". According to this account, Krishna was at one time the only being in existence. Desiring to create the universe, He divided Himself into two parts, the left being female and the right male. That female was none other than Radha, the eternal consort and Shakti of Krishna, who is described as being the Mula Prakriti, or the root source of all existence. From the conjugal sport of Radha and Krishna a golden egg was born that was the repository of the material from which our universe was created.

Creation, then, is depicted in the Devi Bhagavata Purana as proceeding from Krishna, through Radha. The feminine, Shakti, is shown to be crucial and indispensable in the process of creation. This fact very clearly demonstrates the mutual dependence in which god and goddess hold one another. The relationship that is enjoyed between the gods and goddesses in Hinduism is one of the wielders of power (shaktiman, the masculine principle) and the power itself (Shakti, the feminine). Each is meaningless without the existence of the other. While the possessor of power is the guiding force as to the power's direction and purpose, it is the power itself which provides the ability to perform any task. To use a crude example, we might say that the deva is the computer while the Devi is the electricity that makes the computer's functioning possible. Shaktiman is the principle that gives guidance and direction to power. Shakti is the vital life-giving force of the god, as well as the personification of his particular power. As Shrivatsa Goswami explains this concept:

On the transcendental plane this functional duality implies the split of the Absolute into power or potency (Shakti), the subjective component, and the possessor of power (shaktiman), the objective one. On the phenomenal plane too there exists such a duality. (Goswami, 1985)

Together, the deva and Devi, the god and goddess of Hinduism, are the able and the ability, respectively. Moreover, this concept is not relegated solely to the realm of the Divine. What is true on the macrocosmic level is also the rule on the microcosmic. Human beings too are said to also participate in the interplay of Shakti and shaktiman. For in Hinduism, every woman is said to be a manifestation of the divine Shakti. The power of Shakti, the feminine principle, is believed to be directly present in creation in the form of our mothers, sisters, daughters and wives. As the contemporary feminist author Elinor Gadon explains, "The truth of the Goddess is the mystery of our being. She is the dynamic life force within. Her form is embedded in our collective psyche..." While she is primarily present as personified in woman, however, Shakti is also present in man.

There are several traditions of spiritual unfoldment in India that teach the notion that Shakti resides within each and every human being, and that liberation can be achieved by the proper utilization of the feminine principle within. One example of such a tradition is the path of Kundalini-yoga. According to Kundalini-yoga philosophy, Shakti resides at the base of the spine in the form of the kundalini energy. The goal of this path is to raise this energy through the various energy centers (chakras) of the subtle, or astral, body. As each energy portal is open, the yogi achieves newer and higher levels of spiritual realization and power. Once this Shakti has reached the top chakra located at the crown of the head, full liberation and self-realization are achieved. This very process is described as the union of Shiva and Shakti.

In addition to Kundalini-yoga, there is an entire denomination of Hinduism dedicated to the realization of the Great Goddess, known as Shaktism. The tradition of Shaktism is most influential in West Bengal and Assam. Its influence, however, has been felt throughout the length and breath of South Asia. While some references to Shaktism can certainly be found in the ancient Vedic literature, it is the works known as the Tantras which are considered most authoritative by adherents. Philosophically, the teachings of Shaktism seem to occupy a middle position between the dualism of Samkhya and the extremely monistic interpretation of Vedanta posited by Shankara.

Unlike with Shankara, for the Shakta the world is not seen as being merely an illusion; it is in fact extremely real. In Shaktism, it is believed that Shakti (the goddess Prakriti) evolves her own being into 36 tattvas, or constituents of reality, in order to create the universe. The present diversified universe is nothing less than the creative manifestation of the uncreated goddess Prakriti, or Shakti. Prakrti, both in the form of this world and the human body is in fact the vehicle for salvation. In practice, Shaktism stresses the sacramental nature of the human body due to its being the locus of spiritual unfoldment. For Shaktas, as for the majority of Hindus, women are greatly respected as being the personifications of Shakti in human, and therefore very spiritually accessible, form.

How has this view of the feminine affected the Hindu perspective on the nature and role of women in the Hindu community? Traditionally, Hinduism teaches that, while women and men naturally share much in common, their different psychological states and outlooks should not be overlooked. The belief is that, in general terms, while men are more aggressive, cerebral and self-promoting, women tend to be more nurturing, intuitive, mature and giving. Interestingly, it is precisely these feminine qualities which are aspired toward in Hindu spiritual life - by both men and women. Like every other religion and culture known to history, individual Hindus have sometimes had difficulty putting their high spiritual ideals into actual practice. Overall, however, the record of Hinduism vis-à-vis the treatment of women has been a very good one. As a result, according to Klaus Klostermaier: Traditional Hinduism is still strongly supported by women; women form the largest portion of temple goers and festival attendants, and women keep traditional domestic rituals alive and pass on thefamiliar stories of the gods and goddesses to their children.

As we will see, Hindu women have not only historically enjoyed the status of being the repository of Shakti, but have often actually had the opportunity to wield some actual power. Unlike what is clearly observed in the majority of Western literature, Hindu literature is full of accounts of heroic, strong and brave women. There are many accounts of such women in the *Mahabharata*. For example, we find Draupadi, who is depicted as a brave and iron-willed woman. There is also Kunti, who perseveres with her honor and her faith intact despite a life riddled with tragedies. In the Ramayana, we meet Sita, the wife - and Shakti - of Rama, an incarnation of God. Though arranged marriages are the norm in Hindu society, we find that Sita chooses her own husband in a svayamvara ceremony. Also of her own free will, she chooses to accompany

Rama to the forest when he is sent into exile, thus exhibiting her strength and commitment to loyalty. While living in the forest, she continues to display her independent nature, as when she convinces Rama to chase the gold-spotted dear. Hindu literature is full of such examples of strong, heroic women. Images of powerful women in Hinduism are not limited to the realm of literature.

They are also witnessed throughout the living historical record of India as well. Hindu women have historically easily risen to heights of power within various monastic and religious hierarchical structures, parallels of which would have been unheard of in Western religion and society until only recently. In the earliest Vedic eṛa, for example, women were awarded the sacred thread of priests (brahmanas) and one text of the Rig Veda (V, 28) mentions that there was a female *rishi* or revealer of sacred truth known as Vishvara. There were also women philosophers such as Vachaknavi, who debated Yajnavalkya, of Upanishadic fame.

The famous Sanskrit grammarian, Panini, observed the distinction in the Sanskrit language between "acaryani" (the wife of a teacher) and "acarya" (a lady teacher), indicating that women were accepted as spiritual teachers. Such women saints as Andal and Mirabai were leaders of the devotional Bhakti movement "...that initiated the religious liberation of women [and] was largely promoted and supported by women devotees". Women have continued this long tradition as leaders of various Hindu communities to this day. Such examples of this phenomenon can be seen in the forms of Gurumayi Chidvilasananda, Amritanandamayi, and Meera Ma, among many, many others.

Considering that Indian culture has always been a culture in which religion has always been the most important social institution in society, it is no small accomplishment for women to have risen so high in the echelons of Hindu leadership.Such respect for the feminine has not been as readily visible in the history of the Western world, unfortunately. The Western religions of Judaism, Christianity and Islam have not had the same abundant degree of examples of women in leadership throughout their respective histories. To this day, for example, women are barred from the priesthood in the Roman Catholic Church.

It has only been in the latter third of the twentieth century that a reemergence of the feminine has begun to take place in European and American societies. Recognizing the terrible price that this gaping deficiency has wrought upon the world in the forms of war, the environmental crisis and the exploitation of women, many present day women thinkers are openly calling for a reclaiming of feminine values in many different sectors of life. In the words of Eleanor Rae: "while the feminine is not limited in its context, there are nevertheless certain key places where it is most appropriately rediscovered. These are in women, in the Earth, and in the Divinity". By recognizing the sacred nature of women as personifications of the feminine aspect of divinity, and by seeing the Earth, not as a lifeless object, there solely for our exploitation, but rather as the living personality of our collective Mother, we can end much of the needless violence and suffering brought about by denying the feminine.

Agreeing with this assessment, Vandana Shiva has written: The violence to nature as symptomatized by the ecological crisis, and the violence to women, as symptomitized by their subjugation and exploitation, arise from this subjugation of the feminine principle. In an crystal-clear display of the ancient concept of Shakti coming full circle to occupy the center stage of current academic debate, it has finally been recognized that the feminine aspect of the very Divinity Him(Her)self has been too long neglected. In the works of such people as Matthew Fox and Vicki Noble, we are now witnessing a call for the reemergence of the concept of the sacred feminine power of God, of Shakti. In such interesting developments as these, I venture to say that we are not so much witnessing the "Hinduization" of Western thought, as we are the rediscovery of the feminine principle as an integral and inseparable part of our very being.

These more recent developments is the West, as well as the long and positive history of the concept of Shakti in India, have shown the idea of a sacred feminine power originating from Divinity and, therefore, necessarily inherent in all things, to be a very relevant subject for further exploration - both on an academic, as well as on a personal, spiritual level. While seemingly arising from the misty and esoteric depths of the philosophy and sacred stories of Hinduism, Shakti is actually a force which also has the ability to affect all human culture: politically, socially and at the deepest levels of our psyches - if we will only let Her.

Bibliography

Ahmad, Aziz. *Islamic Modernism in India and Pakistan*. London: Oxford University Press, 1967.

Bagwe, Anjali. *Of Women Caste: The Experience of Gender in Rural India*. Calcutta: Zed Books Limited, 1995.

Brown, Judith M. *Modern India: The Origins of an Asian Democracy*. New York: Oxford University Press, 1994.

Cartier-Bresson, Henri. *Henri Cartier-Bresson in India*. New York: Thames and Hudson Incorporated, 1987.

Crossette, Barbara. *India: Facing the Twenty-First Century*. Indianapolis: Indiana University Press, 1993.

Desai, Neera. *Women in Modern India*. Bombay: Vora and Company, 1977.

Dietrich, Gabriele. *Reflections on the Women's Movement in India: Religion, Ecology, Development*. New Delhi: Horizon India Books, 1992.

Everett, Jana Matson. *Women and Social Change in India*. New York: St. Martin's Press, 1979.

Gandhi, Nandita and Nandita Shah. *The Issues at Stake: Theory and Practice in the Contemporary Women's Movement in India*. New Delhi: Kali for Women, 1992.

Ghosh, S.K. *Women in a Changing Society*. New Delhi: Ashish Publishing House, 1984.

Jacobson, Doranne and Susan Wadley. *Women in India: Two Perspectives*. New Delhi: Sunil Composing Company, 1977.

Jeffrey, Robin. "Matriliny, Women, Development, and a Typographical Error." *Pacific Affairs*. Fall 1990. Volume 63, Number 3. 373-7.

Kaushik, Susheela, ed. *Women's Oppression: Patterns and Perspectives*. New Delhi: Vikas Publishing House, 1986.

Khan, Mumtaz Ali and Noor Ayesha. *Status of Rural Women in India: A Study of Karnataka*. New Delhi: Uppal Publishing House, 1982.

Khanna, Girija and Mariamma Varghese. *Indian Women Today*. New Delhi: Vikas Publishing House, 1978.

Liddle, Joanna and Rama Joshi. *Daughters of Independence: Gender, Caste and Class in India*. New Delhi: Kali for Women, 1986.

Mukhopadhyay, Maitrayee. *Silver Shackles: Women and Development in India.* Oxford: Oxfam Print, 1985.

Nanda, B.R.,ed. *Indian Women: From Purdah to Modernity*. New Delhi: Vikas Publishing House, 1976.

Randhawa, T.S. *The Last Wanderer: Nomad and Gypsies of India*. Ahmedabad: Mapin Pubin Publishing, 1996.

Roy, Buddhadev. *Marriage Rituals and Songs of Bengal*. Calcutta: Nayak Printers, 1984.

Stern, Robert W. *Changing India: Bourgeois Revolution on the Subcontinent*. Cambridge: Cambridge University Press, 1993.

Tellis-Nayak, Jessie B. *Indian Womanhood: Then and Now*. Indore, India: Sat Prachar Press, 1983.

Thakur, Rekha. "Women's Seat." *The Times of India*. Volume 71, Number 9, June 6, 1997.

Vanita, Ruth and Madhu Kishwar. "In India, a Women's Place is..." *World Press Review*. September 1986. Volume 33, Number 9. 56.

INDEX